The GREEN

A New England Guide to Planning, Planting, and Maintaining the Eco-Friendly Habitat Garden

ELLEN SOUSA

with a Foreword by William Cullina

BUNKER HILL PUBLISHING

Acknowledgements

I dedicate this book to Robert, for without his support and love (and incessant nagging!), I could never have completed this book. Thanks also to best friends Suzanne, Jen and Laura, my parents for providing an upbringing in nature, and to my publishers Ib and Carole Kitchel Bellew, for believing in an unknown author. And on behalf of native plant gardeners everywhere, I am grateful to Bill Cullina and the great people at New England Wild Flower Society for helping enable a new generation of gardeners working in harmony with nature.

www.bunkerhillpublishing.com

First published in 2011
by Bunker Hill Publishing Inc.
285 River Road, Piermont
New Hampshire 03779, USA

10 9 8 7 6 5 4 3 2 1

copyright ©2011 Ellen Sousa

Library of Congress Control Number: 2011925663

ISBN 10: 1-59373-091-8
ISBN 13: 978-1-59373-091-8

Published in the United States by Bunker Hill Publishing

Designed by Louise Millar

Printed in China by Jade Productions

Contents

Foreword

I believe that, just as we have social responsibilities to our human neighbors, communities, and those in need, we have an ecological responsibility to the plants, animals, insects, and natural communities that we share this earth with. For a good part of the last century, gardening and horticulture centered on the control of nature through science with the help of a seemingly limitless arsenal of insecticides, fungicides, rodenticides, chemical fertilizers, and large, gas-guzzling machines. Though we still carry on the legacy of this age in both our bloodstreams and our behaviors, I believe we are truly evolving a more sane and responsible view of the natural world and our place in it. This ethical shift from war to diplomacy, domination to stewardship has been slow and not without setbacks, but the rewards are worth any trouble. I am grateful that my own children do not have to play on pesticide-drenched lawns. I am grateful that there are moths flying through the darkened sky in my backyard. I am grateful that I live in a place where the melodies of the hermit thrushes are not drowned out by the din of mowers and blowers. I am grateful that there are others out there grateful for these things, too.

I first met Ellen Sousa when she was a student in several of my courses at the New England Wild Flower Society. When she told me about her idea for a manual on ecologically responsible gardening in New England, I imagined a small handbook or even a series of blog posts. I had no idea the project would grow into such a comprehensive, engaging, and personal work that traces her own journey toward stewardship and tolerance while providing a clear and compelling road map for others embarking on this path. Bravo, Ellen, and bravo to you as well for caring about all the life we share this small blue marble with!

William Cullina
Southport Island, Maine

Treat the earth well:
It was not given to you by
*   your parents,*
It was loaned to you by
*   your children.*
We do not inherit the Earth
*   from our ancestors,*
*   we borrow it from our*
*   Children.*
OGLALA SIOUX PROVERB

Opposite: ***Like to eat? Thank a pollinator!*** *Many food crops and flowering plants require bees, wasps, flies, and beetles for pollination. Pollinators are "keystone" species, meaning their loss has a cascade effect throughout the entire ecosystem.*

Preface

The message from scientists is clear. Our climate is changing, much faster than it should be, according to historical cycles. Expect increasingly severe weather patterns to disrupt our landscapes and lives, as well as snowballing wildlife extinctions. One quarter of American bird species are in decline, and pollinating insects and pest-eating bat populations are in a free fall. Widespread losses of these species destabilize the natural processes we all rely on for survival. On top of that, a corrupt political climate has placed much of the control of our nation's food and energy production in the hands of a few mega-corporations, who favor short-term profits over long-term environmental stability and health. Our children and grandchildren will wonder why today, when faced with this knowledge, we did not do more to slow the losses, to protect what we still had.

If these things concern you, and you're still reading after all this doom and gloom, and are looking for ways to "green" your landscaping, reduce energy usage, and protect the health of your family, your community, and the planet, this book is for you. "Beneficial" gardening has taken on real urgency, and with just a few changes, you can transform your property—whatever its size—into a natural habitat to protect the remaining birds, insects, and other vital "ecosystem workers" that help maintain a stable, functioning environment that supports us all. Sifting through the ideological and technical complexities of greenscaping, combined with the widespread "eco-washing" in the media can make converting to earth-friendly landscaping feel overwhelming. I hope this book provides clear facts, solid ideas, and real-life inspiration for anyone looking to lower their environmental footprint and protect biodiversity in their backyards.

Opposite: *The balsam fir and red spruce forests of northern New England are ravaged by the effects of acid rain, as well as increasing average temperatures worldwide. If this unique habitat disappears, the* **Bicknell's thrush** *(left) will probably disappear as well.*

Toward a Natural Gardening Style

Conventional gardening has generally reflected an ideal of order and controlled nature; of "subduing" the land, as the Puritans called it. A few trees dotting a large expanse of sheared lawn. A small selection of clipped evergreen shrubs placed to cover the foundation. A few exotic flowering plants encouraged to bloom heavily by using fertilizers and irrigation. Obsessive mowing, weeding, and deadheading to keep nature perfectly groomed and unblemished. And zero tolerance for any insect life.

This type of garden may faintly remind you of nature's beauty, or evoke a feeling of exotic, faraway places. In fact, it is profoundly unnatural, as it generally requires large amounts of fuel, water, and chemical inputs to thrive.

But the tide has turned. As we look for ways to reduce energy consumption and protect natural resources, gardeners and landscapers now understand that the way they garden can have a positive impact on the environment—and on their wallets. Educated plant choices and nontoxic yard maintenance techniques means being able to have a beautiful garden—even a formal one, if that's your style—while at the same time promoting biodiversity and a safe and healthy environment right in our own yards.

A natural habitat garden allows your garden to act in the way nature does. This means choosing plants that are naturally suited to your site and soil conditions so that they can thrive without too much help from you. And where your garden plants do need a little help, instead of overfeeding them with chemical shock treatments, you feed the soil instead, allowing nature's organic processes to nurture your plants.

Opposite: *Cooperating with nature, we get a free ticket to winged wonders such as this beautiful* **Eastern tiger swallowtail butterfly**.

It also means developing tolerance for some of the wildlife (yes, even bugs) that appear in your yard. In fact, most bugs are either innocent bystanders or are beneficial in some way. By learning some of the pest control and crop growing techniques passed from generation to generation before the age of synthetic fertilizers and pesticides, you'll keep your lawn and garden in healthy balance, without harmful chemicals.

In a natural habitat garden, biodiversity is encouraged and celebrated. Wildlife is not just welcomed as something nice to look at, but recognized as essential to a stable and functioning environment. Without abundant pollinating insects, we'd lose many food crops and our landscape would quickly degrade. Without birds, dragonflies, frogs, toads, bats, and other predators, pest populations would spiral out of control. Without frogs and small fish to eat insect larvae, we'd be swarmed with mosquitoes and infected by diseases they carry. Without chipmunks, squirrels, and ants to spread seeds and nuts across the landscape, we would have fewer plants and trees to purify our air and water. Without flies, fungi, beetles, and bacteria to break down dead lifeforms, we would soon be buried alive in detritus.

A natural gardening style means combining plants roughly according to how they would be found in nature. This allows plant communities to form, encouraging the mutually beneficial relationships among plants and wildlife that have evolved over thousands of years, forming a web of interconnected life.

A natural habitat garden includes plants native to New England and its environs, restoring and celebrating the unique ecology and history of our landscape.

A natural habitat garden invites serendipity into your design, allowing plants to set seeds, which are then eaten by birds, who distribute them across the landscape through their droppings. Seedlings are integral to biodiversity, to a larger gene pool, and to helping ensure the continuation of species.

A natural habitat garden recognizes that people are a part of nature, and supplies places for us to explore, relax, observe, and participate. It caters to the needs of everybody who uses the area, with open areas for children as well as secluded areas for quiet contemplation.

When the cherries bloom, enjoy **northern orioles** *and* **hummingbirds** *drinking sweet nectar from the blossoms.*

Why a Habitat Garden?

Protecting the "web of life"

All life on our planet is linked through a web of life known as biodiversity. Every species, from the tiniest soil microbes to plants, birds, mammals, reptiles, amphibians, and invertebrates, plays its own part in a complex yet fragile interaction of natural processes that allows life on earth to thrive. The air that we breathe, the water that we drink, and the soil in which we grow our food all depend on the strength and health of this web of life. Each species contributes in its own way. And, just like a spider's web, if enough strands are missing, the entire web collapses.

As weather patterns become more severe from accelerating climate change, and our land and natural resources are increasingly in demand for food, housing, recreation, energy, transportation, and industry, the web of life is dangerously frayed. Humanity has become an independent force of nature, causing rapid transformation of natural processes that have traditionally taken thousands of years.. The rate at which we are impacting our environment does not give wildlife time to adapt to the changes.

Scientists know that declines and losses of large numbers of species will cause major instabilities in our natural processes, and other rapid changes that we can't even predict. Climate change can seem overwhelming, and fixing it often seems beyond our individual control. But we have an urgent need to try to slow down or stop the rapid declines and extinctions of many plant and animal species. If we don't, our environment could degrade to a level incapable of supporting human life. By creating habitat in your backyard, you can help repair the damage being done to our web of life and start to offset the damage already done. You can make a difference.

Environmental stability depends on fully functioning ecosystems, an intact "web of life."

Every backyard helps

Each of us is a steward of our own tiny piece of the Earth, and the landscaping decisions we make on our properties can restore food, shelter, and nesting places for many creatures. With just a bit of planning and knowledge, you can turn your own property—whatever its size—into a natural haven for the various species that are being increasingly crowded out of our world. Encourage your neighbors to do the same, and your contiguous backyards can form a connected network of wildlife coridors full of life and biodiversity. To do so is to make your contribution to what could be the largest, most valuable nature reserve in an increasingly urbanized planet.

Nature isn't somewhere you go or something you watch on television.

We are all gardeners

For thousands of years our forebears (both European and Native American) lived with acute awareness of weather's impacts. We are just a few generations removed from producing our own food, but since the Industrial Age, we've become mostly urbanized, fed by food grown elsewhere, and have largely forgotten how stable weather, healthy soil, and clean water are fundamental to our survival.

Anybody who farmed during the Dust Bowl of the 1930s, or grew potatoes to feed their family in 1840s Ireland, understood—too late—that extreme weather and a reliance on the same few crops can lead to disaster on a large scale. Those who survived migrated to better lives elsewhere, but we have no New World or Western lands left to explore or exploit, nowhere to simply "start again." And the grim truth is that a few large industrial-agricultural corporations now control most farmland and food crops in the US, owning the patents to a few seed crops, genetically altered to contain bacterial insecticide and resistance to Roundup, a carcinogenic and neurotoxic weed killer systematically sprayed all around us.

The good news is that we do have one final frontier that we can control, which is our own "backyards," including schoolyards, public places, apartment balconies, even the areas surrounding our companies and businesses. We can protect our health and remaining biodiversity by redefining the way we use our local landscapes, We can also return to local self-sufficiency —by growing more of our own food as well as supporting New England family farmers who have a vested interest in caring for the land, instead of simply profits.

Help your health and feed your family

Whatever your age, digging in the dirt and playing outdoors are good for you! Gardening provides the moderate exercise and fresh air that lower your risk of many chronic diseases, and scientists have recently discovered what most gardeners knew already—that exposure to certain soil-dwelling bacteria releases brain chemicals that reduce stress and make us feel happy! Gardening is highly therapeutic, providing a creative outlet, a place to relax and unwind from our bustling lives. And when we grow our own food, we enjoy the health and flavor of fresh, pesticide-free vegetables and fruits that arrive on our table right from our doorstep, not transported large distances.

Doctors have been telling us for years to improve our health by eating "lower on the food chain," by consuming more fresh fruit, vegetables, and whole grains. Plant-derived phytonutrients are known to help prevent a host of medical issues, but at the same time many common foods contain traces of toxic pesticides with known links to various cancers and neurological issues. Some are systemic, meaning they can't be washed off,

"Everything that slows us down and forces patience, everything that sets us back into the slow circles of nature, is a help. Gardening is an instrument of grace."

MAY SARTON

Converting your lawn to low-care grasses gives you a green lawn without toxic chemicals.

Right: *Using empty local spaces to grow fresh, nutrient-packed food can dramatically improve our health.*

Whenever we consume food made from genetically modified corn or soybeans, or eat meat from livestock fed on GM alfalfa and corn, we ingest microscopic traces of toxins which can build up over time in our cells. Wild seafood accumulate toxins such as mercury and lead, adding to the load. Most common pesticides are relatively new chemical compounds, only tested for short-term effects, but scientists are finding disturbing cellular-level impacts on people, domestic animals, and wildlife, including fetal cell death and birth defects. The long-term interactions between the increasing numbers of biological toxins in our environment are still untested, and we are wise to limit our exposure to these unnatural substances in every way we can.

Fresh, organically grown fruit and vegetables are expensive to buy, but growing your own (or buying from a local organic farmer) helps reduce your family's dietary exposure to pesticides. It is possible to grow vegetables anywhere in New England, as long as you have a space that receives full sun in the summertime. Plant **blueberries**, **strawberries**, **raspberries**, **grapes**, and other delicious fruits and share some of them with birds such as **thrushes**, **orioles**, and **flycatchers**. They'll return the favor by dining on your garden pests. Grow culinary herbs such as **sage**, **oregano**, **thyme**, **coriander**, and **mint** to flavor your meals and provide their natural health-giving benefits. Their pungent foliage deters many pests, and their flowers attract many beneficial insects to your garden. Grow tomatoes in bags of soil on a warm, sunny porch, or join a local community garden. Share hands, and harvests, by combining your garden space with neighbors.

Blueberry flowers awaiting buzz pollination by local bumblebees, who are in steep decline across the nation.

Pollinators enable flowering plants (including many of our food plants) to reproduce, in a fascinating example of the mutually beneficial relationships between plants and wildlife. Pesticides are contributing to major declines in pollinator species.

What kind of butterfly? Jeb tries to identify a caterpillar through the magnified lid of a "bug viewer."

Below: *Nature sometimes isn't pretty, but seeing nature up close provides kids with teaching moments about life.*

Get out and play!

Addicted to virtual reality, and too busy to participate in an unstructured world, American kids are increasingly disconnected from nature—and increasing obesity statistics reflect that children are spending too much time indoors, contributing to poor health.

Outdoor time is essential. Unstructured outdoor play helps kids develop critical thinking skills, stimulates creativity, and improves academic success. Outdoor education improves self-esteem, confidence, and cooperative behavior.

Habitat gardens invite nature into your backyard, allowing you to share its daily miracles with the kids in your life. Give a child a small area of garden to tend, and help foster a lifelong connection to the outdoors. Or volunteer to help start and maintain a schoolyard garden, where a natural outdoor classroom will reinforce lessons taught indoors, while encouraging and engaging kids in the processes of growing and eating healthy foods.

Save energy, water, and money, and help the environment

With energy conservation a priority and the cost for cleaning and treating municipal water rising, we're all looking closely at the resources that go into maintaining our home landscapes. The good news is that we have plenty of alternatives to toxics and technological processes that depend on fossil fuels such as oil, natural gas, and coal.

Chemically treated lawns consume huge amounts of petro-chemicals to keep them looking golf-course green throughout the year, besides leaching chemicals into groundwater. Is it really worth it, when there are Earth-friendly, locally available alternatives?

You can still have a lawn and a beautiful garden, but without risking your health, killing pollinators, hastening wildlife declines, poisoning soil life, and polluting water. Switching from a synthetic chemical-based lawn and garden treatment, to an organic approach that feeds the soil's natural life (instead of suppressing it), means few—if any—toxic substances are needed. For lawns, that means less overall maintenance over time. Planting native species, which have naturally evolved to thrive in our changeable climate, and matching plants to your site conditions, means few fertilizers and less water are necessary.

And because native plants supply vital resources to almost every bird species and to beneficial insects, bats, amphibians, and reptiles, just by adding a few native shrubs and trees to your garden, you can help threatened wildlife and slow the extinctions.

Planting even one native New England tree is probably the simplest yet most powerful contribution you can make to the planet's health. Healthy trees absorb air pollutants by settling, trapping, and holding floating particulates and allergens such as dust, ash, and pollen, and improve air quality by converting carbon dioxide—making trees especially important in urban areas, where air quality is already poor. Plant and tree roots also filter soil-borne pollutants, breaking them down before they enter groundwater. Situating trees and shrubs near your house insulates it from the extremes of heat and cold, saving money by reducing heating and cooling costs. And native trees are essential to the survival of most of our small but important species that support life at the bottom of the food chain. When we plant trees, we are making a

Plants native to New England support the highest number of native species, from birds to butterflies to beneficial insects.

Above: ***Flowering dogwood*** *in June.*

Chemical fertilizers mostly wash right off lawns and into waterways.

Reduce areas of lawn and replace them with functional gardens, including native trees.

Almost all native insects require a certain plant or plant family to survive.

*When **milkweed** is doused with herbicides and removed, **monarch butterfly caterpillars** lose the food plants they need.*

true long-term investment in the health of the landscape that our grandchildren will depend upon.

Reusing and recycling materials in your landscaping saves the cost of new products, and their associated manufacturing processes and transportation costs. Composting much of your yard and home's organic waste can drastically reduce your waste stream, saving you money and providing free fertilizer for your lawn and gardens. Allowing tree leaves to build up under existing trees instead of removing them restores the fungal, algal, and bacterial associations formed between plant roots and the surrounding soil—an intricate process enabling trees to manufacture their own food. Most landscape plants, including most lawn grasses, grow best in a soil enriched by their own decaying foliage.

Natural inspiration

Habitat gardens offer the budding artist a range of natural subjects to develop skills in the creative arts. Interactions with nature have inspired creative genius from Beethoven to Einstein. American Impressionist painter Joseph Greenwood produced his early works by painting the natural landscapes in and around Spencer, Massachusetts, and Henry David Thoreau used the farms, woodlots, and villages of Concord to craft a science- and philosophy-based environmental ethic that continues to inspire conservationists today. Emily Dickinson grew asters and marigolds in her Amherst garden, to attract the butterflies, bees, and hummingbirds that featured prominently in her poetry.

Development means that birds and other wildlife are steadily losing the natural places and plants they need to survive. Deforestation in Central and South America are also shrinking winter habitat for migrating birds that travel north each summer to breed.

Gazing at nature, with its inherent beauty, its patterns and rhythms, is a soothing experience, a way to calm a busy mind.

> *"I perhaps owe having become a painter to flowers."*
>
> CLAUDE MONET

Plant stems left standing in winter capture snow, protecting plants with "poor man's mulch."

Left: *The diversity of plants in a natural habitat garden provides a profusion of blooms throughout the year, enough to share.*

An ever-changing palette

Aesthetically, a natural habitat garden containing a diversity of plants provides a constantly changing tapestry of color and texture. With their differing blooming times and life cycles, a mix of plants provides varying and distinctive interest, while ensuring a constantly replenishing source of food and shelter for wildlife through the year.

Allergies and the habitat gardener

If you suffer from hay fever or other allergies, consult an allergist. It might be possible to grow plants that won't make you sneeze or sniffle. Certain plants, including birch, maple, and oak trees and some grasses, enable their own pollination by producing puffs of pollen that blow away at the slightest wind. Plants with colorful and conspicuous flowers have evolved to attract bees, butterflies, and other insects; their pollen is large and sticky, designed to make its way to other flowers by sticking to insect parts rather than blowing away in the breeze. A diversified landscape with a variety of flowering plants and trees reduces the amount of pollen released by any one species, and a dense tree canopy can help to intercept and settle windborne pollen and other floating allergens.

Stressed plants produce the rapid green flesh that attracts aphids, which secrete a sticky liquid called honeydew, on which allergy-causing mold spores can multiply by the billions. Choosing the right plants for your garden conditions and using natural soil amendments instead of chemical fertilizers will keep your plants healthy.

If you have allergies to specific local plants, find a source for local honey to alleviate your symptoms. The more local, the better, as the honey is likely to contain pollen from the plants that bother you. Local honey modulates your body's immune system. Buying local honey is also a great way to support farmers who raise at-risk honeybees in hives.

Goldenrod does not cause hay fever. This yellow stunner is an unfortunate victim of guilt by association because it blooms at the same time as **ragweed**, whose airborne pollen is the real culprit. Although some varieties of goldenrod are too aggressive to grow in smaller gardens, goldenrod is one of New England's most valuable wildlife plants.

Beyond Pachysandra – Discovering New England's Native Plants

Until recently, American gardeners had access to just a small number of cultivated plants and shrubs. Since the mid-20th century, the typical residential landscape has consisted of a mix of the same homogenized plantings of clipped **European yew**, with flowering **azaleas** and **forsythia** from Asia, surrounded by a monoculture of **Kentucky bluegrass** (actually a Eurasian native) or, in shady areas, perhaps a mat of **Japanese pachysandra**, **English ivy**, or **European periwinkle** (*Vinca*) chosen for their "pest-free" foliage. We have far more plants to choose from now, but generally still see the same few plants in the home landscape. However, a breathtaking array of native plants grow naturally, and in the past decade, homeowners, municipalities, and landscapers have embraced the value of regionally native plants as a lower-maintenance and environmentally beneficial option.

A New England *native plant* is one that grew in the region prior to European settlement and colonization. Native plants are adapted to the challenges of the climate, with a built-in resistance to common diseases as well as temperature and moisture fluctuations. And because they have co-evolved alongside our native wildlife, native plants maintain the vital and irreplaceable links among plants and animals.

Native plants adapted to your garden conditions reduce water usage.
Right: ***Great blue lobelia*** *at Coastal Maine Botanic Gardens*

Less work, less water

Severe weather plus a seemingly constant battle against diseases and pests can make gardening in New England a frustrating experience. Instead of giving up, or trying to force a plant to live where it can't thrive without being watered, fertilized, and sprayed, gardeners are discovering that native plants can be just as beautiful, but often less fussy than the expensive plants from Europe and Asia that fill garden catalogs and magazines.

All gardens need occasional maintenance. But if you take some time to match your site conditions to plants that live naturally in those conditions, you'll find that your garden eventually needs little to no irrigation, fertilizing, and no pesticides. Whatever the conditions in your yard, nature has a beautiful plant that will thrive there. Instead of trying to change your growing conditions, why not choose a plant that grows there naturally?

If you have a sandy or rocky slope in full sun, planting **bearberry, wild blue lupine, butterfly milkweed** and **juniper** will protect the area from erosion and attract rare butterflies. Shady woodland? Grow **mountain laurel, ferns, foamflower, wild blue phlox,** and **black cohosh.** A wet area of lawn where grass just refuses to grow? Allow **mosses** to fill in, and plant native stunners such as **swamp rose mallow, lobelia, sedge** and **Joe-Pye weed** for a glorious summer display filled with color, beauty, and life.

Below left: *Rose mallow grows wild in the marshes of southern New England.*

Right: *Even a vertical rock wall can support a plant community.*

Definitions: Native versus Invasive versus Naturalized Nonnative Species

Discussions involving native and nonnative landscape plants quickly become confusing, especially when the definition of "native" depends on a plant's location, genetics, or history. The following generally accepted definitions should help you understand how plants interact with their landscape.

Native

A plant that was growing in the region prior to European settlement, including **violet** *(pictured)* and **goldenrod**, and also many trees such as **hemlock, pine, oak, chestnut, elm, beech, hickory**, and **maple.**

Introduced nonnative

A nonnative plant (also called an "exotic") was introduced into a region for use in agriculture and home gardens, or accidentally brought in as seeds or roots in ship ballast or imported soil. Ornamental or edible plants such as **cosmos**, **peonies**, **nasturtiums** *(pictured)*, and **cabbage** are examples of introduced nonnatives. Often they provide some benefit to native wildlife, such as nectar, pollen, or seeds.

Naturalized nonnatives

Naturalized nonnatives are introduced plants such as **ox-eye daisy** or **Queen Anne's lace** *(pictured)* that have since spread into natural areas, mostly through seedlings carried by wind or birds. They are not necessarily ecologically destructive or overly aggressive, but many people assume they are native because they have been around for centuries. Some forms of wildlife have adapted to utilize their nectar, pollen, seeds, and foliage, making some naturalized nonnatives valuable to pollinators and birds. How a naturalized nonnative behaves in your landscape and its means of reproduction (seeds or roots) will determine how urgently you need to control its growth.

Invasive nonnatives

An invasive species is a nonnative plant that spreads at many times its evolutionary rate, crowding out native species and forming monocultures that sustain little other life. **Purple loosestrife** *(pictured)* and **Asiatic bittersweet** are familiar invasive species seen across New England. The USDA determines if a species is invasive within certain regions. Invasive nonnative plants tend to host far wildlife species than native plants, reducing overall biodiversity.

Native wildlife need native plants

Over thousands of years of evolution, plants have developed specialized relationships with local wildlife. Many plants grow only where a specific pollinating insect is available. Spring-blooming wild flowers rely on early-season **bumble bees** and **syrphid flies**, and many insects, including **butterflies** and **moths**, exist only where particular flowers thrive. Some insects are generalists, able to use a variety of plants for food or other resources, but most are specialized, requiring a specific plant or plant family to survive. Plants protect themselves by manufacturing chemical compounds that are poisonous to any who dare take a bite (including us!). Over thousands of years, local insects have evolved their own immunity to those leaf toxins and become capable of eating and digesting the leaves of those plants.

A recent book by entomologist Douglas Tallamy points out that most popular landscaping plants, including European lawn grasses and Asian ornamental trees, evolved along with different sets of insects and natural controls than native plants that co-evolved here with local insects. In many cases, foreign plants are popular precisely because of their "pest-free" foliage, but Tallamy illustrates how, because 96 percent of our native insects feed only on co-evolved plants, alien plants support very few leaf-eating insects. You might think that's a good thing until you realize that large numbers of caterpillars and insect larvae are key to the survival of most birds, bats, and other lifeforms. Because most human and natural landscapes in the US are now filled with foreign grasses, food crops, and ornamentals, areas that support healthy populations of native insects are few and far between. Tallamy's message is simple. Regionally native plants, especially trees such as **oak**, **willow**, **birch**, and **maple**, support much higher native insect species diversity than most foreign plants. Just by planting more natives, we support the lower lifeforms that are key components of an ecosystem, protecting our remaining biodiversity.

By providing native insects with the native plants they need, you promote the insect diversity that supports the food chain. A garden with Asian plants and shrubs will support a few co-evolved species (including destructive Japanese beetles), but very few of our native specialists, which simply disappear.

*This **spicebush swallowtail butterfly caterpillar** needs to eat the foliage of native **spicebush** and **sassafras** to survive until it can morph into a beautiful butterfly.*

Don't worry too much about leaf-eating caterpillars defoliating your expensive shrubs and trees. Most healthy plants can withstand a certain amount of leaf damage, and areas planted largely with a variety of native plants attract enough birds, predatory insects, and other natural enemies that tend to keep any single insect from dominating an area and becoming a pest.

*The endangered **Karner blue butterfly** (left) needs **wild blue lupines** to survive. Unfortunately they cannot live on the hybrid lupines growing on roadsides of New England.*

Instead of planting Japanese maples, which few native insects eat, plant one of New England's own maples, which support countless native species.

*Think this "wild" white rose at left and think is native to New England? It's actually **Japanese multiflora rose**, a nonnative invasive plant crowding out native wild roses such as the pink **Virginia rose** at right.*

Many nonnative berry shrubs do feed birds, and some birds readily use nonnative shrubs for nesting. But, without ample supplies of caterpillars and insects when birds are feeding their nestlings, busy parents need to travel farther from their nests to find food, leaving eggs and nests much more vulnerable to predation.

A sense of place

Scientists believe that rising average temperatures mean the sugar maple will disappear from New England within decades.

A garden based upon native plants is perceived as belonging here. As New England's regional identity disappears, maintaining our distinctive native landscape helps preserve some of what makes New England unique.

A weed is just a wildflower in the wrong place

Gardening with native plants doesn't mean your garden has to look weedy and wild. If you live where homeowner restrictions dictate your landscaping style, or if you simply prefer a formal garden, many well-mannered natives are perfectly at home in a cultivated garden.

The beauty of New England's native plants is the wide variety of textures, colors, and growth habits they have developed in response to specific climatic conditions. Spring ephemerals are showy wildflowers that grow in wooded areas, but take advantage of early spring sunshine before trees leaf out to put on a spectacular show of color before going dormant in the heat of summer. **Butterfly weed's** nectar-rich, neon-orange summer blooms are a beacon for newly emerging adult butterflies, and **New England asters'** showy blooms compete with **goldenrod** to attract late-season **hoverflies**, **bumblebees**, and migrating **monarch butterflies**. **Ferns'** lush foliage provides a wonderfully lacy texture and green filler to a shady garden. Many gardeners simply don't want to tend to a formal garden, and native plants, chosen and planted wisely, can be the ideal solution.

Left: *When planted without a barrier near woodlands, **Japanese pachysandra** can spread quickly, crowding out native plants.*

Right: ***Running foamflower*** *has pretty spring flowers important to early-season pollinators, and makes a great native alternative.*

From top left, clockwise: **Maidenhair fern, New England aster, butterfly milkweed, virgin's bower, black cohosh, Dutchman's breeches.**

What's next . . . a politically correct garden?

Although using local native plants is probably your optimal route to encouraging the widest biodiversity, you're no eco-criminal if you grow nonnative plants, as long as they are not potentially invasive here. Many beautiful nonnatives behave politely in New England gardens, can thrive with minimal care, and attract birds and insects. **Japanese crabapples** attract butterflies, hummingbirds, and pollinators when they bloom in spring, and many butterflies have adapted to them where the closely related hawthorn or wild cherry has disappeared. **Black swallowtail butterflies** are still abundant in New England—although most of the native plants they have evolved to eat (**wild parsley** and **golden Alexanders**) have disappeared, their caterpillars have adapted to eat introduced plants in the same family such as **dill**, **carrot**, **parsley**, **cilantro**, **fennel** and **Queen Anne's lace**.

Black swallowtail butterfly caterpillars eat only plants in the carrot family, including *cilantro* (below left).

Below right: *Hollyhock* is an heirloom plant that your grandmother probably grew. Pictured: *Gardens "with a view" at Saint-Gaudens National Historic Site, Cornish, NH.*

In biodiversity, there is strength and flexibility, and an area planted with native plants may show greater resilience and adaptability to serious environmental disasters such as as flooding, drought, or imported pests.

Cultivating heirloom flowers, herbs, and vegetables also preserves elements of our agricultural history, and by saving seeds from heirloom vegetables you grow, you can contribute to your own food security. Seed from open-pollinated plants represents a genetically stable food resource at a time when our food supply is based increasingly on a few genetically identical, bioengineered food crops owned by large corporations,

Cultivars (short for *cultivated variety*) of native plants are an easy way to start gardening with natives because they are readily available. A cultivar is a plant selected for a certain characteristic, such an abundance of berries or beautiful flower color. However, because cultivars are generally selected for aesthetics and not necessarily wildlife value, you should always plant some straight species if your main goal is to support wildlife. Many cultivars are genetic clones of the parent plant, contributing little to the genetic diversity of the species.

Rethinking Lawns

The grassy, manicured lawn is a relic of our British ancestors, whose aristocrats favored large expanses of green lawns, clipped by grazing sheep, to show off their magnificent stately homes. Lawns found favor in suburban American landscapes in the early 1900s, encouraged by a dominant Euro-culture in which even the American Garden Club lectured its members that keeping a large lawn was a civic duty. Since then, mostly due to the availability of cheap chemical lawn treatments, larger lawnmowers, and the rise of the "mow and blow" landscaping service, enormous lawns have become a tradition, and a golf-course-green lawn has come to symbolize suburban status, homogeneity, and conformity, the pride and joy of many a new homeowner. However, our summers are hotter and drier than in England, and most of us don't have sheep. Keeping a traditional bluegrass lawn green through a hot New England summer requires regular irrigation, frequent mowing, and fertilizing in the form of a chemical-by-the-bag assault on our environment.

Traditional lawns require at least an inch of water per week, frequent mowing, and lots of fertilizer to keep them green. Grow a lawn containing fescue and clover to reduce mowing and help protect our water supplies.

The price of chemlawn

Some facts about traditional lawn care that put it all into perspective:

- 30 percent of all water consumed on the East Coast is used for lawns.
- Using a gas-powered lawnmower for one hour emits as much hydrocarbon as driving a car 350 miles.
- Chemical lawn treatments require large amounts of fossil fuels to produce and transport.
- Millions of pounds of chemicals are used to control lawn weeds, much of it washing *unused by your lawn*, right into nearby waterways.
- Twenty-four of the most common lawn pesticides are toxic to fish, sixteen are toxic to birds, and eleven are toxic to bees.
- More than half the nitrogen from lawn fertilizers never reaches plant roots but disappears straight into the atmosphere to form nitrous oxide, ranking behind only CO_2 and methane as our worst greenhouse gas.
- A growing pool of research links exposure to lawn, garden, and agricultural pesticides to chronic illnesses such as leukemia, Parkinson's disease, and cancer, as well as learning disabilities in children.

A lawn with healthy soil created without pesticides and chemical fertilizers will host earthworms and other soil-dwellers that feed birds.

Pictured: *The* **northern flicker** *is a ground-feeding woodpecker that eats grubs and other insects.)*

Lawns will probably always have a place in our residential landscapes, providing areas for kids to run and play as well as a contrast to flower borders, tree groves, and other areas. However, the good news is that you can still have a lush, green lawn without polluting the earth and endangering your family's health.

Chemical fertilizers feed your grass with quick dosages of some of the nutrients that all plants need: nitrogen, phosphorus, and potassium. But when your grass receives its nutrients directly from synthetically produced chemicals, most of the beneficial, naturally occurring organisms that live in healthy, living soils simply disappear. When plants don't need to find their own food using their roots (which partner with soil microbes to mine soil for nutrients and moisture) roots grow shallow and weak, leaving grass susceptible to drought, pest damage, and diseases.

For a green, safe, traditional lawn without chemical dependence, shift your thinking from feeding your lawn to feeding your soil. A healthy soil teems with a mostly-invisible army of organisms that work together to supply grass with all it needs to stay healthy. Feed the benign soil microbes, and they'll repay the favor by feeding your grass, encouraging root growth, and suppressing the destructive pathogens that attack grass. By adding organic soil amendments, earthworms and other soil residents will break them down into nutritious plant food, delivered directly to the root zone, at the same time aerating the soil to improve root penetration and improve soil drainage. Healthy soil grows dense, healthy grass that easily outcompetes weeds.

Chemical-free lawn care—the basics

Mow high, by raising the mower blade to at least three inches. Longer grass blades have more surface area for photosynthesis, allowing grass roots to grow deeply into the soil. Taller grass also helps shade the surrounding soil, slowing evaporation and discouraging weed seeds from germinating. During the last mow of the year, in fall, lower the blade and cut low, to make your thick lawn less hospitable to winter voles that eat plant roots.

Use a mulching mower and chop grass clippings directly into the lawn instead of carting them away. Decomposers will break them down right away into nutritious plant food, and clippings alone can supply more than half the nitrogen needs of your grass. If you don't have a mulching mower, use clippings to build a compost pile along with another organic material, such as dried leaves. Or, use 1 inch of grass clippings as an organic mulch in your vegetable garden to control weeds.

In the fall, use your mulching mower to chop some of your fallen tree leaves right into your lawn to continue feeding soil life. Rake the rest into nearby beds to break down over the winter, or add to your compost pile.

Raking compost into your lawn once a year is one of the simplest ways to keep your lawn green and healthy.

Feed your soil with liquified organic fertilizers that include compost, sea kelp, humates, and other ingredients that feed soil micro-organisms, applied with a hose-end sprayer. Oxygenating the liquid with a small pump before application vastly speeds up nutrient uptake. Many lawn care companies now custom-brew aerated liquid fertilizers based on your soil's individual needs.

For smaller lawns, you can simply rake a thin layer of compost into the soil once a year and let rain and earthworms work it into the soil. You can apply organic fertilizers to your lawn at any time of the year, they don't burn plants, but applying before rain will speed up absorption. Never use fertilizers with "N-P-K" numbers higher than 10-10-10. Anything higher will kill or displace beneficial soil microbes and disrupt the soil ecosystem.

As beneficial bacteria, fungi, and other microbes begin to build up in your soil, their combined activities loosen it, opening up soil pores compacted from foot traffic and snowpack. When you first convert your lawn to organics, you can use plug aeration to create two-inch long holes to open small pockets and allow water, food, and oxygen to reach the root zone of your grass. In high-traffic areas, install an alternative to grass such as gravel, sturdy mulch like bark or wood chips, or hardscaping such as flagstones or porous materials, to allow rainwater to drain.

Let your grass go dormant in summer drought. It's not dead, just dormant, and fall rains will green it up again.

*Scorned as weeds, **dandelions** tell you about your soil. If you don't like dandelions, use natural fertilizers to boost soil microbial populations.*

Have your soil tested for pH, nutrients and soil life. If the results show nutrient deficiencies, or a low soil pH, apply soil amendments as recommended by the soil test. Calcitic limestone and wood ash helps raise soil pH and adds calcium, but you can skip a step and save money on limestone by mixing a much smaller amount of lime (usually less than one-quarter the recommended amount) to compost that you apply to your lawn (or use to produce compost tea). It will raise the pH more quickly than applying limestone directly to the lawn.

For weed control, **hand-pull** or **spot-treat weeds** (see page 164) instead of treating the entire lawn with herbicide. After removing weeds, overseed with grass seed to fill in the bare spots. As you improve your soil over time, grass becomes healthy and vigorous, and weed problems will diminish.

Replace with low-mow, no-water grasses

For a lower-maintenance, thick and green lawn, overseed your lawn with a mix of perennial **ryegrass** and a variety of fine-leafed, slow growing **fescue** grasses. These grasses are deep-rooted and drought-tolerant, require less frequent mowing than bluegrass, and grow even in sandy or clay soils without watering or fertilization. Fescues need mowing only once a month instead of once a week, and grow only to about four or five inches. Use tall fescues for sunny lawn areas, and red fescues for areas with more shade. Sold under names such as Eco-Lawn, a dense mix of cold-climate grasses should easily outcompete common lawn weeds. Seed some **Dutch white clover** into your lawn. Clover adds nitrogen to the soil, stays green even through drought, and tolerates dog urine better than most grasses.

Grow a "shag lawn"! A lawn of fine low **fescue** grasses requires little fertilizer, grows in shade or sun, and should never need watering once established.
Below: *Pennsylvania sedge* is a short grasslike plant that can be used as a lawn substitute for areas without too much foot traffic.

Left: *This flowering lawn is a mixture of* **fescue**, **clover**, *and native* **violets** *and* **wild strawberries**.

Right: **Bluets** *will often appear on their own, forming a white carpet in spring.*

Encourage a "flowering" lawn

Another simple alternative to a traditional lawn is to allow low flowering plants such as **violets**, **bluets**, **clover**, and **wild strawberries** to seed themselves. These plants are considered weeds, so don't be surprised if they appear on their own without your help! You can also introduce them by overseeding your existing lawn. A lawn blooming with tiny, colorful wildflowers requires very little work, and provides many food resources for pollinators and birds. If dandelions pop up, you can always hand-pull them and add to your compost pile. Their long taproots pull nutrients from deep in the subsoil that will improve the quality of your compost. Leaving just a few dandelions to bloom in early spring supplies valuable nectar to **orchard mason bees**, and other pollinators who need to feed as soon as they emerge from hibernation. **Dandelion** foliage is full of vitamins, minerals, and antioxidants. Rabbits love them too, and the presence of dandelions near your vegetable garden may distract bunnies from eating your prized crops.

Subdivide your lawn

Reduce your mowing by reducing the size of your lawn. Divide lawns into planted areas, islands, and pathways, bordered with small areas of lawn. Or give up part of a front yard as an edible habitat, and grow some healthy superfoods, including **blueberries**, **tomatoes**, **carrots**, **cherries**, and **spinach**. Include some tough and colorful flowering herb plants to attract pollinators and tiny flying pest controllers.

Convert some lawn into a garden, and grow fresh vegetables. Or plant a small patch of wildflower meadow containing tough and colorful cottage garden–style plants.

Replace grass with groundcovers

Plant drought-tolerant, low-growing groundcovers to create a green, fresh mat that requires no mowing or irrigation once established. This is not always a low-maintenance option, though, as even dense areas of groundcovers may require some weed removal. When replacing grass with groundcovers, start with areas where grass doesn't do well. Choose plants based on soil conditions and exposure, and try to plant groupings of single plant varieties together, but give them enough space to mature without crowding each other out. In large areas, weave these plantings to nearby shrubs and trees.

Barren strawberry.
All wild strawberries make excellent groundcovers. Some varieties serve up a sweet treat for wildlife and people too!

Moss makes sense in cool, damp, shady areas where grass does poorly and mowing is awkward.

Sunny areas

Moss phlox *(Phlox subulata)* *
Barren strawberry *(Waldsteinia fragarioides)* *
Wild strawberry *(Fragaria virginiana)* *
Yellow Star Grass *(Hypoxis hirsuta)* *
Bearberry *(Arctostaphylos uva-ursi)* *
Crowberry *(Empetrum nigrum)* *
Sedum spp. **
Pinks *(Dianthus spp.)*
Moss campion *(Silene acaulis)*
Hardy yellow ice plant *(Delospermia nubigenum)*
Woolly speedwell *(Veronica pectinata)*
Creeping thyme *(Thymus serpyllum)*
Common oregano *(Origanum vulgare)*
Fragrant sumac *(Rhus aromatica)* *

*Indicates New England native plant

Shade/Part-Shade

Running foamflower *(Tiarella cordifolia)* *
Wild ginger *(Asarum canadense)* *
Mayapple *(Podophyllum peltatum)* *
Anemone *(Anemone spp.)* **
Canada mayflower *(Maianthemum canadense)* *
Huckleberry *(Gaylussacia spp.)* **
Bunchberry *(Chamaepericlymenum canadensis)* *
Golden star *(Chrysogonum virginianum)*
Wintergreen *(Gaultheria procumbens)* *
Partridgeberry *(Mitchella repens)* *
Allegheny spurge *(Pachysandra procumbens)*
Sedge *(Carex spp.)* **
Foxtail clubmoss* *(Lycopodium clavatum)*
Dwarf scouring rush *(Equisetum scirpoides)* *
Woodland horsetail* *(Equisetum sylvaticum)*

**Indicates some varieties are native

41

Habitat Essentials

Habitat gardening is just like planning and designing the interior of your home. You consider the everyday needs of those you invite into your space, furnish or rearrange the space accordingly, and stock the cupboards well. No matter what types of wildlife you would like to attract, remember the basics. All living things require food, water, shelter (from weather and predators) and a safe place to raise young.

Plant it, and they will come

Plants supply the seeds, berries, nuts, cones, buds, twigs, leaves, sap, flowers, nectar, and pollen that feed many birds and mammals. Plants shade the ground and drop their foliage, feeding soil-dwelling invertebrates and tiny decomposers that break down organic matter into rich soil. Plant foliage feeds many insects that are essential foods for birds, bats, dragonflies, spiders, and other wildlife. Plants also provide shelter from the elements, protection from predators, and safe places to build nests.

Opposite: *Gardens with a mix of old and new trees, evergreen and deciduous vines, shrubs, perennials, grasses , rocks, and other natural objects provide food, nesting, and protection for birds, pollinators, and small creatures that comfortably coexist with us.*

Below: *Insects and their larvae (caterpillars and grubs) are staple foods for most birds.*

Photo © Copyright Pat D. Hemlepp. Used with permission of the photographer

*Can you tell which of these will sting? Not easily. The **sweat bee** (bottom left) are gentle pollinators who won't sting you unless you swat at them. The **braconid wasp** (top) is parasitizing a **gypsy moth caterpillar**. These small and inconspicuous wasps don't have a communal nest to defend, so are unlikely to sting. Pollinating insects that visit flowers are often gobbled by hungry predators, so it's no coincidence that many (**hoverfly**, below right) have evolved stripes like their stinging relatives.*

A toxic-free zone

It might seem counterintuitive to a new gardener, but the presence of a variety of insects in a garden is what keeps it healthy. Insects support most higher lifeforms, either directly or indirectly, and their presence attracts natural enemies such as birds and predatory insects who control their populations naturally. Short-term, pesticides may reduce a pest problem, but most don't discriminate between target pests and beneficial insects, and they destroy an ecosystem's natural balance. Control pests by filling your gardens with a diversity of plants that feed birds and other predators. Birds feed hundreds of insects to their nestlings each day, and in an area with breeding birds, most pests don't stand a chance of multiplying.

Although some microorganisms can adapt and even thrive in toxic habitat, most higher life forms are extremely vulnerable to the presence of pesticides, fungicides and herbicides, and pesticide buildup is increasingly linked to major bee die-offs. Imidacloprid, widely used in the US for grub control, has now been banned in several countries for its impact on honeybees. Many pesticides bioaccumulate through the food chain, with higher members carrying heavy loads.

Plants become a stage for the frenzied dance between prey and predators.

Pictured from top left: **Cedar waxwings** *gorging on berries. A beautiful* **great spangled fritillary butterfly** *sips nectar from the flowers of* **swamp milkweed***, also one of one of the essential foods for the* **monarch butterfly caterpillar** *(middle left). Middle right:* **Monarch butterfly** *in chrysalis form, just before its emergence as an adult.*

Left: *This driveway's edge looks untidy, but birds consider it fine dining! Leave seed stems standing through fall and winter for them to forage.*

45

*The structure of your plantings is important in a habitat garden. In winter, the evergreen **hemlock**, **juniper**, **rhododendron**, and **mountain laurel** provide safe places for birds to shelter. Juniper, with its scratchy foliage that cats dislike, is a good place for a summer birdbath.*

There's safety in thickets

Birds and other wildlife will visit your yard only if they feel safe from cats, hawks, and other predators. And they'll usually only build their nests in spots they instinctively know are safe. Plant groupings of trees, shrubs, and other plants to form thickets where birds can safely feed, take cover, and build nests. Include evergreens such as **spruce**, **juniper**, **pine**, **hemlock**, and **rhododendron** to provide cover and shelter in winter, as well as plants with thorns or twiggy branch structures to protect small songbirds and their nests. Climbing vines connect the ground with the upper tree canopy by traveling in, around, and up any surrounding plants, providing a link between lower and higher levels of the habitat. Connect garden beds, woodland edges, and other boundaries to link habitats and create corridors that provide safe travel between feeding, nesting, and watering areas.

*Many birds have very specific nesting requirements. The **wood thrush** (above left) nests only in shrubs surrounded by tall shade trees. This songbird with a beautiful flute-like song migrates from Mexico and South America to New England's forests in spring, and is suffering population declines because development in northern US forests increases populations of nest predators.*

Above right: ***Bluebirds, tree swallows**, and **wrens**, prefer to nest in tree cavities, but will live in a suitable nest box.*

To create the most biodiversity in your garden, mimic the layered effect found in nature by underplanting large trees with smaller trees and shrubs, adding vines, and covering the ground layer with shorter plants that protect and nurture the soil. Each layer of vegetation you add to your habitat increases the niche habitat conditions available and the number of species your area will support.

Death is an integral part of life. Top: *This **yellow-bellied sapsucker** taps a hole in thin-barked trees, slurps the sweet liquid, and eats insects.* Above: *Climbing vines such as this **trumpet honeysuckle** increases the habitat value of fence posts and bird nesting boxes.*

Kids love to build brushpiles! Many birds and other creatures use brushpiles for cover

Right: *This "high rise" made of old wood provides habitat for birds and nesting for solitary bees that lay eggs in tiny holes.*

Dead or dying wood

In the formal landscape, dead trees are cut down and dead branches removed. However, snag (dead or dying trees) and fallen logs are important microhabitats, providing food and homes for a myriad of living creatures, most of them very tiny. Insects, arthropods, and a host of fungal organisms all make use of old wood, as well as many birds. Try to find opportunities to integrate the shapes and forms of dead or declining trees into your landscape. For a badly damaged tree, cut off only those branches that pose a danger should they fall, and leave as much stump as you can. Fungi will rot down the dead wood into soil; you can speed up the decomposition process by drilling holes or sawing crosscuts in the stump and keeping it moist. Buy edible or medicinal mushroom spores from a supplier and inoculate the stump to create your own edible mushroom factory, at the same time hastening the stump's demise. Use its broken branches to build a log or brushpile as protective shelter and safe sanctuary for wildlife. **Chickadees** and **thrushes**, as well as **chipmunks**, **turtles**, **toads**, and **salamanders** will all use a brushpile for cover, at the same time dining on the **centipedes**, **pillbugs**, and other decomposers working to soften and break down old wood. **Winter wrens** and **white-throated sparrows** nest inside brushpiles, and towhees on the ground underneath. **Hummingbirds, dragonflies,** and **American phoebes** like to perch on the twigs and small branches that protrude from brushpiles.

A relaxed garden style makes yardwork easier on you and better for wildlife. Seed clusters left standing on stems are important bird forage when the snow has buried other food sources

*Gardens mulched with leaves host many insects that feed ground-feeding birds such as **eastern towhees** (above right), **ovenbirds**, and **brown thrashers**.*

A living soil

Lawns and gardens free of chemical fertilizers and pesticides contain soil that feeds and houses life at the base of the food chain. A living soil contains billions of microorganisms, plus larger life forms such as **earthworms, beetles, ants, centipedes, millipedes, slugs, springtails,** and **mites,** which feed on organic and mineral matter and recycle their nutrients back into the soil. Feeding and mulching gardens with any plant material, including compost, dry leaves and bark mulch, builds healthy populations of these beneficial soil organisms. Instead of cleaning your gardens in the fall, allow plant stems to remain in place through the winter and allow leaves to accumulate under trees and shrubs and in beds. Seeds feed hungry winter birds, and many beneficial insects hibernate in leaf litter and hollow plant stems. Leaf litter is also important for declining amphibians such as **toads, frogs** and **salamanders,** who help control soil-dwelling insects.

In spring, you can clean up your beds by gently raking out large debris, but leave some of the plant remains (chop them up with a pruner or a shredder for a neater look) as a nutritious soil mulch. Nature's cleanup crew will break them down into plant food.

*Can you spot the well-camouflaged **American toad** in the leaves? Toads love to eat slugs and other pests! Attract them to areas where garden slugs are a problem with daytime shelter such as a broken terracotta pot turned upside down.*

*Spring-flowering **moss phlox** and **candytuft** thrive with the excellent drainage and shallow soil at the top of a sunny rock wall. **Pinks** bloom afterward.*

Left: *A beautiful streetside garden makes creative use of the rocks uncovered during excavation in this Massachusetts subdivision.*

Leave a few areas of soil undisturbed and untilled to protect underground nest structures excavated by ground-nesting pollinators, including **sand**, **digger**, and **sweat bees**, which lay their eggs in tiny tunnels excavated in bare soil, sandy banks, or under leaf litter. Loose, sandy soils, are nesting habitat for a variety of rare birds and turtles, but, because of shoreline development, recreational use of sandy beaches and dunes, and vehicle traffic in old sandpits, they are among the most heavily disturbed and endangered soil habitats in New England.

Bare and dusty areas are also used by birds to take a dust bath, which they do to balance the oils in their feathers and control parasites.

Rocks and stone walls

Thanks to Ice Age glacial action and our more recent agricultural history, rocks and stone walls are ubiquitous in New England's landscape. Frustrated colonial farmers built stone walls from the rubble that filled their fields. Many are still standing today, providing homes and passageways for wildlife, as well as a visible link to a historical way of life. Unmortared or dry stone walls provide many nooks and crannies where **frogs**, **salamanders**, and **snakes** can hide, and nocturnal mammals such as **bats** can rest during the day. Walls provide protective cover for small mammals and turtles

and other reptiles. Try to incorporate existing rocks and boulders into your landscaping, or "plant" locally sourced rocks into your landscape. The soil underneath will eventually host soil-dwelling arthropods and microbes that live on the minerals leaching from stones, recycling the nutrients for nearby plants to use. Over time, your rocks will develop interesting lichens and mosses that form their own microhabitats. Even steps and paths made of stone slabs can provide homes for invertebrates that tunnel underneath rocks, including **ground beetles** and **pillbugs**, both beneficial decomposers and foods for many creatures.

Water

Without clean water, very wildlife cannot survive for long, especially during winter freezes when many water sources are inaccessible. At the other extreme, a stream, pond, or even a boggy area on or near your property immediately increases the number of wildlife species that can use the area. Best of all, the many beautiful plants that grow in and around water make waterside gardening a joy.

Water isn't difficult to add to your landscape, and birds will usually appear almost immediately if you install a water feature. Water also attracts, **turtles**, **frogs**, **toads**, **salamanders**, **dragonflies**, **damselflies**, **bats**, and other beneficial wildlife. A simple hole dug in the ground, lined with PVC or rubber, can get you started with

*Soft or fluffy materials from **milkweed**, **dandelions**, **thistles**, and **moss** provide nesting materials for birds. **Hummingbirds** use the soft brown fluff from the fronds of **cinnamon fern** to line their nests.*

The sound of moving water is soothing for human visitors, but a landscaped water feature will also attract winged visitors.

Doesn't water attract mosquitoes?

Mosquitoes need standing water to breed. As long as your water circulates (using a pump in an artificial pond, or moving water in a natural waterway), or is refreshed at least once a week, it won't breed mosquitoes. Clean ponds support populations of fish and frogs, which eat mosquito larvae.

a backyard water feature, or you can buy preshaped ponds and waterfalls from garden supply stores. (See page 136 for details of installing a water feature.)

Or place a birdbath under a window, add a solar fountain or dripper, and sit back and enjoy the show. Birds love the sound of moving water and will investigate as soon as they dare.

A muddy area or a sandy seep is habitat to amphibians and many pollinators. Butterflies often gather in mucky or wet areas where they seek mineral salts

Top: *A stone birdbath is shallow enough to provide a perfect drinking hole for* **butterflies** *and other tiny pollinators attracted to nearby flowering plants.*

Above: *Plant foliage collects rainwater and dew that butterflies and other tiny insects can drink. The* **cup plant** *is so-named because the way its leaves intersect the stem, forming a cup that fills with rainwater.*

Pollinators in peril

The honeybee is our best-known pollinator, living in managed hives in orchards or trucked around the country to pollinate food crops. Catastrophic declines in recent years are causing concern about food production and availability but honeybees are not native. They were first brought here from Europe in the 1600s to pollinate crops, because they were familiar and efficient pollinators, and more easily managed than wild bees, which are often solitary and do not live in hives. In New England, however, we have many native pollinators, including **bees**, **wasps**, **butterflies**, **moths**, **beetles**, and **flies**, which not only contribute to crop pollination but are essential to many of our native plants and wildlife. Some are more efficient crop pollinators than honeybees.

Orchard mason (mud) bees forage earlier in the spring, in colder and wetter weather than honeybees, making them especially valuable to fruit tree growers at higher elevations in New England. **Bumblebees** perform something called *buzz pollination*, in which they vibrate their flight muscles inside flowers, dislodging pollen in a way that honeybees cannot. Buzz pollination improves yields for many important crops such as **tomatoes**, **potatoes**, **cranberries**, and **blueberries**. **Leafcutter bees**, so called because they build their nests using small rounded pieces cut from leaves, are valuable pollinators for **carrots** and **legumes**. Studies show that the presence of wild bees in crops that require cross-pollination between male and female plants dramatically improves yields – the presence of other insects makes honeybees restless and more likely to move between flowers. If you grow food crops, diversify your plantings with areas of pollinator-friendly plants to support beneficial insects of all kinds.

Native bees currently don't exist in sufficient numbers to take over pollination of large-scale crops, so they may never replace honeybees in modern agriculture. However, for local-scale crops where they have suitable habitat to live and nest, native bees represent a backup plan for food crop pollination if honeybee populations continue to collapse. Whether or not you grow food crops, planting pollinator-friendly plants and providing undisturbed nesting sites will support thousands of native pollinator species.

American bumblebees have fur, helping them survive cold snaps and trap more pollen than honeybees. Bees have a bad reputation, but most are gentle and will not sting you unless provoked. Most native bees are solitary nesters, laying eggs inside tiny underground tunnels, within plant stems, or behind tree bark, and don't defend their nests.

Choosing Plants for a Natural Habitat Garden

The encouraging news is that, although many birds and other wildlife species are in decline, they can often rebound quickly when their environment improves. However big or small your space, adding as many bird- and insect-friendly plants and trees as possible, especially natives, will immediately support existing populations. Accommodate a variety of appetites and lifestyles by including the following types of plants in your habitat:

- Plants that supply edible seeds, nuts, cones, sap, and fruits at various times of the year
- Flowering plants and trees that produce nectar and pollen
- Plants and trees whose foliage is eaten by caterpillars and other insects, which in turn feed birds, bats, dragonflies, and other insectivores
- Plants that provide cover and protection from predators and the elements, as well as safe nesting opportunities

Flower and grass seeds feed many birds.

Seed and nut plants

Popular garden annuals such as **sunflower, cosmos, calendula, zinnia,** and **cleome** produce lots of seeds to feed birds, and are easy to grow from seeds pushed into the ground in late spring. Perennials and grasses native to our region such as **Joe-Pye weed, aster, liatris, perennial sunflower, goldenrod, little bluestem,** and **switchgrass** are reliable seed producers, and our native birds depend on them for food. See page 59 for the best plants to grow for the benefit of New England birds.

*The **mourning cloak** is one of just a few butterfly species that hibernate in their adult butterfly form in New England, often wintering in wood piles or sheds. When they emerge in early spring, they use flowers such as these pussy willows for nectar.*

*Small berries from spring-flowering native shrubs such as **serviceberry** and **elderberry** (left) are gobbled by **mockingbirds**, **finches**, and **bluebirds** as soon as they ripen. Other berry-bearing natives such as **winterberry** (right) keep their berries much longer, providing valuable winter forage*

Fruiting (berry) plants

Sugary fruits and berries supply energy and fat to supplement most birds' main diet of insects and caterpillars. Include a variety of native fruiting shrubs and trees that flower at different times so that ripe fruits are available when birds need them most. **Serviceberries** (also called **juneberries** or **shadblow**) ripen in June, coinciding with the return of **scarlet tanagers** to New England. **Blueberries**, **wild cherries**, and **elderberries** ripen in summer, with **dogwood**, **sassafras**, and **spicebush** berries (all high in fat) ripening in fall when **hermit thrushes** and **flycatchers** need energy for their travels south. **Viburnum**, **rose hips**, **crabapples**, **holly**, **bayberry**, and **juniper** fruits generally don't ripen until a series of frost and thaw cycles have sweetened them, making them valuable to overwintering **robins**, **cedar waxwings**, and **thrashers** returning the following spring. Fallen orchard fruits feed **pine grosbeaks** through winter.

Some butterflies and other pollinators visit flowers only rarely for nectar but prefer drinking from overripe fruit or the sweet sap that drips from cuts and wounds on trees. **Red-spotted purples**, **question marks**, **admirals**, **viceroys**, and other small butterflies are attracted to fallen fruits and woodpecker holes as well as certain **wasps** and overwintering birds.

Nectar and pollen plants for pollinators

Most flowering plants produce nectar (a high carbohydrate food source for many pollinating insects and birds) and protein-rich pollen, which many insects eat and feed to their young. Try to accommodate the widest variety of pollinator sizes, shapes and tastes by including plants of different flower types, colors and scents in your gardens. Plants with packed clusters of tiny shallow-faced flowers (such as herbs) make nectar accessible to short-tongued pollinators such as hover flies and parasitic wasps, larger flowers attract bumblebees and butterflies, and tubular flowers attract hummingbirds and long-tongued bees. Plants with scented flowers attract many bees, flies, and night-flying moths. A variety of plants blooming at different times from early spring til fall supports a diversity of pollinators, who each need nectar at crucial stages in their life cycle. Many of our native trees also produce flowers at various times of the year, and planting them is easy way for homeowners can help pollinators and many other forms of wildlife.

Goatsbeard flowers attract many tiny pollinating insects in June.
New England aster *flowers are an important late-flowering wildlife plant.*

Old-fashioned, single varieties of flowering plants are better choices for pollinators and birds than cultivars or hybrids. The single **marigold** *at right even has flower markings that facilitate pollination.*

Accept a few chewed leaves on your plants, knowing that the culprits are important bird food.

*Right: **Joe-Pye weed** feeds many birds, butterflies and beneficial insects, and **violets** (top) are the only food plant eaten by fritillary butterfly caterpillars.*

Foliage (food) plants for herbivorous insects

Almost every type of insect eats plants, and most are specialized to feed only from specific plants or plant families. The sheer biomass provided by the foliage and needles of native trees, and the diversity of insects they support, makes native trees much more valuable to wildlife than imported trees, although some native insects have adapted to foreigners. **Apple trees**, for example, are not native to the US, but some native insects—adapted to eat native **wild cherries**, **serviceberries**, or **hawthorns**—can survive on foliage of the closely-related **Asian crabapple** hybrids. When in doubt, choose a native variety.

Easy Annuals

Annuals provide a quick and easy way to attract birds and pollinators in a sunny area. Annuals flower and go to seed the same summer you plant them, producing lots of free bird seed, and they're perfect for filling spaces between young perennials and shrubs in the first year or two after planting. Collect seeds from your favorite plants, and replant them every year.

Zinnia spp.

Ornamental millet (*Pennisetum* spp.)

Cockscomb (*Celosia* spp.)

Sunflower (*Helianthus annuus*)

Spider flower (*Cleome hassleriana*)

Salvia spp.

Verbena spp.

Larkspur (*Delphinium consolida*)

Bachelor's button (*Centauria cyanis*)

Cosmos spp.

Calendula spp.

Four o'clocks (*Mirabilis jalapa*)

Marigold (*Tagetes* spp.)

Flowering tobacco (*Nicotiana* spp.)

*Plants with large petals such as **rudbeckia** (below) and **echinacea** provide butterflies with landing pads to rest while they drink.*

*Right: **Calendula** and **cosmos** are easy nectar and seed plants that add color to any garden.*

The fluffy late summer blooms of **Muhly grass** *seed plumes contrast beautifully with* **New England aster** *at Coastal Maine Botanic Gardens.*

Dogwoods (**gray dogwood** *berries, below left) and* **viburnums** *are excellent native shrubs for birds.*

Below right: **Virginia creeper** *is a twining native vine perfect for sprawling over an old wall, and its habit of climbing trees makes it a hit with nesting birds.*

Seed and Nectar Perennials and Grasses

Black-eyed Susan (*Rudbeckia* spp.)
Black cohosh (*Actaea racemosa*) *
Blazing star (*Liatris* spp.) **
Coneflower (*Echinachea* spp.)
Perennial sunflower and Jerusalem artichoke
   (*Helianthus spp.*) *
Agastache spp., including hyssop
Goldenrod (*Solidago* spp.) *
Coreopsis spp. **
Aster spp.*

Joe-Pye weed (*Eutrochium*) and boneset
   (*Eupatorium perfoliatum*) *
Mountain mint (*Pychnanthemum*) *
Wild ageratum (*Conoclinium coelistinum*)
Catmint (*Nepeta* spp.)
Sedum spp. **
Switchgrass, northern sea oats, Indian grass,
   little and big bluestem, muhly grass *
Sedge (*Carex* spp.) **
Rush (*Juncus* spp.) **

Nectar and Fruiting Shrubs and Small Trees

Summer Fruiting

Serviceberry/juneberry
(*Amelanchier* spp.) *

Wild strawberry (*Fragaria virginiana*)*

Red mulberry (*Morus rubra*) *

Blueberry (*Vaccinium*) *

Blackberry, raspberry, bramble (*Rubus*)**

Fall Fruiting

Elderberry (*Sambucus*) **

Spicebush (*Lindera benzoin*) *

Viburnum spp.**

Dogwood (*Cornus* spp.) **

Plum and cherry (*Prunus* spp.) **

Mountain ash (*Sorbus* spp.) **

Sweetbay magnolia (*Magnolia virginiana*)*

Persistent Winter Fruits

Holly (*Ilex* spp.) **

Rose (*Rosa* spp.) **

Highbush cranberry (*Viburnum opulus*) *

Chokeberry (*Photinia* spp.) *

Bayberry (*Morella pensylvanica*) *

Juniper (*Juniperus* spp.) **

Sumac (*Rhus* spp.) *

Crabapple (*Malus* spp.)

Hawthorn (*Crataegus* spp.) **

Snowberry (*Symphoricarpos albus*) **

Nectar, Seed, Berry and Nut Perennial Vines

Trumpet honeysuckle
(*Lonicera sempervirens*) *

Virginia creeper
(*Parthenocissus quinquefolia*) *

American bittersweet
(*Celastrus scandens*) *

Virgin's bower (*Clematis virginiana*) *

Wild grape (*Vitis* spp.) **

Groundnut (*Apios americana*) *

Plants for Nesting and Cover

Juniper, eastern redcedar
(*Juniperus* spp.) **

Hemlock (*Tsuga canadensis*) *

Cedar, arborvitae (*Thuja* spp.) **

Yew (*Taxus* spp.) **

Pine (*Pinus* spp.) **

Rhododendron
(*Rhododendron* spp.) **

False Cypress, White Cedar
(*Chamaecyparis*) **

Balsam Fir (*Abies balsamea*) *

Rose (*Rosa* spp.)**

Raspberry and blackberry **
(*Rubus* spp.)

Viburnum spp.**

Dogwood (*Cornus* spp.) **

Apple and crabapple (*Malus* spp.)

Hawthorn (*Crataegus* spp.) **

Ninebark (*Physocarpus opulifolius*) *

Cherry (*Prunus* spp.) **

* Indicates New England native

** Indicates some varieties are native

*Plants with scratchy or thorny stems such as **wild rose**, **hawthorn**, and **juniper** make things a little, er, uncomfortable for predators. The evergreen juniper provides protective cover through the year.*

61

Important Butterfly and Moth Caterpillar Food (Host) Plants and Trees

Tortoiseshell	Plants in the *Salicaceae* family, including willow, poplar, cottonwood. Also nettle.
Tiger Swallowtail	Members of the *Rosaceae* family, including cherry, apple, crabapple, rose, raspberry, blackberry, bramble, hawthorn, serviceberry, ninebark, spirea, chokeberry, mountain-ash, potentilla. Also, *Salicaceae family*, magnolia, tulip poplar.
Spicebush Swallowtail	Spicebush and sassafras
Black Swallowtail	Dill, parsley, fennel, carrot, purple-stem angelica, golden alexander, rue
Pipevine Swallowtail	Dutchman's Pipe
Monarch	Milkweed
Underwing	**Heath plants** such as blueberry, cranberry, azalea, rhododendron, Labrador tea, leucothoe, laurel, sweetfern, bearberry.
Blue, Azure and Emerald	*Rosaceae* family. Also, dogwood, New Jersey tea, viburnum, coralberry, legumes, Heath plants, sumac, poison ivy, elm, hackberry.
White and Red Admiral	*Fagacaea* family, including oak, beech and chestnut trees. Also, Rosaceae family, Salicaceae family, nettle
Checkerspot, Pearl Crescent	*Asteracaea* family, including aster, ironweed, helianthus, eupatorium, thistle, hollyhock, pearly everlasting and mallow. Honeysuckle, white turtlehead.
Painted Lady	**Legumes**, including clover, vetch, wild indigo, wild blue lupine, showy tick-trefoil. Also, hollyhock and mallow.
Red-spotted Purple	Rosaceae family, Salicaceae family, Asteraceae family. Also, magnolia, tulip poplar
Luna Moth	*Juglandaceae* family, including hickory, walnut, butternut
Sphinx, Hawk, Tiger Moths	Members of the *Betula* family, including birch, alder, hazelnut and American hornbeam trees. Also, heath plants, conifers, buttonbush, fringetree, viburnum, coralberry, snowberry, honeysuckle, Virginia creeper, grape, sundrops, evening primrose, bee balm, mountain mint, plantain, snapdragon, gerardia, toadflax, nettle.
Silkworm moths	Magnolia and tulip poplar, spicebush, sassafras, Rosaceae family, Fagaceae family, conifers, buttonbush, American wisteria
Common Wood Nymph, Little Wood Satyr	**Native grasses** such as big bluestem, switchgrass, purple lovegrass, and little bluestem. Also buttonbush, Virginia creeper, grape.
Slant-line, pine devil, geometer	**Conifers** including juniper, pine, fir, spruce and larch. Betulaceae family, Heath plants.
Prominent	Members of the *Aceraceae* family, including Maple and Box Elder trees. Elm, hackberry, legumes.

Hairstreak and Elfin	Rosaceae family, Fagacaea family, Betula family, Juglandaceae family, ash, conifers, legumes, heath plants, sumac, poison ivy, wild strawberry.
Sulphur	Legumes,
Mourning Cloak	Ash, elm, hackberry, Salicaceae family.
Viceroy	Elm, hackberry, Salicaceae family.
Checkered and Mustard White	Cabbage, mustard, and peppergrass
Question Mark	Salicaceae family, elm, hackberry, nettle
Comma	Elm, hackberry, Salicaceae family.
Fritillary	Violet
Common Buckeye	Plantain, snapdragon, gerardia, toadflax.
Dagger moth	Aceraceae family, Juglandaceae family.
Skipper, Black Dash, Edge, Duskywing	Native grasses. Also, sedge, legumes, Salicaceae family, New Jersey tea, Fagacaea family, American wisteria, groundnut.

*Trees improve air quality, prevent flooding, and help keep water supplies clean. The mighty **oak tree** (pictured) is the most valuable native tree in the eastern US for butterfly and moth caterpillars.*

"*Fairy wings...suspended as if by magic...flitting from one flower to another, with motions as graceful as they are light and airy.*"
JOHN JAMES AUDUBON

Inviting Hummingbirds to Your Garden

Hummingbirds may be tiny, but they are highly territorial, feisty, and chances are, they'll quickly become your favorite summertime visitors! New England's native "hummer" is the ruby-throated hummingbird, which breeds here in summer and migrates south in winter in a grueling flight across the Gulf of Mexico. Hummingbirds measure 3½ inches, with wings that beat dozens of times per second, allowing them fly 50 miles per hour, and swoop in highly agile maneuvers. They can even fly backwards.

Hummingbird need to eat twice their body weight in insects each day just to survive! They eat insects "on the wing," catching them in midair, and they fuel these agile flights by drinking sugary nectar and tree sap. To invite hummingbirds, plant their favorite

Ruby-throated hummingbirds love red flowers, and they go wild for the bee balm in the author's garden.

plants, and hang nectar feeders in an open area near shrubs and trees. Twigs provide perches for hummingbirds, and they will vigorously defend your plantings or feeders from other winged creatures they perceive as threats—including bees!). If you wear red, you might even find yourself eye-to-eye with a hummingbird taking a good look at you.

Hummingbirds love to fly through water. Construct a simple water sprayer for them by fixing a hose attachment set to "mist" onto a trellis. Plant the trellis with cardinal climber or another hummingbird vine, and sit back and enjoy the show!

Starting in March, migrating ruby-throats leave their winter habitat in Central America and fly toward the United States. Eventually many find their way to New England, where just a few months of hot weather provides the lush breeding habitat they favor.

Fill and hang your hummingbird feeders starting on April 1. The first migrating males fly into New England in early April to scope out potential feeding grounds and take advantage of the first blooming nectar plants and sap from newly drilled sapsucker holes. Females arrive several weeks later. If they like what they find, migrants may choose your habitat as their summer home.

Hummingbirds head south starting in mid-August, and the last pass through New England in October. Help them fuel up for their long journey by including nectar plants that flower in late summer and early fall, and keeping feeders clean and filled.

Feeder tips:

Fill hummingbird feeders with a solution of one part sugar dissolved in four parts hot water. Do not use red dye, which is unnecessary, and is not considered safe for hummingbirds.

Clean feeders regularly with a few drops of dish soap and hot water and scrub all parts with a long brush. To prevent mold from forming, immerse the feeder in a solution of one part bleach to nine parts water, rinse, and allow to dry. It's especially important to clean feeders regularly in hot weather when the sugar water can ferment and sicken birds.

A nectar feeder brings hummingbirds where you can watch them. Hummingbirds will investigate anything red.

A habitat garden buzzing with insect life and planted with hummingbird favorites such as **columbine** *provides what hungry hummingbirds need.*

Hummingbirds love drinking the nectar from the flowers of **rhododendron**, **mountain laurel**, *and* **foxglove**. *Look for females picking at spider webs to use as a sticky binding material for their nests.*

The Best Hummingbird Nectar Plants for New England

Annuals
Fuschia *(Gartenmeister Bonstedt)*
Flowering tobacco *(Nicotiana alata)*
Scarlet sage "Lady in Red" *(Salvia coccinea)*
Cigar plant *(Cuphea ignea)*
Scarlet runner bean *(Phaseolus coccineus)*
Cardinal climber and cypress vine *(Ipomoea)*
Jewelweed *(Impatiens capensis)* *

Perennials:
Cardinal flower *(Lobelia cardinalis)* *
Heuchera **
Red columbine *(Aquilegia canadense)* *
Bee balm *(Monarda didyma)* *
Agastache
Foxglove *(Digitalis purpurea)*
Beardtongue *(Penstemon)* **
Canada lily *(Lilium canadense)* *

Perennial Vines
Trumpet honeysuckle *(Lonicera sempervirens)* *
Trumpet creeper *(Campsis radicans)*

Shrubs and Trees
Weigela
Summersweet *(Clethra altinifolia)**
Flowering quince *(Chaenomeles speciosa)*
Rhododendron and azalea *(Rhododendron)* **
Red buckeye *(Aesculus pavia)*
Cherry *(Prunus)* **
Crabapple *(Malus)*

* Indicates New England native
** Indicates some varieties are native

Moths . . . not just invaders of closets

Many fly at night, so you may not always notice them. But American moth species outnumber butterfly species by 14:1, making them an important food for birds, bats, and other species. Some are gray and drab, but New England hosts an amazing array of striking moths that rival the most beautiful butterfly in elegance and color. Although some moths are classified as pests, most of these are imported moths to which our native trees have no built-up resistance. And fewer than 0.01 percent of moth species invade closets! Some moths are important pollinators of night-blooming plants, especially fragrant ones.

Sphinx or hawk moths are common pollinators that visit mostly light-colored fragrant plants that bloom after dark. Some have tongues longer than their bodies, and plants with moth-pollinated flowers tend to have spurs (tubes) just the right length for certain species to access. Moths are often attracted to porch lights, although they can drive themselves to exhaustion in the process. Sphinx moth caterpillars are hornworms, large caterpillars with fierce-looking appendages to intimidate predators. In gardens, leaf damage to tomato plants, as well large fecal pellets on foliage, are a giveaway to their presence.

New England's giant silkworm moths include the lime-green, graceful luna moth, the cecropia, polyphemus, promethea, and io moths. With wingspans up to 5 inches, they are related to the silkworms in China used to produce silk, although attempts to develop an industry around American silkworms were unsuccessful.

Adult silkworm moths live only one week, mating and laying eggs. They lack mouthparts and don't feed on or pollinate plants. Caterpillars eat the leaves of many deciduous trees, and then spin silk threads to attach themselves to twigs or leaves. In winter, look for cocoons in leaf litter or grass under their favorite shrubs and trees, which include oak, maple, birch, hickory, beech, willow, apple, cherry, larch, poplar, sassafras, and ash.

Silkworm moths were more common in New England before pesticide use became common, and their favorite food, the American chestnut tree, was virtually wiped out by a blight in the early 1900s. Populations have also been decimated by a European parasitic fly introduced to this country as a control against gypsy moth caterpillars; the fly unfortunately also developed a taste for silkworm caterpillars.

Large tolype moths (Tolype velleda) *sport a furry scarf and tail. Their caterpillars are generalists, feeding at night on a variety of native trees.*

Hummingbird clearwing moths are day fliers that often visit gardens.

The unmistakable luna moth looks as though it belongs in the tropics.

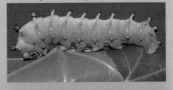

The beautiful but declining cecropia silk moth.

Planning Your Natural Habitat Landscape

Check out the neighborhood

Look around your neighborhood and notice what kinds of vegetation exist. Is it woodsy with houses here and there? Is it urban, but with a few parks and patches of open space here and there? What grows in them? How much habitat diversity is there?

Use a free Internet service such as Google Maps to view satellite photographs of your area. Are you near a river or swampy area? Look at the topography. Are you on the side of a large sloping hill or valley?

Look for realistic opportunities to integrate your site into the natural landscape. Every piece of land has the capability of sustaining a certain number of species, called its carrying capacity. The larger the property, the larger the number of species it can support. But even the smallest city lot can provide "pocket" habitat for butterflies, invertebrates, and insects, along with birds that eat them. Some insects may complete their entire life cycles in an area the size of a shoebox, and some creatures require a minimum of 250 acres to live. By understanding your site's attributes, you can enhance existing microhabitats to increase their size, strength, and ecological value. Or, you can decide to re-create habitat that is locally extinct with native plants that support specialized wildlife such as rare butterflies and moths.

Look for ways to connect existing plants and trees to create screening, privacy, and travel corridors for wildlife. Add understory to your existing trees, and team with your neighbors to create larger habitats that support a wider diversity of wildlife than small, disconnected areas.

In the middle of a new housing development Nothing but a few young specimen trees and lots of lawn? Dot your property with as many large native trees as you can afford, and link them with groupings of flowering native shrubs to feed and shelter birds year-round. Add moisture-loving plants to areas that flood occasionally. Underplant trees and shrubs with groundcovers to create understory habitat. Reduce your lawn by adding beds of edible and flowering plants. Add a water feature with moving water to screen traffic noise and lure birds.

Woodsy area with houses dotted here and there? Try to link your property with nearby natural woodlands. Identify the trees growing in your woods, and encourage them to expand their populations into your yard to contribute to forest habitat communities. If you like a lawn, keep your formal lawn area near the house, but allow a woodland edge to develop near your property line.

In the midst of open fields? If you live in one of the remaining areas of New England dominated by open fields or farmland, consider creating a small habitat island on your property consisting of trees and shrubs to provide cover and shelter for birds. Include evergreens as winter windbreaks. Add a water feature.

On the water? If you live next to a stream, pond, or lake, plant a buffer zone of plants along the water's edge to help keep the water clean and improve habitat for birds and aquatic wildlife. (See page 119.)

Near water or wetlands? Add thickets of native shrubs, vines, and plants to attract the many insect-gobbling creatures that live within ½ mile of a water source. If your property is moist, plant native wetland plants to maintain wildlife populations. (See page 132.)

Got space? If you own a large acreage, manage areas of it as early successional habitat to increase your property's carrying capacity for declining New England wildlife species. Over 250 acres of forest? Keep the forest intact to provide contiguous woods for birds and mammals that require it to nest. (See pages 111-113.)

New England's native turtle populations are in steep decline due to development and roads near their aquatic habitats.

*The Massachusetts Butterfly Club replanted **flat-topped asters** along utility rights-of-way to bring populations of **Harris's checkerspot butterflies** (pictured) back from the brink. If you have sandy soil with sun, plant the native wild **blue lupine** (below) to help endangered **Karner blue** butterflies.*

Sandy soil? Undeveloped areas of sandy soil are rare in New England due to development and suppression of natural fires, which keeps growth low. If you live on a sand deposit or along a sandy coastline, help restore this disappearing habitat by growing plants native to sandy, acidic soils. (See page 125.)

Big development nearby? Although digging up wild plants is illegal, a plant rescue is an opportunity to sustain native plant populations otherwise displaced by development. Arrange to dig up native plants and relocate them. Contact a local native plant society for help and advice (See page 215). Take a note of the habitat being destroyed, and try to replant your refugees in conditions similar to where they were growing.

Take a hike in nearby natural areas for inspiration. Notice how nature keeps every inch of earth covered.

Pictured: ***Blueberry*** *and* ***larch*** *growing in an Ossipee, NH bog.*

Read your landscape

Every yard in New England has its own unique growing conditions that are as variable as New England's weather. Analyze your surroundings so you can most effectively landscape it:

- Use a compass to identify north, south, east and west
- Take some time to learn the daily and seasonal patterns of sunlight as it moves across your property. Look for the amount of sunlight or shade that hits different areas at different times of the year. Is there an area in total shade in winter when the sun is at its lowest in the southern sky? Certain evergreen plants such as rhododendron and hollies can burn if exposed to harsh winter sun.
- Look for microclimates. You may have one area with growing conditions quite different than the rest of the property. Are there areas where the snow melts first? Warmer microclimates occur on the south sides of houses, on south-facing slopes, near water, and next to stone walls and ledge outcroppings. Take advantage of those areas to grow plants that enjoy heat.
- Note areas where wind patterns seem particularly strong. New England's winds come mainly

from the west, but some of the worst winter storms funnel howling wind and moisture from the northeast. Winter winds can damage evergreen foliage. Windbreaks containing shrubs and trees can deflect wind from your house and gardens.

- Send for a detailed analysis of your garden soil. The physical and chemical makeup of your soil is unique, and the results of a test will help you determine the plants and wildlife that can thrive in your habitat.

- Pick up a handful of soil and rub it between your fingers to examine its structure. Sandy soil will feel gritty and will not hold together, and water drains quickly through it. Clay is heavy, sticky, water cannot flow through it well, and it is easily molded. Silty soil is somewhere in between. The best soil for planting crumbles easily and absorbs water quickly, yet drains easily. Darker soil contains more organic matter, and lighter means less organic matter.

- Look for areas that are subject to flooding or become very dry in summer. These are indications of poor or good drainage. Rainwater that persistently puddles or bubbles up can indicate a high water table or underground.

- Is your terrain sloped or flat? Gardens on slopes usually drain well. Note any high and low spots. Low spots are usually colder and moister, but also more protected from temperature extremes. Soil at the bottoms of slopes tends to be deeper and richer from years of soils drifting down from above.

- How much human disturbance has there been over the years? Is this a new homesite on a subdivision where most of the living topsoil has been removed or compacted? Or has your property been mostly untouched by heavy machinery or logging within the last half century?. Undisturbed areas have high ecological value, because they contain stable soil life and vestiges of intact native soil. Subsoil or compacted soil can be rejuvenated with organic material to rebuild soil structure and improve growing conditions.

- Identify the plants and trees already growing on your property.

Get your soil tested

All plants have their own requirements for the soils where they can grow. Soil conditions differ across New England, although most are generally acidic (pH between 5.0 and 5.8). There are pockets of limestone with a higher pH (alkalinity) scattered around the region. Home soil testing kits are inexpensive but are nowhere near as effective as having a detailed soil test from a lab, which provides information on organic content and soil type, as well as specific recommendations for soil amendments based on what you plan to grow. Once you know your soil type and pH levels, you can choose plants that grow naturally in those soils. Or add soil amendments and organic fertilizers to raise or lower the pH levels to one more acceptable. Traditional lawn grasses as well as most nonnative food plants prefer a neutral to alkaline pH, so if your soil is acidic, apply organic soil amendments to increase pH, and inoculate your soil with the soil microbes that help neutralize it. (See page 153) If your property holds builders' rubble containing mortar, your soil may be alkaline.

Remember that different areas of your property may be quite different from each other. So if you plan to landscape in several areas, have the soil tested in each. Take separate soil samples from the highest and lowest area of your property, any gardens where soil has been trucked in or excavated, and any wet or boggy areas.

*If you live in woods, especially in an area rich in limestone, you can grow interesting and pretty woodland plants such as **lady's slipper** (pictured) and **merrybells**.*

Limestone and calcium-rich areas

Pockets of alkaline soil exist in New England, including the Connecticut River and Lake Champlain valleys, occurring around outcrops of calcareous bedrock such as limestone, dolomite, and marble. Soils here have a higher pH, offering opportunities to grow plants that otherwise do not thrive in New England's typically acidic soil. At the same time, don't waste your time trying to grow many of New England's acid-loving natives that won't tolerate your sweeter soil.

Take an inventory

What kinds of plants grow in your neighborhood? Invest in a plant identification guide or find a garden coach to help. Chances are you'll find many (or mostly!) exotic plants with Asian and European origins. Probably lots of invasive plants, too. Look carefully and you may be able to find some native plants still hanging on. Note any existing birds or other wildlife, and the structure of the areas where they spend time.

   If you do find native plants, try to integrate them into your landscape design. Each native plant population, however small, is important to maintaining genetic diversity within its species, and at least some of your plants likely represent remnants of historical plant populations.

   Use existing vegetation to plan your plant choice and design. A plant's presence reveals much about the soil type, light, drainage,

This naturalized meadow is mowed only once every few years to keep it from turning back into forest.

and other conditions. For example, if you see white pine, sweetfern, and pink lady's slipper, the soil there is probably fairly dry and acidic. Hemlock trees, cinnamon fern and Jack-in-the-pulpit indicate soils high in moisture.

Identify any nonnative invasive plants to be removed or controlled. (See page 147.) Removing them from your property makes room for native plants and associated wildlife, and you may be amazed at what natives will rebound once invasives are removed.

Work with what you've got

All plants have requirements for the amount and quality of light they need, as well as soil structure and fertility. After evaluating your property, research plants that match your conditions. It's much easier to grow plants already suited for your garden than to modify your garden to meet the needs of the plants you want to grow. In the Plant Guide (see page 169) are descriptions of each plant's optimal growing conditions. Some species can grow in a wide range of environmental conditions, and this is indicated too.

Become a selective weeder

The passive approach to creating natural gardens is to stop mowing, and watch what seeds itself in. You'll need to remove any invasive plants as they pop up, but you will probably also find asters, ferns, and a few sedges begin to appear, along with a vine or two. Eventually woody shrubs and tree seedlings will appear in the natural process called succession. Depending on your taste, interest, and available time, you need to decide the right level of controlling succession in your backyard.

In New England, the ground never stays bare for long. Our soil is a great seed bank, with seeds from plants of decades ago lying dormant, awaiting the opportunity to grow. Nature never misses an opportunity to fill a niche, so if you stop weeding or mowing, weeds are guaranteed to appear. Although many birds frequent weedy areas, the reality is that most of our common weeds are invasive, nonnative plants. As such, unmanaged wild areas are biologically doomed ecosystems. When an area fills with imports, its natural evolution comes to a screeching halt.

Staghorn sumac is an early successional shrub that can be used for habitat islands in lawns.

*If a sunny area is left unmowed, plants such as **goldenrod** and **Joe-Pye weed** will begin to colonize in the first stage of succession.*

Timeline for creating a habitat garden

Start small, work in phases, and become familiar with your plants and growing conditions. Understand that creating gardens is a process and a learning experience. You may find that your taste and appreciation of how your garden evolves may change over time. What once seemed messy is now alive, dynamic, and beautiful.

Year 1:
Get your soil tested and research plants suitable for your soil.
Identify the plants growing on your property, including any native plants to be encouraged, or invasive plants to be removed.

Start a compost pile.

Plant native trees and shrubs to get them established while you plan other areas. Plant at recommended distances apart so that they will form dense but not overcrowded groupings when mature. Plant young seedlings of native shrubs and trees near existing shrubs or trees nearing the end of their lives to begin the cycle of replacing nonnative exotic shrubs or trees..

Mulch around new plants with leaf mulch, well-rotted compost, or other organic materials such as untreated tree bark or partially decomposed wood chips to promote soil microbial life and suppress weeds.

Start the process of creating a woodland garden by allowing leaves to remain where they fall. Leave plant stems in beds to feed winter birds and provide wintertime shelter for beneficial insects.

In the fall, rake excess leaves into piles or add them to a compost pile. As plants seed themselves in, identify and remove existing invasives, and allow nature to regenerate at its own pace.

Leave an area or edge in your yard unmowed to begin the process of reestablishing native plants.

Try to find an area in your yard that you can let "go wild."

Years 1 – 2:

Use no-till method to convert areas of lawn to garden beds. (See page 155.)

Plant perennials in groups of three, five, or larger.

Sow seeds of annuals in beds before rain is forecast, to add quick color and interest while perennials are establishing, and to attract birds and pollinators. Allow them to reseed, or collect seeds for future sowing.

Install low wire fencing to protect new plants from dogs and kids.

Continue to identify any weeds or plants that seed themselves in, immediately removing any invasives. Allow desirable seedlings to remain where they are, or move them to other locations.

Years 2+

Assess the condition of your plants. Move any unhappy plants to more suitable spots, or replace them with divisions or seedlings from other plants that are thriving. Continue to add more beds and link them to existing gardens.

Design Ideas for Naturalizing your Gardens

You may already have a few foundation shrubs plus a flower bed or two with typical garden flowers, but you want your garden to feel less formal, not actually wild but more natural. You may also want your garden to reflect the progression of the seasons, but still provide color and interest year-round.

*A native American cottage garden containing **butterfly weed**, **blue lobelia**, **phlox**, **gayfeather**, **Joe-Pye weed**, **Culver's root**, **columbine**, **goldenrod**, and **violets**.*

Plant large groupings of plants, include a variety of heights and shapes, and try to link with adjoining natural areas. Eliminate straight lines using curving, meandering beds punctuated with vertical elements. Loosen transitions between plant types and colors. Just by adding a few tall, narrow, and wispy plants near the front of a bed creates a more natural effect. Scattering tall annuals such as **Brazilian verbena**, **salvia**, and **cosmos** can also add to a brimming-with-flowers, cottage garden look.

Allow seedlings of your favorite plants to place themselves in your garden. This evokes the random placings of nature, while allowing plants to find the niche areas where they are best suited. Garden author Rick Darke calls this a "directed serendipity to your landscape art." You can edit the scene as needed, by transplanting seedlings or giving them to friends. Reseeding is often the only way to maintain populations of short-lived perennials such as cardinal flower, especially in moist soils where root competition is fierce. And transplanting your favorite seedlings throughout your gardens allows you to create a harmonious design through repetition of a single plant, color, style, or theme.

You evolve as a habitat gardener—it's less about controlling the process and more about editing/guiding. Be flexible. Enjoy the process and always let nature help you along.

Can you reduce the size of your lawn but still keep an open area for kids to play? Situate high-maintenance gardens closer to the house.

Below: Borrow distant views by scattering groupings of shrubs and trees in your lawn to frame views and reduce lawn areas.

Choose plants for interest across the seasons

Traditional gardens have one spectacular season (usually spring or summer) but drop out of the race the rest of the year. Using a variety of plants with multi-season interest, makes the most of your garden space, and keeps it more interesting. Spring-flowering wildflowers ensure your garden a burst of glorious color in early spring, and are often more reliable than tulips and other exotics, which can peter out after a few years or become food for rodents. Some native wildflowers are spring ephemerals, which bloom for a few weeks and then go dormant for the summer. Others retain their foliage through much of the year, keeping the ground covered and fading into the background to allow other plants their moment of glory. Many spring-flowering shrubs produce colorful berries later in the year as well as attractive fall foliage. Evergreen and semi-evergreen perennials and shrubs provide color and interest through the winter. Grasses are a essential components of fall and winter landscapes, when waving stems with seed plumes feed birds. Many perennials form seed heads that provide a dramatic winter effect.

*Spring wildflowers light up a woodland garden and feed early pollinators. **Crabapple** fruits add color to a winter landscape and feed hungry **cardinals** when food is scarce.*

Crisp edges add formality.

Right: *Gardens edged with flat cobblestones make mowing a breeze at Park-McCullough in Vermont.*

Top: *this vegetable garden at Tower Hill Botanic Garden illustrates how flowering plants and colorful garden implements can unify the chaotic color and textures of a vegetable plot.* Below: *Scatter herbs such as dill throughout your garden to attract beneficial insects, and for cooking.*

Define edges and lines

Any type of edging adds "formal" to a scene, and a crisp mowed edge to a naturalized area suggests a deliberate effect rather than neglect. Hard edging keeps grass out and soil or mulch in. Flush bricks with lawn to reduce the need for hand trimming. Spade-cut edging needs seasonal recutting, but is simple and neat. Even a small rustic garden fence enclosing a wildlife garden helps define the area.

If you like a cultivated, manicured garden, in which plants are arranged in a formal style with sharp contrasts of form and color, straight lines, and geometric patterns, you'll have to be religious about weeding, but it's possible to naturalize even a formal border. A natural Zen-style garden based on minimal plant material and contrasting hard structures can create an ordered look, and by using natural materials such as bark mulch, stone, moss, and boulders you can discourage weed growth and create an attractive, natural landscape that needs minimal weeding.

Combine edible and flowering plants

Vegetable gardeners know marigolds in a vegetable garden not only make the garden beautiful, but also help repel pests. Interplanting vegetables with flowering plants, herbs, and annuals attracts pollinators, ensuring good vegetable crops, as well as attracting birds and bats that keep your crops pest-free.

Grow vertical with vines

Grow flowering vines up a wall, trellis, arbor, or pergola to create privacy and supply nesting for birds. By their very nature, vines like to travel in search of light, so choose vine species carefully for the space available. **Virginia creeper** *(above left)* is a native vine with spectacular fall foliage that can be used to cover a brick wall, but it will creep under wooden siding unless trimmed. Vines such as eastern **native honeysuckle** are less aggressive, and excellent for creating a habitat thicket in a shrub border or along a fence. Annual vines are even safer for creating quick, temporary, vertical habitat .

*Above right: This **American wisteria** at Arnold Arboretum in Boston is a beautiful southern US native flowering vine that makes a less aggressive alternative to Asian wisteria, which can destroy buildings when left unchecked.*

Annual Vines:
Sweet pea *(Lathyrus odoratus)*

Cardinal climber and **morning glory** *(Ipomoea spp.)*

Scarlet runner bean *(Phaseolus coccineus)*

Nasturtium spp. (vining types)

Moonflower *(Ipomoea alba)*

Black-eyed Susan vine *(Thunbergia alata)*

Perennial Vines:
Dutchman's pipe *(Aristolochia spp.)*

American bittersweet *(Celastrus scandens)* *

American wisteria *(Wisteria frutescens)*

Virginia creeper *(Parthenocissus quinquefolia)* *

Fox grape *(Vitis labrusca)* *

Groundnut *(Apios americana)* *

Trumpet, hairy, and limber honeysuckle
(Lonicera spp.) *

* Indicates New England native plant

Top left: *The photo cannot convey the intoxicating scent of* **summersweet**. *This plant has a strong fragrance to tempt pollinators at a time of year when flowers compete with many others for pollinators.*

Right: **Jack-in-the-pulpit** *is an interesting native plant that tempts pollinators into its flowers by releasing a putrid smell similar to the rotting tissue where some flies lay their eggs.*

Bottom left: **Sweet alyssum** *is an old-fashioned, easy-to-grow, reseeding annual for gardens. It blooms right up until frost, attracting many types of tiny beneficial insects.*

Fragrance . . . and the Act of Floral Deception

We can thank insects for the fragrance that we enjoy in flowers, because plants produce scent to lure pollinators. Bees, especially, are drawn to heavily scented flowers such as **summersweet, lilac, rose, heliotrope,** and **sweet pea.** Plants such as **evening primrose** have adapted to open their lemon-scented yellow flowers only after sundown, when night-flying moths are active. In some cases, plants can even mimic the smell of decaying tissue or animal dung to lure carrion flies and dung beetles looking for nesting opportunities. Highly evolved plants such as **Jack-in-the-pulpit, skunk cabbage,** and **red trillium** even have flask-shaped flowers that trap unsuspecting visitors inside. As flies thrash around trying to escape, they ensure good pollination.

Plant in large drifts

Generous sweeps of plants tend to have greater visual impact than a few dotted here and there, and large drifts of bold colors attract hummingbirds, butterflies, and other pollinators. Although expensive, planting new beds in groups of three or five of the same plant fills a garden much more quickly than single plants. Planting in odd numbers is pleasing to the eye, and for many flowering shrubs, a good landscaping solution is to plant in groupings of three to enable insect pollination, improve fruit set, and create optimal shrub nesting for birds.

Butterflies are nearsighted, and are more likely to find a garden full of strong colors than a few plants here and there

Below: *Vermont's Hildene estate*

*The red **bee balm** on this pond bank pulls hummingbirds right out of the sky. Most bees cannot see red flowers, but the red blooms of bee balm reflect ultraviolet light, which attracts long-tongued bees to pollinate the blossoms.*

Solitary ground-nesting bees don't see well, but can easily spot light-colored flowers contrasted with surrounding green, such as this **white boneset**.

Old-fashioned single **Korean mums** (Dendranthema) *bloom right through November in this central Massachusetts garden.)*

Sex...shrub-style! *Planting berrying shrubs in groups of three improves berry production and creates the twiggy shrub habitat that many birds prefer. Many shrubs, including the native* **viburnum** *family (pictured) berry best when their flowers are cross-pollinated between flowers from genetically different members of the same species growing nearby.*

Create a wildflower meadow

A wildflower meadow is an open space planted with colorful perennials and grasses chosen for their ability to maintain their own populations over time without fertilizer or irrigation. If you choose plants suited to your soil conditions, you should only need to provide supplemental water to a wildflower meadow. Ongoing maintenance involves controlling weeds for the first few years, so that the clumping grasses and perennial wildflowers that dominate a meadow planting will gradually cover the ground thickly. Mowing once a year (in spring) prevents woody shrubs and trees from overshadowing and overtaking the sun-loving wildflowers.

Your biggest challenge is to prevent weeds from dominating your meadow in the first few years. Most of what pops up will be invasive thugs that must be removed. Soil preparation is key. Remove or smother all existing vegetation, then allow any remaining weed seeds in the soil to germinate. Gently till these weeds when they emerge, then sow seeds in spring after your last frost and keep moist until germination. Thin seedlings to no less than eight inches apart. Or buy or raise plants as plugs or containers, and plant randomly at 8-inch intervals. This is the best method for clay soil.

A new meadow takes about three years to mature to the point where plants are not crowded out by weeds. In the first few years, plant a nurse crop of annual rye grass, other wildlife-friendly annuals, or short-lived perennials to prevent weeds. As the

A wildflower meadow is a low-cost, low-maintenance alternative to a lawn. You can tuck a meadow into any size property.

meadow matures, certain plants will dominate; you may choose to do some thinning to level the playing field and prevent them from crowding others. Mow some walking paths through your meadow and include a bench for wildlife observation.

Annual wildflower meadows
A quick way to create wildlife habitat is to grow an annual meadow of bird- and butterfly-friendly annuals and grasslike plants that bloom gloriously in summer. Although they bloom and die within one season, they should produce enough seed to keep their populations returning year after year. By mixing various annuals together, you can create a meadow effect even in a small area.

Plants for Wildflower Meadows
Choose a seed mix from local, ecologically aware seed suppliers who can verify if a mix is suitable for your site. Only buy seed mixes with itemized contents. Often, "meadow in a can" seed mixes are made up of invasive nonnative plants.

Annuals:
Marigolds *(Tagetes)*
Sunflower *(Helianthus annuus)*
Ornamental millet *(Pennisetum glaucum)*
California poppy *(Eschscholzia californica)*

Perennials and grasses for moist meadows:
New York ironweed *(Vernonia noveboracensis)* *
Gayfeather *(Liatris* spp.) **
Aster spp.*
False aster *(Boltonia asteroides)*
Milkweed *(Asclepias syrica and incarnata)* *
Swamp sunflower *(Helianthus angustifolius)* *
Coneflower *(Echinacea* spp.)
Mountain mint *(Pycnanthemum)* **
Sedge *(Carex)* **
Rush *(Juncus)* **

Small shrubs that tolerate occasional mowing:
New Jersey tea *(Ceanothus americanus)* *
Gray dogwood *(Cornus racemosa)* *
Yellow wild indigo *(Baptisia tinctoria)* *
Snowberry *(Symphoricarpos albus)* *
Meadowsweet *(Spiraea* spp.)
Steeplebush *(Spiraea* spp.)

Perennials for dry meadows:
Butterfly milkweed *(Asclepias tuberosa)* *
Black-eyed Susan *(Rudbeckia)*
Goldenrod *(Solidago)* *

Grasses for dry meadows:
Indian grass *(Sorghastrum nutans)* *
Switchgrass *(Panicum virgatum)* *
Big bluestem *(Andropogon gerardii)* *
Little bluestem *(Schizachyrium scoparium)* *

* indicates New England native plant
**some varieties native

Create a woodland edge

If you have wooded areas on your property, a woodland edge is an easy way to create quick and beneficial wildlife habitat. Woodland edge is a transition zone where woods turn into another habitat such as open meadow or lawn. A wildlife edge can be as simple as an unmowed buffer between a lawn area and nearby trees.

Many grassy, shrubby plants that thrive in edge habitat are important to butterflies, which need a safe place to rest near nectar sources, as well as food plants to lay eggs. **Song sparrows** and **Eastern towhees** nest in grassy forest edges. In June, turtles travel up to ½ mile from streams, marshes, and ponds to lay eggs in the grassy edges of fields. Edges provide food and cover for small mammals, which in provide food for **owls** and **hawks**.

*Woodland edges support great biodiversity. Plants that tolerate both sun and shade can thrive in the varying light of the woodland edge, including **white wood aster** (below).*

A note about edge habitat. Edge habitat is great for attracting wildlife, but can be detrimental to some of our rare, shy, forest birds, which need large tracts of unbroken forest . Development in New England's forests creates an abundance of edge effect, causing population booms of edge predators such as cowbirds and blue jays.

Remember that a woodland edge is a dynamic environment. Small shrubs grow into trees, and nearby trees may eventually shade out the more sun-loving plants underneath. If you are planting a woodland edge, you should choose plants carefully for eventual height and width. Smaller trees such as sourwood and bur oak have root systems that interfere very little with surrounding plants (unlike beech, hemlock, and maple). Manage succession by thinning out seedlings.

A songbird hedge overflows with color and interest year-round and requires little care after it establishes.

Above: ***Common elderberry***

Create living fences

Hedges make excellent privacy screens, windbreaks, and noise buffers. As an alternative to a traditional hedge, plant a songbird hedge with a mixture of fruiting and evergreen shrubs, planted at correct distances to grow to their mature height without trimming. A variety of bird-friendly shrubs will feed and shelter migrating **warblers**, **vireos**, and **thrushes**.

Landscaping on slopes

A slope or hillside with an angle greater than 20 percent is usually too steep for mowing grass, but many beautiful plants thrive in the good soil drainage. Plant roots help prevent soil erosion by preventing rainwater or flooding from washing soil away, and dense foliage deflects the force of heavy rain. Include a variety of trees, shrubs and perennials, and grasses for a diversity of root depths. Look for plants with deep taproots such as **butterfly weed** or **Russian sage**, and mix with other plants with fibrous or spreading root systems. Other plants that enjoy hillsides include **bearberry, moss phlox, stonecrop, juniper,** and many no-mow **grasses**.

When planting a slope, work one section at a time. Don't remove all the existing vegetation on the slope or the next rain will start eroding the soil. Plant small plants or plugs to minimize digging. Dig holes and create small protruding lips to retain rainwater while the plant establishes. You can also terrace your slope to create level areas.

A sunny hillside planted with just a few varieties of no-mow native meadow grasses is simple by design and function.

Below: *Stone slabs set into a shady hill creates a natural stairway where mosses soon begin to soften the edges.*

Perennials and Low Shrubs
Butterfly weed *(Asclepias tuberosa)* *
Bearberry *(Arctostaphylos uva-ursi)* *
Moss phlox *(Phlox subulata)* *
Yarrow *(Achillea* spp.)
Stonecrop & Sedum **
Russian sage *(Perovskia atriplicflolia)*
Juniper **
Raspberry *(Rubus)* **
Dog hobble *(Eubotrys fontanesiana)* *
Grasses such as **wild ryegrass, fescue** and **little bluestem** *

Shrubs and Small Trees
Red alder *(Alnus rubra)* *
Red-osier dogwood *(Cornus sericea)* *
Ninebark (*Physocarpus opulifolius)* *
Snowberry *(Symphoricarpos albus)* *
Roses *(Rosa)* **
Gooseberry *(Ribes* spp.*)* **
Bayberry *(Morella pensylvanica)* *
Yellowroot *(Xanthorhiza simplicissima)* *
Mountain laurel *(Kalmia latifolia)* *

* indicates New England native plant
**some varieties native

PPacking your garden full of plants keeps weeds at a minimum! If left standing in fall, these plants become standing mulch to feed the soil and the birds.

Foundation plantings

Chosen wisely, placed close to your house provide cooling shade in summer and insulation in winter. Even a shrub strategically placed near an air conditioning unit can help it run more efficiently. But avoid the common mistake of planting large shrubs and trees too close to your foundation. As they mature they will require constant pruning to avoid damaging siding or causing mold. Don't forget to include some twiggy or evergreen foundation shrubs to lure shelter-seeking winter birds close your house.

Work 9 to 5? Plant a fragrant moon garden

If you're able to enjoy your garden only during evening hours, plant what Victorian gardeners called a *moon garden* of fragrant white flowering plants. White flowers glow at twilight, and their perfume is a beacon to night-flying moths and fireflies. Look for white varieties of the following nectar-rich plants, which are all easy to find and grow:

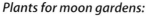

*The thick fragrance of **phlox** always seem to bring back childhood memories of country gardens in summertime.*

Plants for moon gardens:

Spider flower (*Cleome hassleriana*)

Phlox spp. **

Feverfew (*Tanacetum parthenium*)

Tobacco flower (*Nicotiana alata*)

Obedient plant (*Physostegia virginiana*) *

Crabapple (*Malus* spp.)

Actaea spp. **

Sweet alyssum (*Lobularia maritima*)

Cosmos spp.

Summersweet (*Clethra altinifolia*) *

Moonflower (*Ipomoea alba*)

Four-o-clock (*Mirabilis jalapa*)

White indigo (*Baptisia alba*)

False aster (*Boltonia asteroides*)

* indicates New England native plant
**some varieties native

This berm sits on the Rose Kennedy Greenway in Boston, where new parks have brought new life to the city's waterfront..

Plant a rain garden

If you have an area where water typically flows quickly at certain times of the year from roofs or driveways, shallow swales filled with moisture-tolerant plants help slow the water, filtering it before it leaves your property. Some kind of rain garden belongs in every New England garden. If you have dry soil, a rain garden also provides opportunities to grow beautiful moisture-loving plants that you otherwise would not be able to grow without irrigation. (See page 141.)

Create privacy with a berm

Berms are useful for creating privacy, blocking views, or framing distant ones. A berm is simply a mound of earth that absorbs rainwater and directs water flow across an area. A landscaped berm can quickly add vertical depth to an area and even an eighteen-inch berm helps reduce traffic noise.

Keep parts of your garden hidden from view by creating curved paths that invite the visitor to investigate.

Below right: This rustic bench at Garden in the Woods is a cool place to sit on a hot summer's day.

Flagstones can be dropped right onto existing grass to form new patio areas in lawns and benefit soil lifeforms. Decking allows rainwater to drain, and is ideal for creating flat or stepped observation areas on slopes, uneven ground, or wetlands.

Create a destination

Create destinations with paths and benches. Part of the joy of a habitat garden is wildlife right in your backyard. From a landscaping perspective, this means adding private places to sit and observe, preferably using locally available materials. Flagstones can be dropped right onto existing grass to form new patio areas in lawns and provides hiding places for tiny invertebrates such as predatorial ground beetles. Decking allows rainwater to drain, and is ideal for creating flat or stepped observation areas on slopes, uneven ground, or wetlands. Be sure to use non-chemically treated lumber from a sustainably managed New England source.

Trees and Shade in the Habitat Garden

Trees, and lots of them, are vital to life on our planet. On the global stage, trees suck enormous amounts of carbon dioxide from the atmosphere (storing it long-term in their trunks) making them an important tool for mitigating carbon emissions and slowing climate change. Trees cool homes in summer, insulate us from winter cold, and improve air quality by trapping particulates. Tree roots are important soil support structures, preventing erosion, landslides, street flooding. Because of the specialized dependencies between New England's trees and wildlife, native trees are essential to slowing the rapid decline of bird and wildlife species.

The circa 1727 farmhouse at Tower Hill Botanic Garden in Boylston, Massachusetts. Colonial farmers knew that planting **evergreens** at the north side of the farmhouse would shelter their homes from winter winds, and that **sugar maples** and **elms** kept the house cool in summer.

The best trees?

A mix of evergreen and deciduous trees promotes biodiversity, but always choose trees based on available space and soil conditions. Urban trees are almost guaranteed to fail without ongoing maintenance, and a common mistake is to grow large trees too close to homes and power lines.

Deciduous trees provide wildlife with resources through the year, from spring and summer nectar and pollen, to nuts or fruits, foliage for insects, and leaves that fall and enrich the soil. Evergreen shrubs and trees such as pine, hemlock, and cedar keep their foliage through the year, but their dense shade allows fewer understory plants than deciduous trees. Evergreens provide valuable cover and shelter to birds and wildlife, especially in winter, and many insects and birds rely on needles and cones for food and nesting. Take your cue from what you see in your neighborhood to determine what types may be in short supply. (See page 200 for the best wildlife-friendly shrubs and trees for New England landscapes.)

If you live in a new development with at least a ¼ acre of land, consider reintroducing some large native trees back into your neighborhood. This can be as easy as collecting acorns or nuts from nearby trees and planting them in a suitable location in your yard. Some young native tree saplings grow surprisingly fast, and future generations will continue to enjoy the many benefits of the trees you plant now. Trees may take decades to mature but will generally live a long time, much longer than some of the widely-planted imported flowering trees such as the **Asian Callery pear**, which grows so quickly that eventually the trees crack under their own weight. When it comes to trees, quick growth often means quick death, making replacement expensive. Growing native trees also adds to the genetic repository of New England's tree species, helping protect species against the increasing number of pests, pathogens and environmental imbalances that threaten their future survival.

Left: *Some fungi such as these mushrooms form on tree trunks and, like lichens, do not harm the trees.*

Although this mowed, parklike woodland is green and attractive, allowing the understory to develop would improve the health of the trees, as well as dramatically increase the number of species that can live here.

"Tree trash" such as fallen leaves, needles, branches, and stumps becomes nature's nursery for wildflowers and tree seedlings.

Add an understory

The area underneath your existing trees holds many opportunities to restore the multi-layered habitats of healthy woodlands. If you have a wooded area on your property, you already have an area where the soil is cool and moist from the shade, and a free supply of leaves, needles, and twigs replenished annually that break down into deep, rich soil full of the fungi that tree roots love.

If trees could talk, they'd tell you that their favorite fertilizer is their own leaves! Start by leaving tree leaves where they fall. It may take a few years to break down, so you can add some leaf mold (decomposed leaves aged for a year or two) to speed up the process, or a few cupfuls of soil from healthy woodland soil. (See page 153.)

A natural woodland understory typically contains a mix of flowering and fruiting shrubs such as **dogwood**, **serviceberry**, **spicebush**, and **wild cherry**. Herbaceous plants and mosses cover anything bare. The soil is itself a complex ecosystem filled with beneficial fungi, and other tiny soil life forms that are an essential food source for at-risk salamanders and wildlife that spend much of their life underground.

Capture the essence of a woodland ecosystem by underplanting your existing trees with shade-tolerant perennials and shrubs.

*Below: Drifts of native wildlflowers such as **red columbine** and **wood phlox** bloom in early spring, before deciduous trees develop their leaves.*

The distinctive peeling bark of **river birch**. New England has a native birch for every situation.

Right: **Mountain ash** berries in early October.

Evergreen trees usually have dense, thick canopies, so not much light reaches the forest floor, and your plant choice is limited to those that tolerate heavy shade. Or, you can limb up some trees by removing their lower branches to admit more light to the forest floor. Strategic limbing of trees near your house can also help direct more sunshine into your home in winter, saving on heating costs.

A periwinkle "desert"! (Vinca minor) If your garden borders a woodland, don't use aggressive nonnative groundcovers such as **Japanese pachysandra**, **English ivy**, or **Vinca** as groundcover. They spread aggressively by roots (stolons) in moist shaded soil, and strangle native plant seedlings, halting natural succession wherever they root.

The best shade plants

Woodland gardens may not have the traffic-stopping allure of a sunny flower bed, but shade plants offer a wide variety of textures, shapes, and shades of green to create subtle appeal. Plants that evolved in low-light conditions tend to have larger leaves (to capture as much sunlight as possible) and make a bold statement that can become your shade garden's defining factor. You'll notice that many of our native wildflowers that evolved in shady settings have light-colored flowers, probably to make them visible to a variety of pollinators with poor vision.

*The soil under **white pine** trees is usually acidic, supporting mostly acid-loving plants such as **moss**, **ferns**, **blueberry**, and **huckleberry**. Moss colonies combined with rocks, ferns and tree trunks are a simple Japanese-style garden, and a newly-installed moss garden (above) immediately supplies a Zen quality to any outdoor space.*

Perennials and Grass-like Plants:

Ferns **

Sedge *(Carex* spp.*)* **

Moss *

Foamflower *(Tiarella cordifolia)* *

Trillium spp.*

Dicentra spp.**

Celandine poppy *(Stylophorum diphyllum)*

Virginia bluebells *(Mertensia virginica)*

Trout lily *(Eurythnonium americana)* *

Bunchberry *(Chamaepericlymenum canadense)* *

Wild blue phlox *(Phlox divaricata)* *

Goldenseal *(Hydrastis canadensis)* *

Goldthread *(Coptis trifolia)* *

Twinflower *(Linnaea borealis)* *

Bloodroot *(Sanguinaria canadensis)* *

Shrubs and small understory trees:

Serviceberry *(Amelanchier* spp.*)* *

Dogwood *(Cornus* spp.*)* **

Viburnum spp.**

Wild cherry *(Prunus serotina)* *

Spicebush *(Lindera benzoin)* *

Canadian redbud *(Cercis canadensis)*

Rhododendron and azalea **

*indicates New England native plant

** some varieties are native

Bunchberry is a wonderful native groundcover for a partial shade location interplanted with ferns, columbine, and lowbush blueberry.

Moss and rocks for simple shade gardens

You may have a mostly shady area on your property that is somewhat damp and where nothing seems to grow except moss. Actually, moss is wonderful plant to fill in between other plants or as a background plant. A thick colony of moss suppresses weeds, stays green all winter, and requires very little maintenance except for an occasional yank of invasive weeds.

If you already have healthy mosses growing, you can transplant healthy pieces to other areas. The best time of year is between May and October, after rain has fallen and the ground is moist. Dig up a piece of moss along with the soil adhering to it, and press it into the new location, watering several times in the first week or two. Mix some buttermilk or beer with water, and sprinkle it over the moss to help moss establish. Or, buy propagated moss from a sustainable moss farm (See page 215.)

Regenerating forest, or, "weeding the woods"

A forest is the easiest of all landscapes to cultivate in New England. If you sit and wait, eventually trees will cover an area! If your goal is to allow part of your property to return to forest, your job is not that of gardener but of steward. Weed out any invasive plants that might take root, and monitor for seedlings over time. Otherwise, nature will guide the evolution of your forest habitat, but you can help out by watching for, and protecting, seedlings of native wildflowers and trees. If you live in an area crowded with deer, protecting native plants from deer browse will be your great challenge.

Don't trash your leaves! They are among your most valuable gardening resources. Just add water to a bagful and wait a few months for a bag of free compost. Rake up and store fallen leaves and let them sit until they have partially decomposed. The resulting leaf mold makes great mulch that will improve your soil.

The woodland understory comes alive in early spring at Garden in the Woods in Framingham, Mass., with celandine poppy and blue wood phlox in bloom.

Owls of New England

People don't always think of owls when they think of common New England birds, because owls are nocturnal and shy, and difficult to spot. But New England has many species. Most eat small mammals so they are very useful for keeping voles, mice, and rats under control.

If you have trees on your property, allow buildup of "tree trash" such as broken branches or twigs, or build a brushpile to house nests for the small creatures that owls rely upon for food.

If you have an open area nearby, you can provide nesting habitat for barn or screech owls by hanging wooden nest boxes that simulate tree cavities. Hang your box on a pole or a building at least ten feet from the ground to protect the nest from predators. If you hang the box on a building or barn, face the inside of the box toward the inside of the barn.

*The **Eastern screech owl** (above) is well camouflaged, so it's hard to spot in its favorite daytime resting place, a tree cavity.*

*Some owl species, such as the beautiful **barn owl** (below), are in decline.*

Habitat Gardening in Small Spaces

Any water feature with dripping water is irresistible to birds.

A well-used bat roosting box on an old barn provides daytime roosting opportunities for bats. Hang bat houses at least ten feet off the ground, with the opening facing south or southeast, where it will receive at least six hours of sunshine.

Whatever the size of your garden space, you can beautify your surroundings, help protect water supplies, and even grow your own food, while supplying habitat for declining birds and pollinators. Especially in metropolitan areas, even the smallest habitat can add to the mosaic of green oases across your city.

Remember the habitat garden basics. Include evergreen shrubs for cover and protection from the elements. Deciduous trees provide food and nesting opportunities. Dense flowering plants and grasses attract pollinators and other insects. And a living soil, amended with organic ingredients to feed soil organisms keeps plants and trees healthy and thriving, especially in urban areas where plant roots are subjected to great stresses from soil compaction, heat, pollution, and poor drainage.

Use your property's existing structural elements to incorporate more plants into your garden space. A fire escape, fence, or brick wall can support a climbing vine, or a tree next door that hangs into your property can become the canopy for a woodland shade garden that also helps keep your home cool. Supplement nature by hanging bat boxes, bird feeders, nesting boxes, and clean water sources for visiting songbirds. Hang a bird nesting "goody bag" of materials such as leftover yarn, cotton drier lint, or pet hair from brushes near a window and watch **chipping sparrows**, **finches**, or **orioles** pick out bits and pieces for constructing nests.

Bats devour huge numbers of insects each night in summer, but they are headed for extinction, dying by the millions during hibernation from a fungal disease called "white-nosed syndrome". Pictured is an infected bat in a cave.

Shade from buildings or structures

Shady areas next to buildings are ideal for growing native woodland plants because of the absence of tree roots competing for nutrients and moisture. As long as the soil is moisture-retentive and you mulch plants with leaves or partially decomposed wood chips to inoculate soil with beneficial fungi, this kind of shade is perfect for a shady nook with a woodland garden and seating area. If the soil is dry, consider creating a rain garden to channel rainwater from your roof into a moist area where many shade plants will thrive. (See page 139.)

Some birds can survive and even prosper in an urban setting, including house wrens, chimney swifts, and hawks.

Habitat Pots, Planters and Window Boxes

Fill your patio or balcony with containers of pollinator and bird-friendly plants grouped together to create a larger habitat. Some birds will even nest in hanging baskets on a balcony. Many plants thrive in the good drainage of a container, including culinary herbs, which are ideal for growing in pots because they don't mind short periods of drought. Many butterflies, hummingbirds, and tiny pollinators visit flowering herbs such as **mint**, **sage**, **rosemary**, **lavender** and, **hyssop** for the flower nectar. Grasses add a vertical element to container plantings, and many small grasses are also host plants for skippers and other small butterflies.

Drape nectar and foliage plants out of a sunny window box for a colorful display that attracts hummingbirds and other pollinators.

Containers overflowing with plants add color to a patio garden. Note the vine growing up the gutter trellis.

Compact shrub cultivars can be grown in a large container if repotted every three or four years and overwintered in a garage or unheated basement. Compact cultivars of wildlife-friendly shrubs such as **Virginia sweetspire**, **summersweet**, and **weigela** are readily available at nurseries. Several **dwarf blueberry** dwarf cultivars are available for growing in pots. Note that compact varieties are not necessarily shorter; often a cultivar is called compact because of its denser habit. Control the growth of shrubs in containers by pruning their roots every few years.

In summer, pots often need daily watering and fertilization, so self-watering planters can minimize the amount of care required. If you are growing your garden in containers, pay extra attention to the soil's pH levels. Measure soil pH regularly and amend as needed with compost tea, greens and, and other organic amendments as required. Changing leaf color or undersized leaf shape often indicates a soil deficiency. Ask at a nursery for a locally available organic supplement.

The best wildlife-friendly plants for growing in pots and tubs

Annuals:

Floss flower

Button zinnia *(pictured right)*

Marigold

Nasturtium

Impatiens

Salvia

Wax begonia

Fuschia 'Gartenmeister'

Petunia and million bells

Phlox drummondii

Verbena

Candytuft

Calendula

Heliotrope

Lantana

Cigar plant *(Cuphea ignea)*

China pink *(Dianthus chinensis)*
Coleus (if allowed to flower)
Culinary herbs such as **parsley, borage, coriander,** and **basil**

Perennials and grasses:
Coralbells *(Heuchera)* **
Agastache
Sedum **
Beardtongue *(Penstemon)***
Heath aster *(Aster ericoides)**
Culinary herbs such as **sage, lavender, rosemary, mint,** and **thyme**
Native grasses such as **Little Bluestem** and **northern sea oats** *
Grasslike plants such as **sedges** *(Carex)* and **rushes** *(Juncus)***

Shrubs and Small Trees:
Blueberry *(Vaccinium* spp.*)* *
Coralberry *(Symphoricarpos orbiculatus)* *
Virginia sweetspire "Little Henry" *(Itea virginica)*
Weigela "Midnight Wine"

Evergreens for Shelter/Cover:
Dwarf Alberta spruce *(Picea glauca 'Conica')* *
Juniper (dwarf varieties) **
Mugo pine "Slow Mound" *(Pinus mugo)*
Hinoki false cypress "Nana Gracilis" *(Chamaecyparis obtusa)*

*indicates New England native plant
** some varieties are native

With enough sunlight, even a high-rise balcony can support vegetable and fruit plants and attract hummingbirds, butterflies, pollinators, and songbirds.

Top left: **Cherry tomato** plants grow in containers on this sunny deck, along with flowering companion plants such as **nasturtium**, **marigold**, and **calendula**.

Top right: This pretty container of shade-loving tiny ferns, mosses, and lichens provides a bundle of resources for chickadees and hummingbirds collecting nest-building materials, as well as food for insects that feed on lichen, such as the **scarlet lichen** moth (right).

If you have poorly draining soil or live where industrial toxins still exist in the soil, use raised beds to grow vegetables and other plants that need good soil.

Your soil may be so poor and compacted that water won't drain and few plants thrive. Or you may be working with clay soil, which although often quite fertile, is like cement, draining poorly and rotting plant roots. A few plants can thrive in clay, but adding organic matter such as compost, compost tea, or leaf mold is the best way to improve soil conditions. As earthworms and other decomposers eat your soil amendments, they create tiny passages that loosen soil and allow moisture and nutrients to pass through.

Or, use raised beds or containers to provide the moisture-retentive but well-drained soil that most plants love. Raised beds filled with clean soil, replenished with compost, give roots a better chance to establish. Multilevel raised beds allow you to create a terraced garden effect against a wall. Use plants that spill over the edge, hiding the borders.

*Plants in the legume family, including **clover**, **lupine**, **baptisia** (pictured), **peas**, and **beans** grow well in impoverished soils because they are "nitrogen fixers," able to absorb atmospheric nitrogen and convert it to a usable form. Legumes turned into a vegetable garden in fall supply nitrogen to next year's crops.*

Plants that grow in clay soil

Perennials and Grass-like Plants:

Columbine *(Aquilegia* spp.*)* **

Daylily

New York Aster *(Aster nova-belgii)* *

Hosta

Peony

Black-eyed Susan *(Rudbeckia Goldsturm)*

Dead nettle *(Lamium maculatum)*

Giant bellflower *(Campanula latifolia)*

Astilbe spp.

Masterwort *(Astrantia major)*

Siberian bugloss *(Brunnera macrophylla)*

Jacob's Ladder *(Polemonium)* **

Goldenrod *(Solidago)* **

Goatsbeard *(Aruncus)*

Actaea spp.**

Joe-Pye weed *(Eutrochium)* *

Delphinium

Swamp Sunflower *(Helianthus)* *

Oxeye, False Sunflower *(Heliopsis)* *

Sneezeweed *(Helenium autumnale)**

Dutch white clover

Fine-leafed fescue grasses

Shrubs and Trees:

Cockspur hawthorn *

Larch *(Larix laricina)* *

White pine *(Pinus strobus)* *

Shrubby cinquefoil *(Potentilla fruticosa)* *

White Spruce *(Picea glauca)* *

Meadowsweet and steeplebush *(Spiraea alba, S. tomentosa)* *

Honeysuckle *(Lonicera)* **

Elderberry *(Sambucus)* **

Gooseberry *(Ribes)* **

Virginia sweetshrub *(Itea virginiana)*

*indicates New England native plant
** some varieties are native

Give your New England garden an Old World feel with a cobble or brick path with native mosses growing between the stones. Cobble pavers are available at stoneyards, or use flat cobbles that you may have in your existing soil. If you control weed growth, common native mosses may develop on their own.

Above: *Even if you don't have room for trees, woodland props evoke a feeling of a woodland in a shady spot.*

Plants for tough urban sites

Even a single tree planted in a city garden can provide food, shelter, and nesting for a variety of creatures. Native trees also contribute to a larger canopy of natural habitat in cities and towns. For roadsides and other tough urban growing conditions, choose salt- and pollution-tolerant plants. Where sidewalks or pavement leaches lime into surrounding soil, choose plants that tolerate a more alkaline soil (look for the pH+ icon in the Plant Guide). Note that evergreen needle trees do not do well near roadsides, as the pores that line the needles clog with salt and pollutants. Trees in urban settings or clay soils need particular care to keep their roots healthy. Air spade to aerate soil in the root zone—adding plugs of compost mixed with soil. Slower but better in the long term is to inoculate soil with mycorrhizal fungi used by tree roots to mine surrounding soil for nutrients. Avoid fertilizers high in phosphorus, which inhibit the growth of these mycorrhizae.

Perennials:

Sedum **

Stonecrop

Bee Balm *(Monarda didyma)*

Black-eyed Susan *(Rudbeckia hirta)*

False aster *(Boltonia asterioides)*

Grasses such as little bluestem, big bluestem, switchgrass *

Shrubs:

Viburnum **

Elderberry *(Sambucus)* **

New Jersey tea *(Ceanothus americana)* *

Gray dogwood *(Cornus/Swida racemosa)* *

Bayberry *(Morella pensylvanica)* *

Hawthorn *(Crataegus phaenopyrum)* *

Plum, cherry *(Prunus)* **

Common snowberry *(Symphoricarpos albus)* *

Juniper **

Sumac *(Rhus)* *

Trees:

Carolina silverbell *(Halesia carolina)*

Red or sugar maple *(Acer* spp.*)* *

Tuliptree *(Liriodendron tulipifera)* *

Black gum *(Nyssa sylvatica)* *

Red, white, and pin oak *(Quercus)* *

American hornbeam *(Carpinus caroliniana)* *

Crabapple (some cultivars)

Hackberry *(Celtis occidentalis)* *

American elm *(Ulmus americana)* *

River birch *(Betula nigra)* *

Redbud *(Cercis canadensis)*

Flowering dogwood *(Cornus florida)* *

White and green ash *(Fraxinus)* *

American hophornbeam *(Ostrya virginiana)* *

Serviceberry *(Amelanchier grandiflora)* *

American holly *(Ilex opaca)* *

Sourwood *(Oxydendrum arboreum)* *

*indicates New England native plant
** some varieties are native

Planting a Green Roof Garden

Gardening on a balcony or roof? Create a green roof oasis and reestablish the green space swallowed by your building's footprint. Rooftops are ideal for flower gardens because they are usually in full sun, and few weed seeds blow up that high. A rooftop garden can consist of a few containers with plants, or a layer of soil over a waterproof barrier on which a garden can be planted. Rooftop gardens provide valuable habitat for migratory birds (even ducks), butterflies, and other beneficial creatures.

Choose plants such as grasses, alpines, or plants native to coastal areas which don't mind wind and sun (see page 125). Desert plants are also suitable. Because of New England's moist climate, we do not have many native plants suitable for a rooftop garden without requiring you to provide either irrigation or deeper (two to four feet) soil.

Your green roof is disconnected from other terrestrial habitat, so you need to coax it along to encourage natural processes. Include as much organic material in your soil as you can, to encourage soil microorganisms and in turn provide insects and worms for birds. Vary the depth and structure of the vegetation to provide diverse habitat for species with varying needs. Encourage native solitary bees to take up residence by leaving a few open gravelly or sandy areas for them to nest. Or include terracotta pots filled with sand or gravel.

Plant a natural buffer along the edges of driveways and roadsides to absorb stormwater runoff. Choose rugged and durable plants such as **black-eyed susan**, **goldenrod**, **anise hyssop**, **sedum**, **juniper**, *and* **ornamental grasses**.

Green roof on a dorm at WPI in Worcester, MA. The insulating layer of a green roof can substantially increase a building's energy efficiency.

105

Abandoned relics of the Industrial Age have been transformed from urban blight to life at the Bridge of Flowers, Shelburne Falls, Massachusetts.

Several plots at Northampton Community Garden are planted as bird and butterfly gardens, supplying not only gorgeous scenery but also free pest control for surrounding food plots.

No Garden of your Own? Try Community Gardening or Support Local Farmers

You can also support sustainable agricultural use of open spaces by shopping at farm stands, or by purchasing shares in a local Community Supported Agriculture (CSA) program, in which your subscription supplies you with fresh, seasonal vegetables, fruit, meat, eggs, and other farm products directly from local farmers. Some CSAs also incorporate working discounts for farm helpers in school vacations, offering opportunities to learn lifelong values of hard work, patience, and cooperation.

Winter bird feeders bring nature close up

If you have only a small area to help birds, hanging a few bird feeders in a location visible from indoors provides the opportunity to enjoy nature watching during the long winter months. Even if your gardens have plenty of bird plants, a bird feeding station can provide a reliable food source in the worst weather, when natural food sources are buried under snow. Remember to clean your bird feeders regularly to prevent the spread of disease among your avian visitors, by rinsing feeders in a mixture of one part liquid chlorine bleach and nine parts warm water. When buying feeders, look for easy-clean designs that can be dismantled and scrubbed clean.

The type of bird feeder and the food source determine the birds you will attract. Tube feeders with tiny holes containing niger seed attract **finches** and **chickadees**. Tray or platform feeders attract birds such as **cardinals** and **grosbeaks**. Feeders containing suet blocks nourish **woodpeckers** and **Carolina wrens**, which prefer an insect-based diet, and provide valuable fat and energy in early spring when insets are scarce. To prevent warm suet from spoiling and causing beak rot, don't use it in temperatures above 40 degrees.

Use single seeds instead of a mix. Feeding a single variety of seeds in each feeder is a good way to discourage domination at your birdfeeders. Generally, invasive birds such as house sparrows are attracted to the millet found in cheap seed mixes, but don't eat safflower seed. **Squirrels** and **grackles** are also uninterested in safflower, but it does attract a wide variety of other birds, including **cardinals**, **chickadees**, **white-throated** and **song sparrows**, **finches, woodpeckers,** and **nuthatches**. Sunflower seed and split peanuts attract many birds, including **blue jays**, but also every **squirrel** in the neighborhood. Sunflower seed shells contain a substance that is toxic to plants, so feed hulled sunflower hearts, or move your feeder around periodically.

Buy good-quality birdseed. Not all birdseed is created equal. Inexpensive birdseed has usually had the oils pressed from its grains, reducing its quality as a food source for birds.

Welcome winter birds such as the **carolina wren** *with its beautiful song* (top) *or* **downy woodpeckers** (bottom) *by making your own homemade bird feeder. Fill a mold with beef suet and seed, or roll a pine cone in melted peanut butter, place in a plastic bag with cornmeal and birdseed and shake. Freeze and hang from a tree branch using wire which squirrels can't chew through.*

*The **Eastern bluebird, tree swallow** (pictured), **chickadee, nuthatch,** and **tufted titmouse** all build nests in tree cavities or holes, but where old trees are scarce, they will also use nesting boxes. Right: This **chipping sparrow** nest is lined with dog and horse hair woven together using dried grass and mud.*

Nesting Box Guidelines for Common Bird Species

Bird Species:	Entrance Hole Size:	Height above Ground:	Type of mount and preferred location
House Wren	1"	5-10'	Post or tree in part (60 percent) sun
Chickadee	1 1/8"	4-8'	Post or tree in part (40 to 60 percent) sun near large trees
Tree Swallow	1½"	6-15'	Post in open area within two miles of a pond
Bluebird	1½"	4-5'	Post in full sun facing an open area, at least 300 from another bluebird box.
House Finch	2"	8-12'	Post in partial (40 to 60 percent) sun
Tufted Titmouse	1¼"	4-10'	Post near wooded area
Northern Flicker	2½"	6-20'	Post, best with 4" of sawdust for nesting
Purple Martin	2½"	10-20'	White-painted house on a post in full sun, in an open space (no vegetation under the pole) near water and human habitation.
Nuthatch	1¼"	12-20'	Large trees. Box with a side entrance, a narrow, deep bottom and steeply slanted roof. Add 1" of wood shavings.
Wood Duck	4"	4-6'	Place in or beside water, facing the water

Project: *Bird Nesting Boxes*

Whether you live surrounded by nature or in the middle of a city, nesting boxes can supplement natural nesting sites and bring wildlife close to your home. Safely sited nest boxes that simulate the natural holes of old trees and wooden fence posts will almost certainly encourage birds to consider building a nest.

A birdhouse can be as a simple as a small basket or container with a small hole, or even a hollowed-out dried gourd. You can find manufactured birdhouses at most stores, or build your own. Remember that eggs, baby birds, and nests are all at risk from predation, including from European starlings and cowbirds, which destroy nests, or lay their own eggs in the nest to be raised by the unknowing adoptive parents. To prevent this, choose a species you want to attract, and make sure the entrance hole is narrow enough to keep out the birds you want to discourage. Or buy a nest box specifically designed for the species you want to attract. See page 108.

- Use boxes made of ¾" rot-resistant, untreated wood such as cedar.
- Don't stain or paint the inside of the box, to prevent poisonous vapors from sickening birds.

- Leave the wood rough to help nestlings climb out when they are ready.
- Don't add perches, which help predatory birds gain access.
- A tight roof with a two-inch overhang keeps out rain and prevents cats from reaching inside the box from overhead.
- Add a predator guard such as a small wooden block about an inch wide in front of the entrance hole to prevent raccoons or cats from reaching in.
- Include two 5/8-inch ventilation holes and several drainage holes.
- Hang boxes out of prevailing winds and facing away from roads, toward a tree or shrub within 100 feet to provide a safe place for fledglings to land when they first leave the box.
- Metal poles are better at deterring snakes and other predators from climbing inside.
- Always clean out your nesting box after a brood has fledged, removing old nesting materials.

Use the chart opposite to determine the size, height, and location of houses for birds you want to attract.

Project: *Boxes for wood-nesting pollinators*

Many of our native bees, including mason, potter, and carpenter bees, nest in tubular structures such as hollow plant stems or tiny woodpecker holes. Where dead trees are scarce, make up the difference by adding some "prefab" housing to your habitat.

To build a solitary bee nesting box, use a 5/16-inch drill bit to drill a series of six-inch holes into a piece of untreated softwood such as pine or fir. Mason bees will nest only in holes that are open on one side only, so do not drill all the way through. Place this three to six inches off the ground on a post, tree trunk, or the side of a building where mud collects. Mason and potter bees use mud to construct the partitioned cells of their tiny nests.

Bind bundles of dried hollow stems together with wire or twine. Cut stems to six to eight inches and close off one end of the stems with wax, or cut below a stem node so that one end is blocked. Choose stems from plants such as bee balm, purple-stem angelica, blackberry, stinging nettle, Siberian iris, bamboo, or reeds. Use a wooden dowel to drill an opening in the stems where necessary. Place securely in a sheltered spot such as an evergreen tree or under the eaves of a house, where it can receive southeastern sun but afternoon shade.

Constructing nest boxes for wildlife is a great project for kids. This nesting box is made from a block of wood drilled with different length and size holes to accommodate beneficial insects and solitary bees who don't live in hives.

Invasive, Nonnative Birds of New England

If you hang bird feeders, you might notice only a few bird species that visit and hog all the food. Some of the most common birds that visit feeders are **English sparrows** and **European starlings**. These are nonnative birds introduced to the US over the last century, and they are notorious for consuming large amounts of birdseed, leaving none to less aggressive native birds. In towns and cities where little natural habitat exists, English sparrows and starlings form large populations, and, just like invasive plants, bird populations without natural controls can increase to where they outcompete other birds.

Since the mid-1990s, populations of invasive birds have increased significantly in New England. English sparrows and starlings are the only backyard birds not protected under federal laws. If you want to discourage their nest predation in your yard, be persistent in removing their nests, and you can eventually persuade them to give up and move on.

House (English) sparrows. These may be the only birds you see at your feeders if you live in a built-up area. They thrive on food scraps and remnants of human activity and are often spotted in parking lots near big-box stores. House sparrows commonly destroy the nests of native songbirds, contributing to their population declines. **Control:** *To discourage house sparrows, use perchless feeders and don't feed seed mixes containing millet. Feed safflower, or thistle seeds, which house sparrows dislike, but which attract many other birds. If they take over songbird nests in boxes, immediately remove the nests and monitor the area because they may try several times before giving up.*

European Starlings. In the late 1800s, Eugene Schieffelin, fascinated with birds mentioned in Shakespeare, released 100 European starlings in New York City. Today, over 200 million European starlings thrive in North America, where they outcompete other cavity-nesting birds for living space and food— threatened native species such as bluebirds, flickers, purple martins, woodpeckers, and tree swallows. Starlings are a particular threat to nesting songbirds, as they will eat the eggs in nests and throw hatchlings out. **Control:** *Use an external hole guard on nesting boxes to increase the depth of the entrance hole to prevent starling access. If you hang suet blocks for birds, cut out just the bottom of the suet container and hang it upside down. This allows other perching birds to feed, but not starlings.*

Managing Forest Habitat

If you own a large parcel of forest and are cutting it for firewood, or leaving it "to wildlife," most likely it is being invaded by invasive plants and is contributing to the steady decline in quality wildlife habitat across the Eastern deciduous and Northern coniferous forests. But there are some ways you can manage your forests for the benefit of wildlife.

Cut timber outside of bird breeding season

Wildlife officials deal with many cases of birds injured or orphaned when trees are cut during nesting season. Try to avoid harvesting during bird breeding season (roughly between April and August 1 in New England) to protect canopy-nesting birds such as **warblers**, as well as ground-nesting birds.

Leave some mature trees

Old trees are essential to healthy forest ecosystems. With their peeling bark, broken branches, and natural cavities (often oozing with sugary sap), old trees supply important feeding, nesting, roosting, and hibernation opportunities for birds, insects, mammals, amphibians, and reptiles.

Don't fragment forests over 250 acres

Large areas of unbroken forest are increasingly rare across the region, but are critical to many bird species. Cool, shaded moist forest soils provide rich habitat for underground invertebrates and amphibians, which in turn feed ground-nesting birds such as **ovenbirds**, **veeries**, **wood thrushes**, and **hermit thrushes**.

Try to minimize the width of roads or clearings through any forest interior to reduce the "edge habitat" that creeps in. Many birds will not nest where there are edge predators.

Woodpeckers are considered keystone species because the tree cavities they excavate are used by many other creatures. **Pileated woodpeckers** *(pictured) and* **brown creepers** *need fairly mature trees for nesting and foraging.*

*The gorgeous **scarlet tanager** migrates from South America to New England each summer, where they live and nest in large oak and maple forests containing some understory.*

*Fragmented habitat is disastrous for certain birds such as the shy **yellow-rumped warbler** (right) that require large areas of unbroken habitat to nest.*

The scarlet "tanager…flies through the green foliage as if it would ignite the leaves."

HENRY DAVID THOREAU

Small gaps to promote an understory

Although New England was mostly forested at the time the European settlers arrived, many pockets of open space were caused by fires, tree removal by beavers, and croplands cleared by Native Americans. Over the last century, most of the open spaces in our forests have either been developed or left to grow wild, which too often means the area has been taken over by invasive nonnative plants. Ask a certified forester to produce a timber management plan to help you promote young forest habitat. Selectively cutting trees to create small gaps (from one to three trees to a maximum of ¼ acre) promotes a rich diversity of native trees, shrubs, and plants that thrive in the increased sunlight. As long as you monitor the area to prevent invasive plants from colonizing, your understory gaps will increase the biodiversity of your forest and provide critical habitat for many threatened birds.

Managing Farms and Old Field Habitat

Before farming became highly efficient through mechanization, farms hosted an incredible diversity of wildlife. Fields were edged with living fences with wild plants that housed birds, bees, and other creatures that pollinated crops and controlled pests. Today the wide use of herbicides and the tendency to keep farms tidy have made edges and scrubby areas that once supported wildlife are increasingly rare.

Even if your land is actively farmed, there is much you can do to integrate habitat with your crops and pasture. With a large acreage, you have the ability to support many declining bird species that require large tracts for survival.

Before the days of mechanized plows, New England's farm fields were small, usually surrounded by walls built with fieldstones cleared from the soil. Plants and tree seedlings at field edges that "escaped the plow" provided habitat for birds and other wildlife that helped control pests. Today's fields are larger and many of the edges have disappeared, but allowing wild plants such as this native goldenrod on the edges of farm fields provides food and housing for birds and beneficial insects.

*This old field at Norcross Wildlife Sanctuary in Monson, Massachusetts is made up of native grasses including **little bluestem**. It is mowed only once every several years. Birds such as the **eastern meadowlark**, **bobolink** (pictured), and **savannah sparrow** nest only in grassy fields larger than 15 acres.*

Mowing to protect wildlife

Agricultural grasslands such as hayfields, meadows, and pastures are home to many forms of wildlife. In summer, songbirds such as **northern harriers**, **grasshopper sparrows**, and **eastern meadowlarks** forage, build their ground nests, and raise their young exclusively in grasslands. **Wood turtles** often bask, feed, and nest in hayfields and lawn edges near water. Grasslands support many **butterfly** and **moth** (lepidoptera) species that use field grasses and crops as host plants, and these caterpillars provide important food for birds.

Some hints and ideas for protecting the wildlife that use open fields:

- Defer mowing until after mid-July when ground nesters such as bobolinks are generally finished, and most caterpillars have finished eating plants and pupated. If you need to mow a hayfield before the end of July, leave some patches or strips unmowed to reduce the impact on grassland wildlife and create connective travel corridors.
- If mowing in June or early July (nesting season), raise the mower blade to at least six inches to avoid crushing birds' nests.
- Use a wildlife flushing bar on hay equipment to scare birds and wildlife hiding in the grass out of the path in front of the mower blade.
- Keep an eye out for nesting birds when you mow. Try to mow around areas where birds have been observed. Also watch out for fawns. White-tailed deer often leave their fawns for short periods, and because fawns freeze when they sense danger, you may not notice them until it is too late.
- Divide your grassland area into thirds. Mow one-third the first year, one-third the second year, and the last third the third year. Repeat the cycle. Mow late enough to allow caterpillars time to finish feeding.
- Avoid nighttime mowing to reduce the chance of injuring roosting birds.
- To benefit the most beneficial insects, mow an area no more than once year at a height at least 6 inches, to retain enough vegetation to sustain populations of beneficial insect larvae that spend the winter near the ground at the base of plants.
- Unless you are cutting for hay, leave all cuttings in place to decompose over the winter and feed the soil.

Maintain old fields as early successional habitat for threatened species

Early-growth forests (fields left unmanaged for the past twenty-five years) are endangered habitats in New England, where fields are mowed for hay, developed with houses, or left to grow back into woods. Many wildlife species depend on young, scrubby habitat dominated by grasses, shrubs, and small trees, including declining birds such as the **American woodcock**, **prairie warbler**, **blackpoll warbler**, and **golden-winged warbler**, plus **black racer snakes** and **cottontails**.

If you have old fields on your property, maintain an area as early successional habitat by mowing only once every five to ten years to control the growth of trees, and remove invasive plants that commonly colonize old fields: **common buckthorn**, **autumn olive**, **oriental bittersweet**, and **multiflora rose**.

Plant or encourage native shrubs such as **viburnum**, **dogwood**, **vaccinium**, **clethra**, **hawthorn**, and **spirea**, as well as young trees such as **black cherry**, **poplar**, **spicebush**, **sassafras**, **elm**, **willow**, and **juniper**. All are favorite host plants for many large, showy butterfly species, and provide resources to a wide variety of wildlife.

Luk's Tree Farm, Auburn, Massachusetts. Even if you don't own a farm, you can help protect important bird habitat, as well as help New England's farmers keep their family farms, by buying Christmas trees from sustainable tree farms.

*Leave trees and snags around the edges of fields. Their branches and twigs offer perches for predatory birds such as **hawks** and **falcons**.*

Middle: ***Staghorn sumac*** *colonizes old fields and provides valuable nectar plus winter seeds for birds.*

Right: ***Black cherry*** *is a great small tree for wildlife.*

Create wildlife corridors and hedgerows

Messy brambles and thickets may not everybody's idea of an endearing landscape, but even small wild areas of native shrubby plants can provide habitat for wildlife, including **woodcocks**, **indigo buntings**, **ruffed grouse**, and **warblers** as well as **cottontails** and **snakes**.

On an active farm, leaving corridors and hedgerows of vegetation between your fields, woods, and water links habitats together and provides travel routes, ensuring population continuity for species that might otherwise disappear.

Mow fields on a rotational basis, cutting only one-half or one-third of an area each year.

Leave unmowed strips of twenty-five to fifty feet across hayfields to create travel routes from one natural area to another. Rotate these strips, or mow them every three to five years to prevent invasive species from taking root or trees from shading out your crops.

Old apple orchards

If you own property where old apple trees still grow, you have an incredibly valuable source of food, cover, and nesting sites for many forms of wildlife. Although the apple tree is native to Asia, it has been widely grown in New England since 1629. Apple bark, twigs, buds, leaves, and fruit are used by many forms of wildlife. They provide year-round food supplies, but are especially valuable in winter, when uneaten apples still hang on the trees. Old apple trees often have cavity holes popular with nesting **bluebirds**, and old branches and stubs attract insects for **woodpeckers** and **flickers**. Meadow voles, **woodchucks**, and other small mammals that travel in old orchards attract the **hawks**, **owls** and other raptors that keep their populations under control. Many of New England's **bats** also use orchards .

If you prevent other species of trees from growing and shading your apple trees, even older trees should continue to produce fruit, growing alongside low grasses and herbaceous groundcovers such as **violets**, **wild strawberries**, and orchard **grasses**. This maintains habitat for **kingbirds**, **flycatchers**, and **robins**, which help protect your crops from codling moths and other pests.

*You'll never forget the sensation of touching **stinging nettle**, (above), which grows in damp areas on farms and wild areas. Nettles are food plants for several butterfly caterpillars, including the **red admiral** (pictured), **question mark**, and **Eastern comma**, and their dried stems provide hiding and nesting sites for many invertebrates.*

Left: *Orange jewelweed is a hummingbird favorite, often growing near stinging nettle. To relieve nettle sting, break fresh jewelweed stems and apply the juice to the burn.*

Creating a bluebird trail

Bluebird trails are an example of how people can work together to restore habitat for threatened species. **Eastern bluebirds** have been declining in New England because they rely on holes in old trees and fence posts near open areas to nest. As farmland disappears and wooden fencing with it, and old trees are removed, bluebirds now rely on human-supplied housing for survival. Invasive, nonnative birds chase bluebirds away from available nests. Over the past few decades, farmers and 4-H groups have established bluebird trails in and around open fields to provide bluebird nesting sites. A bluebird trail is a series of bluebird nesting boxes set up in quiet open areas such as farm pastures, golf courses, and cemeteries. Because bluebirds won't nest within 300 yards of other bluebird nests, only large fields can sustain many nests. But bluebirds still need our help. They feed mostly on insects in summer, but in winter they depend on wild berries for food. Nonnative **European starlings** also love berries and in some areas strip berry trees bare. Planting as many berrying shrubs and trees as possible, including **chokeberry**, **viburnum**, and **hollies**, can help supply bluebirds with enough berries.

Keep livestock out of farm ponds to prevent erosion and sedimentation. If you have no other source of water, limit livestock access to a small fenced section of shoreline.

Habitat Incentive Programs

Many programs exist to help landowners restore large properties for wildlife habitat. The USDA's Natural Resources Conservation Service (NRCS) provides funding and planning services to improve habitat on private land, and the US Fish & Wildlife Service can help you promote habitat for specific species. Most states also have programs that link landowners with farmers who maintain land for agriculture and wildlife. These agencies also publicize grant opportunities for habitat restoration projects.

Shoreline Landscaping

Whether you're right on the coast or live on a pond, lake, river, or stream, you probably already know that landscaping directly on the water is tightly regulated by local, state, and federal water quality protection laws, and you'll need an approved plan and permit. Quite simply, functioning wetlands make our existence on earth possible. Wetlands absorb toxic runoff from roads and developments to keep drinking water clean and replenished, and reduce the threat of flooding. And they support a huge diversity of wildlife, including many rare or endangered species.

Chemical fertilizers and other pollutants from roads, lawns, farms, and golf courses, as well as leaky septic systems and wastewater, carry nutrients and toxins through groundwater and storm drains into rivers, ponds, and bays. High levels of phosphates and nitrogen in fresh or salt water cause algae growth that reduces oxygen levels, kills aquatic life, and degrades ocean fishbeds. We pay billions in tax dollars for remediation.

This coastal home on Long Island Sound was thoughtfully landscaped by Oehme Van Sweden to protect the Sound's water quality and link the property with its natural surroundings.

If you have lawn within 300 feet of any water's edge, especially if you use irrigation, always use a slow-release organic lawn fertilizer low in nitrogen and phosphorus to prevent unused nutrients from leaching through the soil into the water. Consider converting your lawn to a mix of low grasses that require no water or fertilizers at all, such as perennial **ryegrass, fescues, little bluestem,** Pennsylvania **sedge,** and **poverty oatgrass.**

Right: The pond at Garden in the Woods (Framingham, MA) is landscaped with colorful native plants, providing rich habitat and breathtaking views throughout the year.

Above: Shorelines are home to some of our rarest wildlife. The **northern parula** *is an endangered bird that nests in* **red maple** *and* **Atlantic white cedar** *swamps near the coastline. They are ravenous caterpillar eaters.*

Even better, reduce your lawn's size and maintain a waterside buffer of shore-adapted plants near the water's edge, as a natural filter and to help prevent erosion. Plant roots bind together soil particles, trapping nutrients flowing through groundwater until they can break down. A wide strip or curve of low native perennials, grasses, and shrubs shouldn't block your view and will provide valuable food and shelter for shoreline birds such as **herons** and **egrets**. Shallow-water freshwater

plants such as native **blue flag irises**, **rushes**, and **sedges** also help prevent erosion by absorbing and dissipating wave action that eats away at the shoreline.

*A manicured lawn on a pond's edge usually attracts only resident **Canada geese**. These geese often stick around all year, leaving ½ pound of nitrogen-loaded manure each day on your lawn and local parks.*

If your existing lawn reaches the water's edge, you can simply stop mowing to the edge, and allow native plants to take root and grow, making sure that invasive plants don't establish. A taller buffer containing shrubs and trees can also serve as a windbreak, often creating a warmer microclimate that gives you the opportunity to grow a wider range of plants.

Retaining wall or seawall?

Especially if your property slopes down to the water, preventing erosion is key to any shoreline landscaping efforts. You may be tempted to install a retaining wall, but walls have none of the filtering properties provided by natural shorelines, and they block water access for many forms of wildlife. If you have an existing seawall or retaining wall in good condition, strengthen it by planting native plants at its landward edge, and adding rock riprap into the water at a 45-degree angle at the base of the wall to break the force of waves. Sediment will gradually collect in the rocks, and aquatic plants should begin to grow there, helping absorb wave action. If your wall is in need of repair or replacement, consider removing it, regrading the shoreline, and reestablishing a sloping shoreline planted with shrubs native to New England's shores.

Remember that you will need a special permit from your local water resources board or conservation commission to landscape directly on shorelines. It's advisable to work with a qualified professional who can help you assess your current plant inventory and growing conditions, and recommend plants and designs that are sensitive to delicate aquatic ecosystems.

Components of wildlife-friendly shorelines

Shoreline plants and trees are important for aquatic wildlife, including many species that spend part of their lives on land. Without plants to provide protective cover, birds and other wildlife are exposed to hawks and owls, which often wait near open water for small birds and animals that come to drink. Tree branches hanging over the water provide breeding habitat for **tree frogs**, and by shading the water, trees maintain coldwater habitats for rare fish. Partially submerged aquatic plants provide habitat for both micro- and macroinvertebrates. Fish and frogs hide in submerged vegetation, and many amphibians lay eggs in the muddy bottoms of shallow pools. When plant foliage dies off in winter, bacteria and fungi break the organic matter into detritus, providing food for aquatic scavengers such as mayfly larvae that hatch in the water. **Mayfly larvae** are preferred foods for fish, and flying adults feed birds.

Don't "clean" your shoreline of rocks, fallen logs, and tree branches. Logs that drop into the water redirect currents, creating riffle pools and microhabitats for many aquatic creatures, including **eastern brook trout** that rest in quiet pools. **Turtles** use partially submerged branches and rocks in rivers and ponds to rest safe from predators. After they hatch underwater, some **dragonfly nymphs** climb onto exposed rocks or logs to complete their transformation into adults. Others climb directly up banks.

Threatened turtles such as the **wood turtle** prefer to use sandy riverbanks to travel from the water to their nesting grounds. During turtle breeding season in June, try not to disturb streambanks or sandbars to allow them safe passage to and from their nesting grounds.

If a wetland area has not been heavily disturbed or taken over by invasive plants, it can restore itself fairly quickly with native plants that originally grew in your area.

*Right: **Wood ducks** began to decline in the early 1900s due to the loss of mature and dying trees providing cavities for their nests. The hanging of thousands of wooden nest boxes by wildlife agencies has led to their miraculous recovery.*

Coastal Soils

Constant wind, thick fog, winter nor'easters, sandy soil, salt spray, and salt water within a few feet of the soil surface make gardening on New England's coastline a challenge. If you live very close to the ocean's edge, only a few plants are rugged enough to tolerate such inhospitable conditions. New England's coastline has a variety of unique ecosystems, including sandy dunes, rocky shorelines, elevated bluffs, and salt- and freshwater marshes. Depending on your microhabitat, your landscaping options vary. Study your surroundings carefully and choose plants that are well adapted to your conditions.

Native plants that have adapted over millennia to grow in the harsh conditions of New England's beaches and sand dunes and can tolerate salt and even occasional flooding include **seaside goldenrod** *(pictured),* **beach heather, broom crowberry, American beach grass,** *and* **sickle-leaved golden aster.**

If you own property on or close to a sandy coastal beach, your soil is most likely pure sand, so be realistic about landscaping. New England beach sand is made up mostly of quartz particles, with almost no nutrients or organic matter. Rainwater passes right through it, and in many cases sand is salt-saturated. Forget about English roses or most other ornamental plants that prefer good, moisture-retentive soil. Unless you truck in quantities of topsoil, compost, and mulch each year, your plant choice is limited to plants that thrive in the almost perfect drainage of sandy soils.

If your soil is mostly sandy but farther from shore, you have more options. Look for drought- and wind-tolerant plants that prefer sandy or free-draining soil such as **sand cherry, switchgrass, false heather,** or **bearberry**. Many plants native to sandy areas (including the deserts of the West) have long taproots that enable them to reach deep into the soil to find moisture. "Succulent" plants such as **hardy ice plant** and **sedum** store moisture in their thick foliage and stems, and can usually withstand the harsh reflected heat of sandy, dry locations.

"The sun has shone on the earth, and the goldenrod is its fruit."
HENRY DAVID THOREAU

*What else but **American beach grass** could grow in salt spray and sifting sands? Increased recreational demand on shorelines threatens many rare species, including **diamondback terrapins** and **piping plovers**, which both nest on sandy beaches. Most New England beaches now restrict vehicle access during breeding season to help protect breeding plovers.*

In rocky areas, look for ways to incorporate rock garden or shallow-rooted alpine plants into crevices and soil pockets. **Sedum, moss phlox, goldenrod, columbine,** and **wavy hairgrass** can all tolerate shallow soil. A rocky coastal bluff where salt water doesn't reach, with a soil containing some organic matter, opens up your selection to more plants, but choose plants that can tolerate both the moist air carried in by fogs as well as drying, salty winds.

Plants suitable for low, moist areas near dunes (swales) are **bearberry, beach plum, bayberry, Virginia creeper, cordgrass,** and **Eastern redcedar,** all of which thrive on the moisture and soil salinity of a high seawater table.

Wildlife-friendly Plants Suitable for Sandy, Well-Drained Soils

Native Perennials:

Butterfly milkweed (*Asclepias tuberosa*)

Seaside goldenrod (*Solidago sempervirens*)

Showy aster (*Eurybia spectabilis*)

Bird's foot violet (*Viola pedata*)

Wood lily (*Lilium philadelphicum*)

Adam's needle (*Yucca filamentosa*)

Heath aster (*Symphyotrichum ericoides*)

Blue toadflax (*Nuttallanthus canadensis*)

Mountain mint (*Pycnanthemum tenuifolium*)

Pearly everlasting (*Anaphalis margaritacea*)

Wild indigo (*Baptisia tinctoria*)

Whitetop aster (*Sericocarpus asteroides*)

Eastern silvery aster (*Aster concolor*)

Pearly everlasting (*Anaphalis margaritacea*)

Sand-plain gerardia (*Agalinis acuta*)

Partridge-pea (*Chamaecrista fasciculata*)

Showy tick-trefoil (*Desmodium canadense*)

Northern blazing star (*Liatris scariosa*)

Sedum

Wild blue lupine (*Lupinus perennis*)

Goat's-rue (*Tephrosia virginiana*)

Hyssop-leaved thoroughwort (*Eupatorium hyssopifolium*)

Colicroot (*Aletris farinosa*)

Showy evening primrose (*Oenothera speciosa*)

Horsemint (*Monarda punctata*)

Nonnative Pererennials:

Sea holly, stonecrop, yarrow, Jupiter's beard, needle palm, blanket flower, lance-leaf coreopsis, maiden pinks, artemisia, evergreen candytuft, globe thistle, Mediterranean herbs, Russian sage

Native Vines:

Virginia creeper (*Parthenocissus quinquefolia*)

American bittersweet (*Celastrus scandens*)

Beach pea (*Lathyrus japonica*)

Native Trees:

Scrub and white oak (*Quercus ilicifolia, Q. alba*)

Pitch pine (*Pinus rigida*)

Sassafras (*Sassafras albidum*)

Native Shrubs and Small Trees:

Running serviceberry (*Amelanchier stolonifera*)

Bearberry (*Arctostaphylos uva-ursi*)

Hackberry (*Celtis occidentalis*)

Sweetfern (*Comptonia peregrina*)

Huckleberry (*Gaylussacia baccata*)

Inkberry holly (*Ilex glabra*)

Eastern redcedar and Juniper (*Juniperus*)

Northern bayberry (*Myrica pensylvanica*)

Beach plum (*Prunus maritima*)

Sand cherry (*Prunus pumila*)

Black cherry (*Prunus serotina*)

Sumac (*Rhus*)

Virginia and Carolina rose (*Rosa virginiana, R. carolina*)

Groundsel bush (*Baccharis halimifolia*)

Beach and false heather (*Hudsonia*)

Fragrant sumac (*Sumac aromatica*)

Native Grasses & Grasslike Plants:

Little bluestem (*Schizachyrium scoparium*)

Big bluestem (*Andropogon gerardii*)

Broom sedge (*A. virginicus*)

Switchgrass (*Panicum virgatum*)

Poverty oatgrass (*Danthonia spicata*)

Beach sedge (*Carex silicea*)

Wavy hairgrass (*Deschampsia flexuosa*)

American beach grass (*Ammophila breviligulata*)

A protected salt marsh at Rachel Carson National Wildlife Refuge in Wells, Maine. Salt marshes are now recognized for their value as storm buffers as well as highly productive ecosystems.

New England's Prairies—the Tidal Salt Marshes

Before European settlement in New England began, our bays and estuaries were fringed with prairies of grassy salt marshes, dominated by cordgrass, sedges, cattails, bulrushes, switchgrass, juncus, salt-marsh asters, and rose mallow. Since then, they've have been filled, ditched, or turned into dumps, and some states have lost half their original salt marshes, along with their contributions to coastal flood control. Hurricane Katrina taught us how coastal wetlands are essential for absorbing storm surges, and large-scale restorations of salt marshes are taking place up and down the East Coast. Salt marshes are heavily regulated and only trained professionals can work in them, but if you are landscaping any open area of moist soil near the coastline, try re-creating a pocket of salt marsh habitat using native plants chosen carefully for your particular space. Even a small area planted with native salt marsh plants can support populations of wildlife that depend on these rare habitats..

Plants for Moist Coastal Soils

Northeast Native Perennials and Shrubs:

Rose mallow (Hibiscus moscheutos)

New York aster (Symphyotrichum novi-belgii)

Perennial salt-marsh aster (S. tenuifolius)

Northern blazing star (Liatris scariosa)

Dull Meadow-pitchers (Rhexia mariana)

Obedient plant (Physostegia virginiana)

Wood lily (Lilium philadelphicum)

Mayflower (Epigaea repens)

Sea lavender (Limonium carolinianum)

Pink coreopsis (Coreopis rosea)

Seaside bluebell (Mertensia maritima)

Mudwort (Limosella australis)

Water-willow (Decodon verticallatus)

Broom crowberry (Corema conradii)

Viburnum

Shadbush (Amelanchier canadensis)

Red chokeberry (Photinia arbutifolia)

Winterberry holly (Ilex verticillata)

Swamp rose (Rosa palustris)

Highbush blueberry (Vaccinium corymbosum)

Inkberry and American holly (Ilex glabra, I. opaca)

Summersweet (Clethra)

Eastern redcedar (Juniperus virginiana)

Northern bayberry (Morella pensylvanica)

Groundsel bush (Baccharis halimifolia)

Sweetbells (Eubotrys racemosa)

Northeast Native Trees:

Oak (Quercus)

Red maple (Acer rubrum)

Pitch pine (Pinus rigida)

Black gum (Nyssa sylvatica)

Sassafras (Sassafras albidum)

Atlantic white cedar (Chamaecyparis thyoides)

Northeast Native Grasses & Grasslike Plants:

Little bluestem (Schizachyrium scoparium)

Saltmeadow rush (Juncus gerardii)

Switchgrass (Panicum virgatum)

Black sedge (Carex nigra)

Bulrush (Scirpus cyperinus)

Chair-maker's rush (Schoenoplectus pungens)

Cordgrass (Spartina)

Seaside plantain (Plantago maritima)

Cattails (Typha)

Roses on the coast

Choose rose varieties in coastal zones carefully. Old-fashioned garden roses (bush, climbing, or shrub roses) tend to be hardier and less susceptible to blackspot and mildew that can blight fussier hybrids in areas with summer fog. The familiar beach rose (Rosa rugosa) with its large red fruits that grows all over New England, is an Asian import, brought to Nantucket for erosion control because of its ability to grow well in pure sand. It is now spreading out of control and crowding out natives. Choose native rose species such as **Virginia rose** (R. virginiana), **prickly wild rose** (R. acicularis), or **Carolina rose** (R. carolina), or use the native **beach plum** (Prunus maritima) for erosion control.

The familiar wild rose seen on Cape Cod is actually an Asian import (Rosa rugosa) whose alarming rate of spread threatens fragile sand dune plant communities on the Cape and in Connecticut.

Some common shoreline invasive plants in New England.

Beautiful view of the Assabet River in Hudson, Massachusetts. The native **cattails** *that once dominated the river's edges, preferred nesting plants for* **redwing blackbirds**, *are now being pushed out by the highly invasive* **common reed** *(Phragmites australis).*

Phragmites australis *along the boardwalk at Parker River National Wildlife Refuge (Plum Island) is an Asian import choking out plants native to the marsh.*

The **Asiatic bittersweet vine** *has established itself in almost every habitat in New England, spread by birds that eat their colorful berries (pictured at Ogunquit, Maine.)*

Landscaping Near Freshwater Ponds, Streams, and other Wetland Habitats

Thanks to a hilly landscape formed by the last Ice Age, New England is blessed with plenty of water, and most of us live in or near a stream, pond, or marsh. Colonial settlers systematically drained wet areas for agriculture, or dammed them for industry, creating lakes and ponds that still dot the region. In the mid- to late 20th century, stagnant ponds and polluted water led to realization of the value of protecting our wetlands, and in 1970 the Clean Water Act mandated that states protect wetlands from further destruction.

Whatever the size of your bit of New England, you can help protect water quality. In fact, a wet area is a habitat gardener's dream. A constant supply of moisture encourages lush plant growth, and wetlands are the most productive and biologically rich environments on our planet. Many of New England's most beautiful native plants grow only in wet areas.

Unless you own a large property or work for the federal government, you probably can't recreate complex wetland habitats in your backyard. Wetland plant communities function on a large scale, and their fragmentation has destroyed connectivity among many vital species, however, gardeners can help maintain some of the vital interactions necessary to support wetland ecosystems.

If you have wet areas on your property, study them carefully before introducing any plants. Above all, avoid planting quick-spreading plants that other gardeners may give you, especially Japanese pachysandra and ditch lilies, which quickly grow out of control in moist soils.

Plants along pond shorelines keep the water clean by filtering lawn fertilizers, oils, and other pollutants from nearby lawns and roads.

Identifying water resources

Wetland habitats vary depending on topography and soil type, which determine the plants and wildlife that can survive there. Water resources you might find in your backyard include low areas that drain slowly after heavy rains, ditches and seeps, fast- or slow-moving streams and rivers, marshes, bogs, fens, swamps, and vernal pools. Less obvious water resources are the rain and melted snow that run off your roof and drain away from your house, or sump pump drainage areas that flood occasionally.

Swamps are low, wooded areas occasionally or permanently inundated with shallow water, often dominated by trees such as **hemlock, cedar, red maple,** and **sour gum,** and shrubs such as **black chokeberry, winterberry,** and **elderberry.** Jack-in-the-pulpit, marsh marigold, turk's cap lily, and **marsh blue violet** are common swamp wildflowers. Many swamp plants tolerate varying levels of moisture and are more adaptable than marsh plants for garden use.

Trees, shrubs, grasses, sedges, wet moss, leaf litter, stumps, rotten logs, and rocks all play their own role in the ecology of healthy wetlands.

This farm pond offers plenty of access for kids and wildlife.

A **marsh** is a wetland containing few trees, usually characterized by plants such as **rushes, cattails, pickerel weed, sedges, irises,** and **marsh ferns.** Marshy wetlands usually have quiet water, and

*Bogs are dominated by sphagnum moss and interesting plants such as these **sedges** and **pitcher plant**s, growing in the bog garden at Garden in the Woods.*

their plants tend to resent disturbance. Because water levels often drop in late summer, marsh plants can tolerate some drought, but not high water (deeper than six inches), so don't plant them too deeply.

Bogs are waterlogged areas where decomposing plants and sphagnum mosses have gradually turned into soil that is very high in acidity and low in nutrients. A few plants, including **cranberry**, **bog rosemary**, **leatherleaf**, **Labrador tea**, **rhodora**, and **bog laurel** have evolved to thrive in bogs. Some, including **pitcher plants** are carnivorous, living on insects to make up for the lack of soil nutrition available.

A **fen** is a bog in an area rich in limestone, with a higher pH that favors plants such as **limestone meadow sedge** and orchids such as showy and small **lady's-slippers**.

A **vernal pool** is a small depression in the ground that fills with snowmelt and rainwater in spring. Because they gradually dry up in summer, they are not always recognized as important wetland habitat, but many rare species depend on vernal pools.

Study existing vegetation

Use plant guides (or a wetland plant expert) to identify what is growing already, which may give you clues to the type of wetland that existed nearby before your house was built. In many cases, selective removal of nonnative and invasive plants will allow existing populations of native plants to repopulate the area on their own. Adding local wetland plants can boost an area's ability to return to a functioning wetland.

Native Plants for Wetlands and Freshwater Shorelines

You can help shoreline wildlife by supporting bylaws in your community and state that protect riparian (waterside) areas from excessive development.

Many wetland plants are adapted to a variety of wetland types, but always check a plant's description in the Plant Guide to determine whether a plant is suitable for your conditions. Remember that many wetland plants are colonizers that will spread aggressively, so choose plants based on your available space, and don't plant too thickly.

Native perennials for open, sunny wetlands:

Bee balm (*Monarda didyma*) and wild bergamot (*M. fistulosa*)

Cardinal flower (*Lobelia cardinalis*)

Great blue lobelia (*Lobelia siphilitica*)

Turtlehead (*Chelone glabra*)

Joe-Pye weed (*Eutrochium*)

New England aster (*Symphyotrichum novia-angliaea*)

New York aster (*S. novae-belgii*)

Swamp aster (*S. puniceus*)

New York ironweed (*Vernonia noveboracensis*)

Pointed blue-eyed grass (*Sisyrinchium angustifolium*)

Swamp candles (*Lysimachia terrestris*) and fringed loosestrife (*L. ciliata*)

Goldenrod (*Solidago*)

Obedient plant or false dragonhead (*Physostegia virginiana*)

Northern pitcher plant (*Sarracenia purpurea*)

Marsh marigold (*Caltha palustris*)

Golden Alexanders (*Zizia aurea*)

Culver's root (*Veronicastrum virginicum*)

Swamp sunflower (*Helianthus*)

Rose mallow (*Hibiscus moscheutos*)

Water arum (*Calla palustris*)

Beggartick (*Bidens*)

Bladderwort (*Utricularia*)

Mudwort (*Limosella australis*)

Marsh blazingstar (*Liatris spicata*)

Blue flag iris (*Iris versicolor*)

Spatterdock (*Nuphar lutea*)

Virginia meadow beauty (*Rhexia virginia*)

Rose pink (*Sabatia angularis*) and salt-marsh pink (*S. stellaris*)

False aster (*Boltonia asteroides*)

Grass pink (*Calopogon tuberosus*)

Showy lady's-slipper (*Cypripedium reginae*)

Yellow lady's-slipper (*C. calceolus*)

Rose pogonia (*Pogonia ophioglossoides*)

Water avens (*Geum rivale*)

Swamp milkweed (*Asclepias incarnata*)

King of the meadow (*Thalictrum pubescens* also *T. polygamum*)

Purple meadow rue (*T. dasycarpum*)

Globeflower (*Trollius laxus* var. *laxus*)

False hellebore (*Veratrum viride*)

Blue vervain (*Verbena hastata*)

Pink coreopsis (*Coreopsis rosea*)

Tickseed sunflower (*Bidens coronata*)

Canada lily (*Lilium canadensis*)

Water willow (*Decodon verticillatus*)

Round-leaved pyrola (*Pyrola americana*)

Flat-topped goldenrod (*Euthamia graminifolia*)

Native Perennials for Wet Shady Areas:

Ferns such as sensitive, cinnamon, royal, and marsh fern

Jack-in-the-pulpit (*Arisaema triphyllum*)

Boneset (*Eupatorium perfoliatum*)

Fringed gentian (*Gentianopsis crinita*) and closed bottle gentian (*G. clausa*)

Cardinal flower (*Lobelia cardinalis*)

Arrowhead (*Sagittaria latifolia*)

Grasses and Grass-like Plants:

Wild rice *(Zizania aquatica)*

Sedge *(Carex)*

Rushes *(Juncus)*

Scouring rush and horsetail *(Equisetum)*

Sweetflag *(Acorus americanus)*

Northern sea oats *(Chasmanthium latifolium)*

Tufted hair grass *(Deschampsia caespitosa)*

Trees for Wetlands:

Red maple *(Acer rubrum)*

Atlantic white cedar *(Chamaecyparis thyoides)*

Black and green ash *(Fraxinus nigra, F. pensylvanica)*

Larch *(Larix laricina)*

Sweetbay magnolia *(Magnolia virginiana)*

Black gum *(Nyssa sylvatica)*

Black spruce *(Picea mariana)*

Sycamore *(Platanus occidentalis)*

Pin and swamp white oak *(Quercus palustris, Q. bicolor)*

Arborvitae *(Thuja occidentalis)*

American hornbeam *(Carpinus caroliniana)*

Willow *(Salix)*

River and bog birch *(Betula nigra, B. pumila)*

Shrubs for Wetlands:

Alder species

Bog rosemary *(Andromeda polifolia)*

Chokeberry *(Photinia)*

Leatherleaf *(Chamaedaphne calyculata)*

Common witchhazel *(Hamamelis virginiana)*

Buttonbush *(Cephalanthus occidentalis)*

Winterberry and inkberry holly *(Ilex verticillata, I. glabra)*

Bog laurel *(Kalmia polifolia)*

Labrador tea *(Ledum groenlandicum)*

Summersweet, Sweet Pepperbush *(Clethra)*

Virginia sweetspire *(Itea virginica)*

Silky dogwood *(Cornus amomum)*

Gray or swamp dogwood *(Cornus racemosa)*

Red osier dogwood *(Cornus sericea)*

Sweet gale *(Myrica gale)*

Mountain holly *(Nemopanthus mucronatus)*

Spicebush *(Lindera benzoin)*

Rhodora *(Rhododendron canadense)*, Pinxterbloom *(R. periclymenoides)* and swamp azalea *(R. viscosum)*

Swamp rose *(Rosa palustris)* and New England rose *(R. nitida)*

Sweetbay magnolia *(Magnolia virginiana)*

Mountain cranberry *(Vaccinium vitis-idaea)*

Elderberry *(Sambucus canadensis)*

Cranberry *(Vaccinium macrocarpon)*

Highbush blueberry *(Vaccinium corymbosum)*

Witherod viburnum *(Viburnum nudum* var. *cassinoides)*

Arrowwood viburnum *(V. dentata)*

Nannyberry *(Viburnum lentago)*

Black haw *(Viburnum prunifolium)*

American cranberry bush *(Viburnum opulus)*

Steeplebush *(Spiraea tomentosa)*

Leatherwood *(Dirca palustris)*

Shrubby cinquefoil *(Potentilla fruticosa)*

*Because a vernal pool doesn't stay wet long enough to support fish, aquatic creatures that lay eggs, such as **wood frogs**, **fairy shrimp**, and **salamanders**, breed almost exclusively in vernal pools.*

*According to the EPA, 46 percent of endangered or threatened species are associated with wetlands. Marshes and wet meadows are the summer home for the **American bittern** (pictured), an endangered species.*

Clear out the invasive aquatic weeds

One of the biggest threats to biodiversity and the health of aquatic habitats is exotic species invading wetlands. New England's wetlands are turning into monocultures of **purple loosestrife** *(pictured below)* or **phragmites**. Riverbanks, swamps, and streamsides are consumed by **Japanese knotweed** and **multiflora rose**, obliterating the habitat of many declining wildlife species. To maintain the health of your wetland, clearing invasive vegetation and allowing native plants to grow is an essential, although sometimes daunting, step—however, it really makes an important difference. In several Northeastern states, farmers are successfully using controlled grazing by farm animals to remove invasive species from open meadows next to shallow watersides, increasing the populations of the tiny, endangered **bog turtle**.

Above: *Purple loosestrife is a nonnative invasive that is reducing wetland biodiversity across the eastern US. If it pops up in your garden, pull it right away!*

Left: *Native Americans loved **purple martins** because they ate mosquitoes and other flying pests and scared crows away from their corn. They encouraged martins to live near their campsites by hanging squash gourds for nesting, which was so successful that martins are completely dependent on human-supplied nesting houses or gourds.*

New England Turtles are in Trouble

Everybody loves turtles. Not only are they fascinating and mostly docile, turtles can even help protect your garden plants by eating slugs and snails. Turtles can live for a long time, box turtles longer than 100 years! However, New England's turtles are in serious trouble. **Box**, **spotted**, **wood**, and **bog** turtles are in sharp decline, and even **snapping turtles** face many risks due to mowing, recreational land use, and an increase in wildlife such as raccoons and coyotes that eat turtle eggs.

If you live on or within a half mile of water, you live in New England native turtle habitat. Because turtles live part of their lives in water, but travel to nearby upland areas to nest, their survival depends on landowners near water preserving the habitat. Look around your property for turtle nesting areas such as sandy banks, gravel roadsides, and grassy areas.

Try to maintain a vegetated buffer growing between these areas and the nearby water, to protect turtles from predators when they travel from water to their breeding grounds. Road mortality also threatens turtles. If you see a turtle crossing the road, gently help them cross the road safely, always in the direction it's headed.

The spotted turtle lives in marshy areas and vernal pools.

Ants are valuable soil aerators, seed dispersers, and occasional plant pollinators when they travel inside plants looking for sweet nectar or aphid honeydew. Right: Bloodroot has red-colored roots that contain bitter compounds very distasteful to deer and other grazers, so bloodroot makes an excellent groundcover for areas where deer are problematic. Below: Close-up view of the seeds of celandine poppy. Ants love to eat the fleshy coatings of the seeds (called elaisomes), but they leave the seeds unharmed.

Adding Water to your Backyard Habitat

Adding aquatic habitat to your property is not as difficult as you might think. You can build a water feature or garden pond from a store-bought kit, or dig a small rain garden where you pipe the rainwater that flows off your roof. Even a small pool provides an oasis for wildlife.

Your goal is to set up an ecosystem by creating the conditions necessary for it to thrive with little intervention. Once it's created, your role is to monitor it for anything that may tip the balance of nature in one direction or another.

You don't necessarily need a pump, filter, and fountain to keep pond water clean. Chosen wisely, plants can keep it healthy by maintaining oxygen levels and absorbing excess nutrients. Floating plants such as water lilies block sunlight, which reduces algae. Fish, frogs, and dragonfly nymphs eat many insects. Fish and snails eat algae and clean waste from the bottom of the pond. Once a pond is balanced with wildlife and plants, algae usually stay at an acceptable level.

When designing your backyard pond, try to mimic a natural pond shoreline. Branches, submerged tree trunks, and rocks provide basking opportunities for turtles as well as water access for kids, frogs, and wildlife.

Although you will need to do some annual cleaning to prevent the buildup up too many leaves and plant materials that can deprive a pond of oxygen, leave a certain amount of dead plant materials. They will break down into organic matter that feeds many aquatic insects and fish, which in turn feed amphibians, reptiles, birds, and mammals. Over time, leaves and plant stems will break down into a layer of mud where turtles, frogs, and amphibians burrow into to hide, lay their eggs, or hibernate.

Vegetation and natural gradients on the edges of your pond link your pond to its surroundings as well as providing opportunities for a variety of creatures to safely approach the water's edge.

Installing a wildlife-friendly garden pond

Many stores sell shaped plastic ponds that you simply place in your yard and landscape around. Or you can dig a hole in the ground and line it with flexible PVC or butyl rubber. A flexible liner is better for a wildlife pond than a prefabricated one, because it is easier to vary the depths by creating sloping areas.

Some tips for making your pond beneficial to the greatest variety of wildlife:

- Situate your pond where it will receive at least a few hours of sunlight per day. A sunny location is best for the flowering aquatic plants that will attract the most wildlife to your pond. However, some shade will shelter fish and other creatures from the hot sun and keep the water cool.
- Vary the depth. A wildlife pond should be at least two feet deep in the center to provide hiding places for dragonfly nymphs and certain plants, and attract frogs, while a three- to four- foot depth is ideal for hosting a wider variety of creatures.

*The sound of the **spring peeper** is one of the first signs of spring in New England! A type of tree frog, peepers lay their eggs on tree branches overhanging water.*

Keep your pond water from becoming stagnant with aquatic plants and biological controls such as mosquito dunks or barley balls.

- Provide a shallow end and add some small stones to simulate a natural shoreline and increase the surface area so beneficial bacteria will form.
- Place partially submerged logs and stones of varying sizes in the pond to provide birds and butterflies a way to access the water.
- Add moving water using a splashing fountain or a dripper to attract birds and keep water oxygenated.
- Include shelves of varying depths in the side of your pond to hold containers of aquatic plants.
- Plant perennials and shrubs along the water's edge to provide safe cover, nesting sites, and perching places for turtles, birds, snakes, and dragonflies. (See page 132 for some good waterside plants.)
- Leave a certain amount of decayed vegetation at the bottom to form a mud layer for hibernating frogs.
- Add containers of water plants, reeds, and sedges to the pond bottom and on shelves to provide cover for aquatic creatures such as frogs and fish.
- Include microscopic life and small invertebrates by adding a bucket of water and mud from a local pond to your pond. Make sure the pond whose water you use appears healthy. Your pond will soon establish its own populations of tiny aquatic creatures to keep it in balance.
- Add native baitfish to your pond to eat mosquito larvae, algae, and organic waste. See page 143 for a list of suitable fish that are easily found at bait shops.
- Keep a hole open in the winter ice to allow oxygen to reach winter pond dwellers, and provide birds access to the water in the most brutal weather.

Note that your tap water probably contains chlorine, which can be harmful to plants. Unless you have well water, allow the water to sit for five to eight days to allow chlorine to dissipate before planting.

After you create your pond, watch how it evolves. Birds will probably arrive quickly, amphibians and reptiles perhaps a bit more slowly. Enjoy the process!

Native Plants for Water Gardens

Use a mix of aquatic plants to achieve a balanced ecosystem. Include plants with floating foliage, such as **water lilies**. Plants with underwater roots and stems with foliage above the surface, such as **arrowhead** and **watershield**, oxygenate the water and consume excess nutrients as well as providing hiding and spawning places for fish and wildlife. Try to cover about 50 to 70 percent of the water's surface with plants to control algae growth and maintain a healthy ecosystem. Marginal plants such as **blue flag** and **rushes** grow best along the edge, usually in a few inches of water.

Golden Club is an interesting native plant that grows in mucky soil and shallow water.

In small ponds, grow vigorous aquatic plants in submerged perforated containers to control their growth. Fill containers with good garden topsoil. Do not use potting mixes or peat moss—they will float right out of the pot. Add gravel to the top to prevent soil from floating out. Place on shelves or bricks to get the height you need.

Some plants float on the surface with dangling roots that are not anchored in the pond. **Water hyacinth** and **water lettuce** are often sold as water garden plants, but they are not native and are considered invasive in the South. However, they cannot survive New England winters, so are not damaging here.

Emergent/Marginal plants:

Northern blue flag iris *(Iris versicolor)*
Pickerelweed *(Pontederia cordata)*
Sweetflag *(Acorus calamus)*
Arrowhead *(Sagittaria latifolia)*
Arrow arum *(Peltandra virginica)*

Grasslike plants for containers in shallow water:

Sedges, including **black sedge** *(Carex nigra)*, **tussock sedge**
  (C. stricta) and **woolly-fruited sedge** *(C. lasiocarpa)*
Tufted hair grass *(Deschampsia caespitosa)*
Softrush *(Juncus effusus)*
Dwarf scouring rush *(Equisetum scirpoides)*

Floating-leaved plants:

Spatterdock *(Nuphar lutea)*
Fragrant water lily *(Nymphaea odorata)*
Water smartweed *(Polygonum amphibium)*
Watershield *(Brasenia)*
Golden club *(Orontium aquaticum)*

This bog garden, placed under the deep shade of tall trees and planted with pitcher plants and other bog plants was made by digging about a foot deep and adding a rubber liner. Ferns and moss from a sustainable moss nursery were added around the edges, and indoor houseplants adds zest to the scene during summer.

Container water gardens

A compact water feature such as a patio fountain provides the soothing sounds of moving water, and preassembled kits make it easy to add a water feature without buying complicated pumps and equipment. Patio fountains are the easiest to install and you can fit onto a small balcony. Or fill an old-fashioned whisky-style barrel with a mix of marginal water plants, add a small pump, and enjoy a lush garden pond on your patio or deck.

You can also create a small container garden holding a miniature ecosystem. Your goal is to bring the system into balance so that the plants and animals control algae and keep the water clean, which takes about a month in warm weather. As water temperatures rise, algae will begin to form, but a few fish and other scavengers will eat it, along with any mosquito eggs. The plants reduce the sunlight that reaches the water, keeping it cool and outcompeting the algae for nutrients..

Bog gardens

Bog plants tend to grow smaller than most wetland plants, making them suitable for creating small garden bogs that evoke the real thing. Create a bog garden in a pond liner or rubber pool liner. Dig an area at least twenty-five feet square and twelve to eighteen inches deep, lining it with sand to prevent punctures. Fill with a mix of builder's sand and wetted sphagnum peat and fill with water to six inches below the top of the soil. Plant your bog, then add some pieces of live sphagnum moss (available at moss nurseries,) to establish a moss layer for weed suppression. Or buy a bale of dry long-fiber sphagnum moss and sprinkle on your bog soil to grow new moss over time. Be sure to buy peat that has been harvested using sustainable methods. When peat is mined using large vacuums, the ecology of the bogs is damaged, often beyond repair.

Native plants for bog gardens:

Pitcher plant (*Sarracenia purpurea*)

Grass pink (*Calopogon tuberosus*)

Rose Pogonia (*Pogonia ophioglossoices*)

Sundew (*Drosera*)

Ladies' tresses (*Spiranthes odorata*)
pictured on page 139

Butterwort (*Pinguicula vulgaris*)

Dwarf scouring rush (*Equisetum scirpoides*)

Labrador tea (*Ledum groenlandicum*)

Shrubby cinquefoil (*Potentilla fruticosa*)

Leatherleaf (*Chamaedaphne calyculata*)

Cranberry (*Vaccinium macrocarpon*)

Sheep laurel (*Kalmia angustifolia*)

Bog laurel (*Kalmia polifolia*)

Birdbaths

Birds need clean water every day, so a birdbath or small water feature, especially with moving water, is a good option. Remember to clean your birdbath every few days to prevent the spread of diseases. Twice a week, scrub the bath with a plastic bristle brush and mild dish detergent, rinsing thoroughly before refilling. Every two weeks, after cleaning the bath, fill with a mixture of nine parts water to one part bleach, pour out, and rinse well. For winter birds, install a birdbath heater or use an inexpensive heated dog dish to keep your water from freezing.

Add rocks of varying sizes to your birdbath to provide access for small songbirds, butterflies, and pollinators. Keep birdbaths at least fifteen feet from trees and shrubs, so predators cannot pounce on visiting birds.

Recycling Rainwater

Gutter/downspout gardens

Thousands of gallons of rainwater run off your roof each year. Find ways to collect this free resource, save it, and use it for landscaping. A quick way to recycle the rain from your roof is to use a section of downspout to carry water away from your home, to a nearby area planted with moisture-loving plants.

You can also direct downspouts into a section of flexible piping buried in a shallow ditch, with holes punched in to allow water to seep into the root zone of surrounding plants. Or add an underground cistern to collect roof runoff, storing it for use for irrigation or car washing.

Introduce aquatic habitat to your property with a rain garden, which directs rainwater to a filter or "buffer" zone.

Left: *Recycle rainwater by piping it from roof gutters into a rain barrel, using it to water your lawn or containers during dry spells.*

Rain gardens

A rain garden is simply an excavated area with a dip at the center, planted to collect and slowly absorb runoff from roofs, paved areas, or lawns, filtering nutrients and pollutants before they reach wetlands.

Choose an area downhill from the water source, channeling it away from your house. The area should already drain well. The idea is to allow water to be slowly absorbed into the surrounding vegetation rather than run off quickly.

Simply lift existing sod and excavate any size area up to about eighteen inches deep, with sloping sides. Add a mix of about 50 percent sand or stone aggregate, 30 percent compost, and 20 percent existing topsoil. Experiment with the moisture collection. If your area does not drain, either backfill the rain garden with clay to slow percolation, or increase its size to absorb more water.

Plants suitable for a rain garden are those that tolerate wet conditions as well as dry periods.

Native Perennials & Grasses:

Bee balm, wild bergamot *(Monarda)*

Aster *(Symphyotrichum* spp.)

Lobelia spp.

Goldenrod *(Solidago)*

Swamp milkweed *(Asclepias incarnata)*

Joe-Pye weed *(Eutrochium)*

Boneset *(Eupatorium perfoliatum)*

Swamp rose mallow *(Hibiscus moscheutos* var. palustris)

Grasses such as big bluestem *(Andropogon gerardii)* and Switchgrass *(Panicum virgatum)*

Native Shrubs:

Summersweet *(Clethra altinifolia)*

Winterberry and inkberry holly *(Ilex verticillata, I. glabra)*

Dogwood *(Cornus)*

Stocking a Garden Pond with Fish

Fish are key to keeping a pond ecosystem in balance. But choose fish species and numbers carefully. Remember that fish eat the eggs and larvae of amphibians, dragonflies, and other species, so overstocking your pond will inhibit other beneficial species. Overstocking also creates excessive waste, causing spikes in nutrient levels and algae blooms. If you plan to introduce fish to your garden pond, choose smaller fish that will devour fewer other species and don't need feeding but can be sustained on the pond's natural resources. Wait until the pond's environment is balanced with plants before introducing fish.

If it is deep enough, most fish can survive the winter at the bottom of your pond and do not need to be brought indoors. But leave a hole in the ice to allow gases from decomposing plants to escape, and keep the pump running to maintain oxygen levels.

Native fish for your wildlife pond

It is not legal to take fish from the wild without a permit, so use native baitfish sold at New England's bait shops.

Small (minnow type) baitfish:
Banded killifish *(Fundulus diaphanus)*
Spottail shiner *(Notropis hudsonius)*
Mummichog or mosquito fish *(Fundulus heteroclitus)*
Golden shiner *(Notemigonus crysoleucas)*
Bluntnose minnow *(Pimephales notatus)*
Pumpkinseed, kiver, kibbie *(Lepomis gibbosus)*
Creek chubsucker *(Erimyzon oblongus)*

Larger baitfish (over 8")
Yellow perch *(Perca flavescens)*
Fallfish *(Semotilus corporalis)*
White sucker *(Catostomus commersoni)*

Avoid using exotic fish such as koi and carp in a wildlife pond. They have voracious appetites and will eat most of the pond life. Instead, use inexpensive native baitfish to try to establish your own fish populations.

*This **blue dasher dragonfly** perches on a twig, watching for mosquitoes with his extra-large eyes.*

Dragonflies . . . our mosquito hawks

Dragonflies eat insects, and mosquitoes are their specialty. They're not called **meadowhawks** or **pondhawks** for nothing! A water feature in your yard will attract dragonflies, which will help keep mosquitoes under control. Both adults and nymphs are also food for birds, amphibians, and fish. Dragonflies hatch and spend their early lives underwater, eating mosquito larvae and other tiny creatures. As adults, they chase flying insects, usually near water.

If you are building a pond with dragonflies in mind, the best size is about twenty feet in diameter, with varying depths, ideally at least two feet in the middle and sloping up to shallow edges. Aquatic plants are essential. Underwater plants give the predatory nymphs places to hide and wait for victims, and some dragonflies lay eggs within the stems of underwater plants. When nymphs hatch, they crawl up the submerged vegetation to begin their transformation into winged adults.

New England's Invasive Nonnative Plants

Although the history of our species is full of invasions large and small, the one invasion that may ultimately defeat us is that of invasive nonnative plants in our natural landscapes. It is a battle from within—many of the invasive plants that now blanket our woods, fields, and cities are here because they were originally introduced for ornamental reasons or to benefit wildlife. Until recently, landowners were encouraged to plant multiflora rose and autumn olive to create windbreaks, provide erosion control, and supply wildlife habitat. Many were so successful as food for birds that they soon spread across entire regions.

Japanese barberry, now "banned in Boston." You can support local biodiversity by removing invasive plants from your property to prevent them from spreading into nearby natural areas via birds.

*Although it may be tempting to plant quick-spreading **English ivy**, **bishop's goutweed**, or **winter creeper**, your children will one day curse you when they eventually strangle your entire yard. Each of these photos shows a double whammy of invasive and potentially invasive plants in residential gardens that pose a threat to the health of New England's woodlands.*

Right: *This looks like a berrying evergreen shrub, but it's **Asiatic bittersweet vine** winding through two varieties of **Asian wintercreeper** (Euonymus fortunei). The resulting tangle is well on its way to covering the entire house. Wintercreeper is not on New England's invasive species lists yet, but do not fall for its charms. It can disintegrate stone walls and even after removal, grows from the tiniest bit of roots left in the soil.*

Natural selection gone bad

The problem with invasives is that they grow so well that other plants don't stand a chance of surviving alongside them. Nonnative invasives have few natural predators or controls, so they reproduce much faster than their natural rate, crowding out native species which cannot compete for water, space, light, and nutrients. Invasives form monocultures, reducing biodiversity and leading to widespread loss of habitat. Some invasives change the chemical makeup of the soil, making it unfit for native plants.

You may see birds feeding on bittersweet berries or nesting in a buckthorn or Japanese honeysuckle and conclude that they are "wildlife-friendly." But nonnative berries did not evolve alongside New England's birds, delivering up the specific nutrition that native birds need. Migrating birds rely on the high fat native dogwood berries to fuel their long journeys, and Japanese honeysuckle berries may not cut it. And with very few exceptions, most native herbivorous insects cannot use the foliage of nonnatives as food. Because most baby birds, plus many other lifeforms, are fed exclusively on insect larvae, an area full of nonnative plants cuts off life at the bottom of the food chain.

The natural process of species migration has historically happened alongside resource changes that occur over thousands of years (glacial movement and cooling/warming cycles) or by natural occurrences such as floods, fires, or droughts. Human activity has brought plants to every corner of the globe, and accelerating climate change is enabling many invasive plants to establish in niches where native plants are unable to adapt.

Invasive plants also hybridize with native plants, changing their genetic makeup so that the original native species becomes rare or extinct, and the hybrids dominate. The invasive Asiatic bittersweet vine (now much more common than the native American bittersweet) is an example of how a native vine is becoming "hybridized" out of existence.

Scientists believe that a quarter of the earth's organisms will become extinct in the next twenty-five years, with invasive plants partly to blame. Once a plant is extinct, it's gone forever. Any potential as-yet-discovered medicinal benefit, such as that elusive cure for cancer, are lost.

Extreme weeding . . . removing invasive plants

Craft an attack strategy based on the life cycle of the plant species. Research the biology of the plant, determine the best timing, and strike when the plant is at its weakest. Rarely will you achieve instant eradication. You'll probably need to monitor the area over time and repeat if necessary.

> *"The worst thing that can happen is not energy depletion, economic collapse, limited nuclear war, or conquest by a totalitarian government.*
>
> *As terrible as these catastrophes will be for us, they can be repaired within a few generations...the one process now going on that will take millions of years to correct is the loss of genetic and species diversity by the destruction of natural habitats. This is the folly our descendants are least likely to forgive us."*
>
> E O WILSON

The "Usual Suspects": New England's Most Common Invasive Plants

Burning Bush/Winged Euonymous *(Euonymous alata)*
How many thousands of burning bushes do you see planted around houses, businesses, and on median strips? They are very popular for their bright-red fall display. However, they also produce tiny berries eaten by birds, which is why burning bush is now seeding itself throughout New England's woodlands and is banned for sale in Massachusetts and New Hampshire.

Japanese and European/Common Barberry
(Berberis thunbergii, B. vulgaris)
Common residential shrubs, including cultivars such as "Crimson Pygmy" are grown for their burgundy foliage. Berries are spread by birds to natural areas and reseed as vigorous green-leafed seedlings. Banned for sale in Massachusetts and New Hampshire.

Autumn Olive *(Elaeagnus umbellata)*
Heavily scented flowers in spring, a silvery underside to its leaves, and conspicuous red berries makes this easy to identify. Its berries spread by birds, and it has invaded fields, woodland edges, and other disturbed areas.

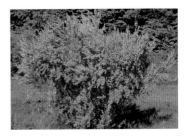

Multiflora (Wild) Rose *(Rosa multiflora)*

One of the major invasive thugs of our region. Originally introduced by the USDA for erosion control and for hedgerows, as well as to supply food and cover for wildlife. Its seeds were distributed widely by birds, and this plant is now colonized in all areas of New England, in large thickets.

Purple Loosestrife *(Lythrum salicaria)*

Everybody has noticed purple loosestrife, because it so beautifully clothes open waterside areas and median strips across the Northeast. It is one of our worst invasives, because aquatic areas are already under threat from pollution and development. Even garden cultivars said to be sterile are not safe—their pollen cross-pollinate with the wild species and reseed across the countryside.

Bishop's Weed/Goutweed *(Aegopodium podagraria)*

Often touted by nurseries as an ornamental shade plant with variegated foliage, this plant spreads aggressively and re-roots from any broken piece of root. It also reseeds, and the seedlings revert to the even more invasive green form. Eradication takes years of persistence.

Yellow Flag Iris *(Iris pseudacorus)*

Poisonous. *Originally introduced as a garden plant suitable for water gardens, yellow flag iris quickly escaped, and can be found in wetlands. It forms large colonies that displace native species such as sedges and rushes, altering wildlife habitat.*

Garlic Mustard *(Alliaria petiolata)*

A biennial herb, it grows in shade, making it one of few invasives that can dominate a forest understory. Root toxins kill natural mycorrhizal fungi used by native plants. Spreads rapidly as a groundcover. A threat to native butterfly species due to crowding out important food plants used by caterpillars.

Dame's Rocket *(Hesperis matronalis)*

Often mistaken for phlox, this is a European import usually growing in wetlands, moist woods, and along roadsides. Sometimes found in wildflower seed mixes.

Lesser and Greater Celandine *(Ranunculus ficaria, Chelidonium majus)*

Spring-flowering invasive to low woods and flood plains, spreading by roots and tubers. A threat to native spring ephemerals.

Tree of Heaven/Copal Tree *(Ailanthus altissima)*

Very common in cities because of its tolerance to air pollution, rapid growth, and ability to clone itself at the roots. Especially damaging because it produces toxins that inhibit the growth of nearby plants.

Border Privet *(Ligustrum obtusifolium)*

Native to Japan, introduced for use as a hedge. Difficult to tell apart from European and Chinese privet – flowers are different.

Common Buckthorn and Glossy Buckthorn *(Rhamnus cathartica* and *Frangula alnus)*

Tall shrub with numerous red and black fruits (both may exist on the plant at the same time) and dull or glossy green leaves. Forms dense stands in wetlands and open areas across New England.

Japanese Knotweed, Mexican Bamboo, Fleece Flower *(Polygonum cuspidatum)*

Shrublike plant with thick, red. bamboo-like stems. Flowers are fleecy white in summer. The stems can spread underground 60 feet in every direction, forming dense stands and popping up even through concrete. A real threat to riparian habitat.

Japanese and Bush Honeysuckle: Morrow's/Amur/Tartarian/Bell's *(Lonicera morrowii, L. Maackii, L. japonica, L. tartarica)*

Introduced for ornamental use, exotic honeysuckle has been spread by birds that distribute the berries. Established across New England.

Norway and Sycamore/Planetree Maple
(Acer platanoides, A. pseudoplatanus)
Commonly planted as a street tree, because of its dense shade and tolerance to road salt and chemicals. Heavily reseeds into nearby gardens, forests, and fields, where it halts understory succession by leafing out earlier in spring than native maples, shading out native ephemeral plants.

Common Reed *(Phragmites australis)*
Grows to fifteen feet and quickly takes over marshland with its thick roots and biomass, crowding out other plants. Forms dense stands containing new growth as well as old dead stems. Difficult to tell from the native Phragmites, but generally the largest stands are the invasive variety.

Canary Reed Grass *(Phalaris arundinacea)*
Native to the US, but cultivars from Europe planted by settlers in the 1800s for hay have become invasive grasses that form dense monocultures covering many acres of wetlands. Variegated variety (called ribbon grass) used in landscaping.

Japanese Stilt Grass *(Microstegium vimineum)*
An annual grass introduced to Tennessee in the early 1900s, where it was apparently brought in as packing material, it has been spreading rapidly north into New England since the mid-1980s. Grows in just about any disturbed soil .

Asiatic/Asian/Oriental Bittersweet *(Celastrus orbiculatus)*
Asian bittersweet is to New England what kudzu vine is to the South. Spread by birds eating its berries, it rapidly twines its way around anything within reach and can quickly engulf a tree, bringing it down from the sheer weight of its woody stems.

Black Swallow-wort *(Cynanchum rossicum)*
Twining herbaceous vine forming extensive patches from rhizomes. Resprouts from roots after mowing. Prevent from seeding by removing seed pods (throw them away) or mowing before seeding. Multiple mows will weaken the plant. Brought into a botanic garden in Ipswich, Massachusetts in 1854, it quickly escaped cultivation and is now found everywhere in Boston.

Quick and Dirty Guide to Organic Gardening

Don't let anyone tell you that you need to use chemicals and poisons to grow a garden. You can nurture your lawn and garden and protect plants from pests and diseases the same way farmers have for thousands of years—without chemicals!

Green gardening is all about understanding and harnessing the life in your soil, and allowing its natural cycles to work for your plants.

What this means to you, specifically, depends on what you are trying to grow. Most plants and trees, when grown in their preferred habitat, can take care of their needs without fertilizers. By shedding their leaves and needles every year and forming root associations with soil bacteria and fungi, plants support themselves by orchestrating complex interactions with their environment. Chemical fertilizers feed plants, but they kill off beneficial soil microbes at the same time. When a plant receives nutrients from synthetic sources, roots no longer need to manipulate the surrounding soil for nutrients, and the lifeforms that naturally colonize plant roots disappear. If we also dig, rototill, and otherwise disturb soil, we destroy the vast interconnected tunnels that funnel moisture and nutrients to roots. The result is soil that is biologically dead and incapable of supporting plants without lots of outside input.

Your job as an organic gardener is simple: Instead of feeding plants with fertilizers, feed the soil life, and they will take care of your plants.

The kitchen gardens at Salem Cross Inn, West Brookfield, Massachusetts.

Feed the soil, not the plants

Compost is the best soil amendment of all. When added to clay soil or an area with heavy soil compaction, compost helps lighten soil structure and improve drainage. In sandy soils, compost helps soil retain nutrients and moisture.

Healthy, living soil is made up of countless micro and macro-organisms that work together to benefit plants. Known as the "soil food web", they range from single-celled microbes to tiny arthropods and earthworms, and feed on and break down organic matter, minerals, toxins, even each other, Microbiological soil activity is key to "unlocking" soil and atmospheric nutrients and turning them into a form that plants can use. Compost, farm animal manure, wood ashes, tree leaves and plant debris are traditional, effective soil amendments used by New Englanders to feed and enrich soil, but they can be labor-intensive to apply. The modern, efficient equivalent is aerated liquid fertilizer, containing a blend of ingredients, oxygenated with a pump to vastly increase microbial activity. Applied to plants as a soil drench and foliage spray, these "teas" supply soil and plants with populations of living microbes, as well as a variety of trace elements and nutrients that plants need, in a form easily and quickly absorbed.

Whether you apply soil amendments in liquid or solid form, the best, readily available microbe foods for lawns and gardens include:
- Good quality (finished) compost
- Seaweed (kelp) and fish-based products
- Earthworm castings (from a worm bin)
- Hot-composted or pasteurized farmyard animal manure
- Coffee grounds
- Alfalfa or other grain-based animal feed (such as rabbit or horse feed)
- Meals made from animal byproducts including blood, feather, and bone meal.

Liquid fertilizers blending these products are increasingly available at nurseries, but you can also brew your own plant fertilizer by soaking good compost for a few days in water (in cheesecloth or a porous bag). For optimal results, use a small aquarium pump to aerate the solution for a day or two and apply using a garden sprayer.

Concoct your own nutrient-rich "tea" blends using whatever ingredients you can find. Fresh foliage and roots from nutrient-mining weeds such as dandelions, yarrow and nettles contribute their cache of accumulated nutrients, and their foliage feeds bacteria that help fight disease. Sea kelp and earthworm castings promote beneficial fungi that help fight black spot and other foliage pathogens.

The catch for New England gardeners is that plants usually

prefer to grow in soil dominated by the specific microbes they evolved with, either fungi or bacteria. Plants that originate outside our region (which includes most annual vegetable plants, lawn grasses, and annual flowers) generally need a sweet (more alkaline) soil with high bacterial populations, and don't thrive in the naturally sour (acidic) soil of New England without help from us. Perennials, shrubs and trees tend to be acid lovers, thriving in soils rich in the beneficial fungi that grow naturally in eastern US woodland soils. So, depending on what you are growing, and the results of any soil testing, you can tailor your soil amendments to encourage the "right type" of soil microbes, either bacteria or fungi.

Feeding lawns, annual flowers, and vegetables. The fungi that dominate New England's soils produce acids that inhibit the growth of the bacteria these plants need for rapid growth and high yields in a short season. Give them a boost with fertilizers containing the sugars that bacteria love, including coffee grounds, fruit, food grade molasses and sea kelp. You can also apply calcitic limestone or wood ash from fireplaces to raise the soil pH and add calcium and magnesium, essential plant macronutrients often missing from garden soils. Well-composted animal manure and corn gluten meal are good nitrogen sources.

Note: Never use fresh livestock manure as a plant tea or soil amendment in vegetable gardens—manure needs to be composted to reach a temperature of 150-160F to kill harmful pathogens such as *Escherichia coli* (E. coli) and *salmonella*.

Feeding perennials, woody shrubs, and trees. Most trees, shrubs, and perennials prefer a woodland-type soil where fungal microbes outnumber bacteria. These plants evolved to feed on nutrients they mine from the surrounding soil using mycorrhizal fungi which are attracted to their roots. You can buy mycorrhizal spores to inoculate your soil, or apply a layer of leaf mold (partially composted, shredded, or whole) or other tree by-products (such as bark or wood chips) over root zones to add fungi. Or simply allow leaf litter to remain under the drip line of trees and shrubs to encourage the natural mycorrhizal associations to form. For a quick boost for stressed trees, concoct a fungally-dominated tea with ground oatmeal, soluble kelp, and a cup of soil from healthy woodland soil. Most herbaceous perennials, especially native woodland plants, also prefer to be fed with compost-based fungal foods, with the exception of meadow-type plants that are adapted to sweeter soils (including rudbeckia and most native grasses).

Get to know the "soil food web"

Farmers have long known that legume plants take nitrogen from the air and convert it to plant food through their roots, but modern microscopes have recently enhanced our understanding of how plant roots interact with microscopic soil organisms to manufacture their own food. We tend to consider fungi and bacteria as bad things, but most fungi and bacteria in healthy soil are beneficial, and in an intact soil food web they usually outcompete the "bad guys."

Mulch for healthy soil

Instead of digging or rototilling gardens, build your soil UP by adding organic matter on top of the soil. Digging exposes millions of dormant weed seeds and disrupts existing stable soil communities by destroying networks of tunnels formed by soil microbes.

Mulch is any organic material, such as leaves, wood chips, shredded bark, cardboard, or straw, placed on top of the soil to inhibit weed seeds and to keep soil cool and moist. Organic mulches also feed the soil food web without disturbance to the underlying soil structure. Add a layer of mulch around root zones of plants, vegetable crops and trees at any time to begin building soil from the ground up.

The best mulch materials for New England:

- Weed-free compost
- Seaweed**
- Leaf mold (decomposing leaves from trees and shrubs)**
- Saltmarsh hay*
- Seashells
- Partially decomposed wood chips (aged at least three months) **
- Shredded bark (not treated or dyed with toxins)**
- Sawdust**
- Pine needles**
- Buckwheat hulls
- Newspaper and cardboard** wetted and covered with a thin layer of bark chips

* bacterially dominated ** fungally dominated

Heavy mulches such as bark and wood chips prevent self-seeding of nearby plants, so avoid them where you want to encourage self-sowing. Wood mulches can also inhibit the natural spreading of some perennials, especially low spreaders that root in the soil. Avoid using mulch on slopes or anywhere that floods.

A tried-and-true New England gardening tactic is to apply a layer of mulch to plants after the ground has frozen in winter. The mulch keeps the soil frozen through the winter, protecting plant roots from fluctuating freeze/thaw cycles which damage roots and heave plants right out of the ground. Winter mulch may attract plant-eating voles, however.

Don't condemn your trees to a slow death with a mulch volcano! Trees take up oxygen and moisture using the roots closest to the trunk, and covering this trunk flare with mulch suffocates the roots and encourages microbes to eat the bark.

Creating No-Dig Garden Beds

To create new beds without digging, simply pile a thick layer of organic materials such as leaves, partially finished compost, and farm animal manure in an area you want to plant. First, smother existing grass or weeds by laying down ten or twelve sheets of newspaper or cardboard. Immediately spray with a hose to thoroughly soak the paper and prevent it from flying away. Overlap the edges to prevent grass from popping through. On top of this layer, pile up as much organic matter you can find, at least 4-6" to ensure that the grass is killed. Use anything you would add to a compost pile. Worms will do their work and within a year, the grass will be gone and the soil wonderful.

You can plant immediately by cutting holes in the layers, but you may need to hand-pull the grass around the edges of the holes. If you've used topsoil or compost as a top layer, wait a few weeks before planting so that you can easily remove any weeds that may germinate.

*Also called **sheet composting** or **lasagna gardening**, worms and other decomposers quickly break down the materials into rich, loose soil perfect for planting, while maintaining the existing soil food web and soil structure.*

Making Compost

Compost is simply organic materials mixed together and left to rot into "black gold". You can buy compost in bags, but even the smallest household can produce its own compost using a mix of kitchen scraps, white paper, tree leaves and other materials that you otherwise pay to dispose of.

Making your own compost can be as simple or complex as you like. Mix materials inside a simple wire bin, or just rake and pile them up in an inconspicuous location. If you don't have much room, a compost tumbler allows composting in small spaces. Or try composting in a worm bin, which you keep indoors and fill with kitchen scraps for redworms to convert into dry, crumbly "vermi-compost".

Look for free sources of organic materials for your compost pile. Fallen leaves and grass clippings (from lawns not treated with pesticides), livestock or poultry manure from local farmers, seashells, garden trimmings such as deadheaded flowers, shrub prunings, and rootballs from dead plants, paper grocery bags, paper towels, and kitchen scraps such as carrot tops, apple cores, corn husks, banana skins, potato and orange peels, eggshells, teabags, and coffee grounds. If you live near the coast, fill buckets with seaweed to add to your compost pile, or collect crab and mussel shells to use as a calcium-rich additive.

For materials to be broken down into the best compost, you need to supply oxygen, water, carbon, and nitrogen. Carbon is any dry, brown material such as old leaves, newspaper, or straw. Nitrogen is supplied by green materials such as weeds, grass clippings, kitchen scraps, and manure. To make sure that any weed seeds or pests don't survive the composting process, you should mix ingredients in such a ratio that the pile heats up to at least 150° F, to kill pests, pathogens, and weed seeds.

The quickest way to create finished compost is to alternate layers of brown (carbon) and green (nitrogen) materials, sprinkling water on each. The pile will heat up and shrink in size as microbes break down the materials. After it has cooled, turn it to add more air, and it will heat up again. When it has finally cooled down and won't heat anymore, your compost is perfect. A pile four feet square is ideal for optimal compost production, and try to include a carbon-nitrogen ratio of 20:1.

Or you can simply pile up your materials, let rain provide the water, and eventually it will break down into usable compost. This takes longer than if you actively manage your pile, and the pile will usually not heat up enough to destroy pathogens and weed seeds. Remember, you can always use partially decomposed compost at any time as mulch or a soil amendment in planting holes.

The quality of any compost depends on its source materials. A pile with a wide variety of raw materials will host the widest diversity of beneficial soil microbes, because each form of organic matter hosts its own set of co-evolved bacteria and fungi. The more "small guys" that inhabit an area, the more higher lifeforms (crustaceans, grubs, earthworms, and others) appear to feed on them, the more levels of decomposition, and the richer the compost.

Depending on what raw materials go in, your compost can be dominated by bacteria or by fungi. Compost made with large quantities of tree leaves, bark, and shrub/tree trimmings will be fungally dominated. Bacterially dominated compost is made up of fresh, green stuff such as kitchen scraps, vegetable garden trimmings, fresh grass clippings, farm animal manure, and the remains of annual plants. If you're really gung-ho about composting, keep two types of compost, one made up mostly of tree leaves, branch, and tree clippings. Use this for your house plants, perennials, shrubs, and trees. Keep another pile with green materials. You'll need to add at least a few "browns" such as dry leaves and coffee grounds to prevent the pile from becoming anaerobic. Use this compost for your lawn, annuals, and vegetable beds.

*Part of your transformation to an earth-friendly gardener is accepting that most insects are either innocuous or beneficial, and their existence promotes a balanced ecosystem. If you see a **hornworm caterpillar** (left) eating the leaves of your tomato or pepper plants, covered in what looks like tiny grains of rice, these white eggs are larvae of a parasitic wasp. Relocate the caterpillar to a "sacrifice plant," another plant the caterpillar can use as food, such as **Nicotiana** (right). Native host plants for hornworms include **ground cherry**, an annual with flowers resembling Chinese Lanterns, and **American nightshade**.*

Tolerate a little pest damage to encourage the predators

Pest problems occur where there is little diversity in plant life. If you plant only roses, the insects that eat roses will explode to take advantage of an abundant food source. Without habitat, their predators cannot reproduce quickly enough to control them. Accept that some plants can and will suffer some insect damage, and that, with the exception of annuals, it usually won't kill healthy plants.

The latest pest is defoliating your plants? What to do!?

But what, I hear you cry, if the latest "invasive" pest is defoliating your plants? Winter moth. Gypsy moth caterpillar. Asian lily beetle. Japanese beetle. The appearance of these imported pests strikes fear into the gardener's heart. They can certainly cause major damage, especially to natives with no natural defenses. A spray program may save a few valuable trees, but usually also destroys beneficial insects and predators at the same time. Keep your landscape plantings diverse and avoid monocultures, so that no single pest can ever destroy your entire garden. Control pest populations by attracting as many insect-eating birds as you can, and plant herbs and other flowering plants to attract parasitic wasps and other predators. As a particular pest's population increases, populations of parasites and predators should eventually increase also, and over time plants develop their own chemical defenses to pests and can control major infestations on their own. In the short term, accept that you may need to sacrifice those plants, until natural controls become effective or plants adapt.

The good news is that Japanese beetles do seem to be on the decline in New England, and a tiny parasitic wasp is believed to be helping. If you spot a Japanese beetle with white spots directly behind its thorax (head), don't kill it! It will infect other beetles and reduce your Japanese beetle populations.

*Before you reach for the spray bottle to kill **eastern tent caterpillars** emerging from their nests in your apple or cherry tree, remember that tent caterpillars are among the **black-billed cuckoo's** main foods.*

157

Some common bio-weapons in our gardens:

Beneficial Insects, Arthropods and Invertebrates

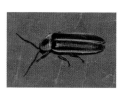

Fireflies (also called lightning bugs or glowworms) are beetles, not flies. They were once familiar nighttime sights in New England, but loss of habitat and pesticide use means that their summer twinkles are rarer. Adults don't feed, but the larvae eat slugs, snails, and cutworms. Keep an area of your yard a little wild (and unlit), to encourage fireflies to light up your summer nights!

Ladybird Beetles (sometimes called ladybugs) love aphids and also feed on thrips, mites, mealybugs, and scale. They often disappear if all aphids are destroyed, but a habitat garden with many flowering plants and shrubs keeps them local.

Tiger Beetles and their larvae eat whatever bugs they can, including flies, caterpillars, ants, spiders, grasshoppers, and aphids. They fly or run quickly after bugs in sunny, open areas, and swarm around lights at night. Adults have a violent streak, grabbing victims in their sharp jaws and killing the prey by slamming it to the ground until it stops moving. They overwinter in undisturbed garden areas or perennial beds. Two types: **Brown tiger beetle** and **six-spotted green tiger beetle**.

Lacewings and their larvae are deadly assassins of aphids, beetle larvae, corn earworms, leafhoppers, mealybugs, caterpillars, and the nymphs of scale insects. Adults look like tiny green alligators, flying around meadows and forest edges in the evening and at night. The eggs are cream-colored ovals found on the undersides of leaves. Lacewings are pollinators and supplement their insect diet with nectar, so attract them with nectar plants.

Parasitic Wasps attack the larvae of many pests. Braconid (shown at left, parasitizing a gypsy moth caterpillar), Ichneumon, and Chalcid wasps. Many species are nearly invisible to the human eye. Many eat nectar and pollen to fuel their flight, so a variety of flowers blooming from early spring through summer will attract them. Most parasitic wasps are solitary and do not sting.

Predatory Bugs include pirate bugs (a pollinator), ambush bugs, assassin bugs (left), minute pirate bugs, damsel bugs, two-spotted stink bugs, and spined soldier bugs These all prey on pests such as tomato hornworms, spider mites, sawflies, thrips, corn earworms, potato beetles, bean beetles, asparagus beetles, and cabbage loopers. They generally live in hedgerows, meadows, fields, and gardens. Stink bugs emit a foul-smelling fluid if disturbed.

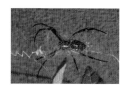

Spiders such as the **black-and-yellow garden spiders** *(left)* feed on insects and are important pest controllers. Garden spiders do not generally enter your house nor are they poisonous. Although many people are frightened of spiders, very few spiders ever bite people. Encourage spiders by providing mulch and a variety of plantings where they can spin their webs.

Daddy longlegs (right; also called **harvestmen**) are common arachnids that feed on insects and tiny spiders, between April and November. They don't spin webs, but hide on tree trunks and in flower heads, waiting to pounce on visiting pollinating insects.

Soldier beetles look like fireflies, but without the glow. Adults and larvae are predatory, eating garden pests such as beetles, grasshopper eggs, caterpillars, root maggots, and soft-bodied insects. They lay eggs in the soil, and the pupae need permanent plantings where they are not disturbed. Adults eat pollen, and milkweed, goldenrod, and nepeta will all attract them

Syrphid or **hoverfly** larvae feed exclusively on aphids. Adult hoverflies are important pollinators. Many people mistake these flies for wasps or hornets because of their yellow/black stripes, but they do not bite or sting! You can identify them by the way they hover around flowers, darting in and out. Attract the adults with flowering plants and herbs. The female hoverfly lays eggs on aphid-infested foliage, and the larvae are sluglike.

Tachinid flies look like houseflies but with more hairs. They are parasitic, injecting their larvae into the immature forms of cutworms, moths, beetles, and sawflies. Introduced species of tachinid flies have helped control gypsy moth caterpillar damage in New England, but they also prey on native silkworm caterpillars. Many native species also exist. Attract them with nectar plants.

Dragonflies and **Damselflies** are flying predators that eat large numbers of mosquitoes. Unfortunately, community spraying for mosquitoes usually also kills dragonflies. Dragonflies lay their eggs in water, so encourage them to repopulate by providing a water supply with many plants nearby. The aquatic nymphs (called naiads) also eat mosquito larvae, and are found under stones or debris next to water. Dragonflies' eyes meet near the top of the head; damselfly eyes are set farther apart. Dragonflies usually perch with wings spread. (See page 144)

Praying Mantis is a nonnative but effective garden predator. Adult butterflies are among their favorite foods.

Amphibians (frogs, toads, salamanders) are predators of slugs, snails, and other small animals. Some help decompose organic matter in the soil. Thin and cold-blooded, they lack scales to keep them waterproof, so they spend most of the year under bark, fallen logs, and wet leaves. In winter, they hibernate in soil where organic materials are allowed to build up.

Reptiles such as **turtles** and **snakes** provide valuable pest control by feeding on voles, moles and mice, as well as amphibians. Reptiles have scales to keep them waterproof and prevent dehydration. Turtles can live for decades, but due to road mortality, development destroying their nesting sites, and a low reproductive rate (eggs are eaten by many predators), their populations are in decline.

Flip a flat rock or paving stone for a peek into a world of subterranean tunnels and burrows made by nature's cleanup crew. You'll see tunnels dug by **earthworms**, **pillbugs**, **ground beetles**, **digger bees**, **mites**, *and* **ants**.

There are probably not many who find slugs attractive. Toads, frogs, salamanders, ground beetles, and blackbirds, thrushes, robins, crows, jays, ducks, seagulls, and owls—all eat them, and native slugs play an important role by eating fungi and algae. The familiar slimy, destructive slugs that ravage our gardens (pictured) are introduced nonnatives.

Soil Friends (Scavengers and Nutrient Recyclers)

Earthworms/redworms ("nightcrawlers") are not native to New England but have been used by gardeners for centuries as effective soil aerators and improvers—their tunneling action opens up soil pores. They usually appear out of nowhere (actually, from deep within the ground) if you build a compost pile. They can be invasive in native forest soils, reducing leaf litter much more quickly than natural processes. Never release red wigglers (also used for fishing bait) into forested areas, and avoid building compost piles in or near forests.

Rove beetles are active scavengers, eating whatever soft-bodied insects and larvae they come across, as well as dead or decaying matter. They eat root maggots so are valuable in the vegetable garden. When disturbed, they raise their tails menacingly.

Ground beetles are shiny, long-legged, dark beetles that hide under rocks and logs during the day. They feed on slugs, snails, cutworms, spider mites, pest beetles, root maggots, and aphids. Provide habitat using rocks, groundcovers, and woodpiles.

Pillbugs (sowbugs) are crustaceans that live under rocks, logs, and leaves, feeding on decaying plants.

Centipedes and **millipedes** are small arthropods with multiple leg segments that live in leaf litter, dead trees, and occasionally buildings where food is available. They feed on decaying plants, fungi, and occasionally plant roots. They roll tightly into a coil to defend themselves, and are eaten by toads, birds, ground beetles, and spiders.

Bacteria are single-celled microscopic plants essential to nutrient recycling. They exist in every habitat, feeding upon just about everything. In turn, they feed many other soil microbes, including nematodes and protozoa. Some are pathogenic.

Fungi form symbiotic relationships with objects in their surroundings, and can be microscopic, or visible, as with mushrooms. Some are pathogenic, but diverse fungal populations usually outcompete them. Fungal colonies spread long distances through soil, feeding on bacteria and other fungi, forming long tunnels, which are then reused by many other members of the soil food web. These tunnels are pathways, recycling nutrients to plant roots. Mycorrhizae are the associations formed between fungi and plant roots, which plants use to manipulate the surrounding soil to obtain nutrients.

Nematodes are tiny and wormlike, ranging from microscopic species to the largest (usually less than $1/10$ inch). Some are parasitic—on humans and on plants—while others prey upon on the destructive soil nematodes.

Protozoa are single-celled microorganisms, which feed on bacteria and other soil life, recycling it into food for larger soil invertebrates.

Buying bugs? Supply habitat instead!

It's possible to buy beneficial insects such as ladybird beetles and lacewings by mail order to release into your garden or greenhouse, but it's not recommended. Beneficial insect farms are responsible for shipping nonnative insects into regions where they impact native insect populations by competing for food and nesting sites. The ladybugs that group by the thousand and make their way into your house in the fall are not usually the native ladybird beetles, but Asian imports introduced to the US for greenfly control. Supply habitat with plants, and beneficial insects will eventually find your garden on their own.

Prevention is the best cure

Practicing good horticulture is your best general defense against pests and diseases, by choosing plants adapted to your garden conditions and planting a variety of plants that support beneficial insects. If your plants are stressed in any way, they have less resistance to pests and diseases. Plant stress can be caused by:

*Hummingbird favorites **cardinal flower** and **boneset** both love the moist soil at the Pond Garden at Tower Hill Botanic Garden in Boylston, Massachusetts.*

- Too much, or too little, moisture. A moisture lover will struggle in soil that is too dry. Some plants cannot tolerate wet feet, and need an area where water drains well. Move plants or improve soil drainage by adding compost and organic matter.
- Incorrect siting of a plant based on its light requirements (sun versus shade). Always research before planting to determine the type of light a plant requires. Move ailing plants around to see if a different light exposure will help.
- Too much mulch. Never pile mulch against the base of plants, as this can rot crowns and stems.
- Overfertilization. Too much nitrogen can weaken plants and actually favors pests such as aphids. Use soil tests to determine what nutrients are missing, and switch to a organic fertilizer.
- Crowding by weeds. Weeds steal nutrients and moisture from nearby plants. The best weed control is to avoid digging and preemptively mulch around plants to deter germination of weed seeds. Second best is to hand-weed when weeds are small.

Don't use bug zappers or light traps! They kill many insects, but only 1 percent are biting bugs such as mosquitoes. More often, they kill night-flying moths (important pollinators of night-blooming flowers), tiger beetles, and other beneficial insects.

Aphids? No need for chemicals; aphids won't usually kill healthy plants. Attract predatory lacewings, hoverflies, and lady beetles (pictured) with flowering plants, and they will devour them. If you find them unsightly, just spray them sharply with a hose to wash them off the foliage (they can't fly back onto plants).

Natural alternatives to chemical warfare

If natural predators are not controlling a pest and you need to intervene, first identify your enemy. Use a bug ID guide to identify your pest, and choose the lowest-toxicity, lowest-impact eradication method. Several New England firms produce natural pest control products designed and packaged for home gardeners.

Natural pesticides, sprays:
- Insecticidal sprays made of dish soap and water or using plant-based ingredients, such as permethrin, garlic, and coffee
- Fungal sprays to help plants fight leaf spot, blight, and other foliage diseases
- Beneficial nematodes, which control certain grubs
- Bacterial toxin (Bt, or *Bacillus thuringiensis*), which kills any caterpillars that ingest it. Use only for serious crop pests, and only in the affected area, to avoid impacting no-pest caterpillars.
- Milky spore to control Japanese beetle grubs, but also impacts beneficial native beetles. Not particularly effective in New England because it takes three to five years to begin working, and does not work at all below Zone 5.

Manual pest control and deterrents:
- Hand-pick pests off plants into a jar of soapy water
- Bitter-tasting or scented sprays to deter pests
- Floating row covers to prevent pests from reaching plants
- Traps such as beer traps (for slugs) or sticky traps
- Scarecrows and other motion devices to scare off pests

The 3 C's of Vegetable Gardening

Companion Planting. Many plants take care of each other by discouraging pests, by exuding natural substances that repel insects. Others act as decoys by attracting pests away from more highly valued plants. Some can even enhance the growth and flavor of other, nearby plants. Research beneficial plant associations for the plants you are trying to grow.

Cover Crops. Planting cover crops of grasses, grains, or legumes in fallow fields or idle vegetable gardens protects the soil from erosion, prevents invasive species from taking hold, and creates a "green manure," which can eventually be turned into the soil, contributing

Marigolds provide an attractive and useful edging for cucumber plants. Their strong scent repels many pests, and helps control certain soil nematodes that can damage your vegetables.

nutrients and food for soil life forms. Cover crops also provide valuable wildlife cover and forage. Good annual cover crops for New England include **buckwheat** (attracting parasitic wasps and hoverflies), **legumes** such as **field peas** or **crimson clover** (which contribute nitrogen to the soil, and food/cover for many pollinators and predatorial insects), and **annual ryegrass** (commonly used for erosion control on building sites, attracting predatorial rove beetles and birds foraging on its seeds).

Crop Rotation. One way to keep a step ahead of pests if you grow vegetables or other crops is to rotate them, never planting the same plant (or close relative) in the same spot as the previous year. Many pests such as corn earworms and cabbage worms are crop-specific, and rotation prevents them from building up populations in a single area.

Irrigation

The essence of an earth-friendly garden is that once established it should survive without irrigation. Any new plantings, however, even of drought-tolerant plants, require supplemental irrigation in their first summer and sometimes into the second year. Vegetable gardens need irrigation during dry spells.

Give plants a deep soaking, and avoid watering too frequently. Occasional, deep watering encourages root systems to grow deep into the soil in search of moisture, whereas frequent, shallow watering causes roots to concentrate near the surface, making plants susceptible to drought stress. Use drip irrigation or soaker hoses in vegetable gardens. And recycle your rainwater. (See page 141.)

Native Americans interplanted **corn**, **beans** *and* **squash** *(the "Three Sisters"). The corn provides a climbing stalk for the beans; the beans supply nitrogen to the soil to nouish the corn, and the squash leaves keep weeds from sprouting.*

Controlling weeds

Forget about spring cleaning your house (do it in late fall instead!), and use early spring to tackle unwanted weeds. Removing weeds when they're small protects the nutrients they would otherwise remove from the soil. Hand weeding in the spring is best, when the moist soil makes removal easy without damaging nearby roots, but specialist tools can make weeding easier for species with long taproots, such as dandelions and thistles. A Weed Wrench is useful for invasive plants and weeds with large rootballs.

Mow or cut stems to the ground repeatedly. Eventually the plant's energy resources will be exhausted. If done before flowers set seed, this can control reseeding. Established plants may require mowing or cutting for several years. Many plants will resprout after cutting, although if done in late fall, this will reduce sprouting the following season. Some plants cannot be controlled by mowing and will resprout even more vigorously.

Avoid tilling, which exposes more weed seeds, and chops weed roots and stems into many pieces, each of which may sprout into a new weed. Some invasive weeds, including bishop's goutweed and Asian bittersweet, regrow from even the tiniest piece of root left in the soil. Even chemical treatment cannot eradicate this problem, and you may be forced to dig up and sift the entire bed, removing each piece of root by hand over the course of several years.

The use of systemic herbicides have been linked to a number of human health problems as well as amphibian deaths and is recommended only where a weed threatens local ecosystems.

Non-toxic weed controllers:
- Natural fungicides, such as acetic acid (concentrated, horticultural-strength vinegar) can be effective if used repeatedly on young seedlings, but are rarely effective for established plants.
- Boiling water
- Weed torches burn hydrocarbon fuels, but offer precision in difficult locations like cracks in pavement or along edges.
- Controlled grazing by farm animals. Cows, goats, and sheep reclaim large areas from non-native invasive plants. Sheep keep grass short, cows clear brush, and goats eat poison ivy!.
- Mulch/barrier method to smother underlying vegetation by inhibiting the light required for photosynthesis. (See page 155.)

Planting

When planting perennials, shrubs, and trees, create a small berm around the perimeter to help contain water in the root zone during establishment, but remove this after the first year. At planting time, inoculate the soil with mycorrhizal spores to kick-start populations of beneficial root fungi. or add leaves, leaf mold from healthy plants. Plant seedlings near mature, healthy specimens of plants, to allow takeup of associated soil organisms.

Pruning shrubs

With some exceptions, most of our native shrubs take on an attractive natural form and don't require pruning. Some shrubs benefit from being cut back to the ground periodically. The plant will then put out vigorous new growth from the base, which is a good way to rejuvenate the plant every few years and also keep its height in check. Cutting shrubs back hard allows them to regenerate as they would in nature if nibbled by deer. Remove older, less vigorous branches and any that block younger growth. Shred the debris and use it as a mulch, to feed the plant and prevent moisture loss. For shrubs such as **elderberry**, **clethra**, and **lilac**, cut down a third of the oldest stems each year for three years to rejuvenate.

A fungus among us. It looks like disgusting dog vomit, but it's actually harmless fungi that occasionally appear on wet lawns or on mulch when conditions favor its growth.

Add shrub prunings to compost, or use the trimmings as mulch under the same shrubs to build up populations of your friendly resident soil fungi. The smaller the trimmings, the more quickly they will break down. Sprinkling the trimmings with water encourages faster decomposition.

Sourcing Plants

"Native plants" is the new buzzword in the horticultural trade, but many plants sold as "natives" are actually grown in other areas, and are therefore adapted to ecosystems different from our own. Try to buy your plants from local growers who propagate plants from local strains. Plants of local provenance are adapted to New England's soil and climate and will grow better than those propagated in other regions. Growing plants from local sources also helps maintain genetic variation within regional populations.

Always look for plants that are nursery-propagated, not picked from the wild. Many rare, native, wild species are threatened due to overpicking by unethical growers. Good nurseries should be able to tell you the source of their plants.

Seedlings vs cultivars?

Cultivars are readily available, and also offer predictable growth habits, which may be important to a specific garden design. However, most are vegetatively propagated from the same original plant, making them genetic clones. Plants grown from seed are genetically unique, each one increasing the diversity of the local gene pool, ensuring that at least some plants have the genetic makeup to adapt to environmental pressures.

Seed Sowing

Landscaping is not always cheap, and growing from seed offers an economical way to establish large numbers of plants. It is also the best method for propagating many native varieties. For some unusual plants or varieties not easily found in nurseries, it's sometimes the only way to acquire them, especially local ones. If you collect seeds from wild plants, be sure to get permission from the landowner and try to collect as few as you need to start your own population—never more than 10 percent of the plant's seeds.

You can try sowing seeds in garden soil where you want them to grow, but you'll risk them being eaten by birds or washed away by rain. A more reliable method is to sow them in flats filled with potting soil or a seedling mix, cover with landscape fabric or place them in a cold frame in early winter. Many plants need a "stratification" period of cold weather before they will germinate, and winter's freeze/thaw cycles help break the seed coat, so spring arrives, they quickly germinate. You can also make your own mini-greenhouses from clear plastic containers, by drilling ventilation holes in the lid and drainage holes in the bottom.

Sow seeds in at least two inches of your chosen planting medium and cover them with as much soil as the seed's width. Research each plant. Some seeds require light to germinate and thus will not germinate if planted too deeply. In spring, when the seeds start to germinate and temperatures go above about 60 degrees, prevent seedlings from frying by propping open your cold frame and enlarging the ventilation holes in mini-greenhouse containers.

Arm yourself with knowledge!
You'll have the best success when you find out exactly what your individual plants and crops need to thrive.

Dealing with Unwanted Wildlife Visitors

Although healthy populations of predators should control most pests, deer, groundhogs, voles, and other mammals in your garden can easily destroy all that you are trying to create. The landscapes of suburbia are notbalanced systems, lacking natural predators such as wolves and mountain lions that once patrolled there and controlled the large mammals.

White-tailed deer overpopulations pose an especially serious threat to residential gardens and native plant populations, especially in suburban areas where hunting is prohibited and backyard gardens and endless edge habitat provide rich pickings for these hungry herbivores. Although starving deer will eat just about anything, some plants are not their first choices. If deer damage is a problem, try growing plants with the "No-Deer" icon in the Plant Guide. Deer use their sense of smell to determine what is safe to eat, so interplanting lots of aromatic plants may confuse them and cause them to seek other feeding grounds. Various deer repellents are also available, which may encourage them to forage elsewhere. If not, deer fencing or wire cages around young shrubs and trees may be your only recourse.

Voles can cause major damage by digging tunnels and feeding on roots and crowns throughout the winter. Snakes are their major predators, and will follow voles into their tunnels to prey on them.

In suburban areas where hunting is prohibited and deer populations are unnaturally high, deer fencing may be your only answer.

Brush, log, and rock walls will shelter snakes during the day and can encourage them to take up residence in your garden. Cats, coyotes, foxes, hawks, and owls also hunt voles. Protect susceptible bulbs, roots and trunks with metal hardware cloth or chicken wire to prevent tunneling, and repeatedly spray castor oil in their tunnels to discourage them. Avoid winter mulch.

Moles and **skunks** also dig tunnels and small pits, but instead of eating plants they're looking for beetle grubs and earthworms. Try to tolerate their presence, knowing they are keeping beetle pest populations under control and that they feed owls and other birds of prey. Simply tamp down their tunnels and fill in their pits. Both animals travel continuously over many acres in search of food, so they should never cause too much damage to any one spot.

Groundhogs and **rabbits** are not as easily deterred by repellents, but wire fencing (four to five feet tall, buried underground eighteen inches to prevent digging) will prevent them from eating your vegetable garden. Chicken wire or hardware cloth placed on the ground around your plants may deter them by making it uncomfortable for them to walk. A diverse garden will reduce the amount of damage these animals can do to any single plant. Rabbits especially love to eat dandelions and common plantain, so these weeds may distract them from your prized plants. Hawks and other raptors also eat rabbits.

*Social (therefore stinging) **wasps** such as hornets and paper wasps build aerial nests made of chewed-up wood, in trees or structures. If you find a papery nest with obvious activity, remove only if located in a high-risk area where it might be disturbed and the wasps will defend themselves aggressively. Otherwise they will not bother humans unless threatened.*

Squirrels are usually not welcome in backyard habitats with bird feeders or where tulip and crocus) bulbs are planted. Use a squirrel baffle on a pole underneath feeders to prevent squirrels from pilfering all the seeds, and place poles at least fifteen feet from the nearest tree or roof . Or put corn cobs onto a squirrel feeder far from your bird feeders to keep them busy and well fed. Squirrels will dig up newly planted bulbs in the fall and eat them. Plant these in wire cages, overplant with the unpalatable *Narcissus* (daffodils), or plant bulbs that are less palatable to rodents. Squirrels are a food source for owls and other birds of prey.

Bears, **raccoons**, **coyotes**, and **foxes** are scavengers and will come into your yard or garden in search of garbage, pet food, and birdseed. Keep garbage safely locked up where they cannot access it and never add any meat scraps or parts to your compost pile. If you live in bear country, take down birdfeeders in early spring, when hungry bears come out of hibernation looking for an easy meal.

The Best Plants for New England Gardens

Key:

Attracts birds	Evergreen foliage
Attracts hummingbirds	Vine
Attracts pollinators	Grows in pH+
Food plant for caterpillars	Grows in sandy soil
Food plant for squirrels and other mammals	Slopes or well-drained soils
Food for amphibians	Tolerant of salt
Grows in full sun	Suitable for growing in containers
Grows in part-sun	Fragrant flowers
Grows in shade	Effective in cottage-garden style gardens
Native to New England	Suitable for shallow soils/green roof/ rock garden
Not a deer favorite	Dioecious – separate male/female flowers on different plants, needs male pollinator nearby for cross-pollinationn
Easy to grow from seed	Plant at least two: Cross-pollination improved between multiple cultivars of same plant (different genetic line
Grows in moist soil	Parts of plant are edible to people and/or have medicinal usages
Aquatic/Water Garden plant	Low-maintenance lawn grass
Bog plant	
Marsh plant	
Groundcover	

Plants in this guide are grouped by plant type, in alphabetical order by genera. Common names are listed in ( ) after each plant genus name. Where a genus name is followed by "spp." this indicates the plant genus contains several sub-species.

Zones listed for all plants (except annuals) indicate plant hardiness zones – see page 214.

An icon indicates that at least one variety of plant within a plant genus has the icon's characteristics. Individual plant descriptions describe the preferred habitat for each variety.

Annuals – Native

Agalinis spp. (False Foxglove)

Wild **gerardia** native to moist sandy fields, shores, and salt marshes. Purple flowers in late summer.

Bidens (Beggartick, Bur-marigold, Tickseed Sunflower)

Native annual or biennial with yellow aster-like flowers. **swamp marigold** (*B. aristosa var. mutica*) grows naturally in moist soils but is adaptable to drier conditions. **Tickseed sunflower** (*B. coronata*) has 2 inch blooms, in late summer and fall. **Beggartick** (*B. laevis*) blooms in summer in swamps and along shorelines. 24 to 60 inches.

Chamaecrista fasciculata (Partridge-pea, Senna)

Legume native to sandy or recently disturbed soils. Yellow pea-type flowers in mid- to late summer. 12 to 24 inches.

Impatiens capensis (Orange Jewelweed, Spotted Touch-Me-Not)

Orange or yellow orchid-like late summer flowers important to migrating hummingbirds. If you're exposed to poison ivy or stinging nettle, break a jewelweed stem and use its juices to provide relief from the rash. Reseeds vigorously in moist areas, but easy to weed out as necessary. 36 inches.

Limosella australis (Mudwort)

Tiny annual with small five-petalled, white flowers. Very rare in New England, it grows in tidal mudflats and open shorelines—both habitats in decline. 1 to 2 inches tall.

Polygonum pensylvanicum (Pink or Nodding Smartweed)

Spires of pink or white flowers attracting many pollinators. Seeds eaten by birds and mammals. 12 to 36 inches. **Kiss-me-over-the-garden-gate** (*P. orientale*) is native to Asia, and is a tall, ornamental heirloom plant good for cottage gardens. 48 to 72 inches.

Sabatia spp.

Rose pink (*S. angularis*) is a biennial with pretty rose-pink flowers that grows vigorously in any open, wet spot. **Salt-marsh pink** (*S. stellaris*) is a rare plant native to southern New England salt marshes. 12 to 36 inches.

Symphyotrichum subulatum (Annual Saltmarsh Aster)

Annual or biennial native to New England's salt marshes. Blue flowers in late-summer. 24 to 36 inches.

Zizania aquatica (Wild Rice)

Tall aquatic grassy plant growing wild in freshwater tidal marshes and other shallow wetlands. Not actually a rice, but a grass, its broomlike flowers yield grains that were an important and celebrated food for Native Americans. Offers valuable forage for many songbirds and shorebirds. 96 inches.

Red bloodflower is an exotic milkweed grown as an annual in New England.

Annuals – Non-Native

Ageratum houstonianum (Annual Floss Flower)

Pretty nectar plant, blooming in purple, white, and pink, excellent for fronts of beds and window boxes. 12 to 24 inches.

Alcea spp. (Hollyhock)

Old-fashioned biennial plant. Requires well-drained soil. Choose single-flowered varieties. Often reseeds. 48 to 96 inches.

Amaranthus caudatus (Love Lies Bleeding)

A favorite in Victorian gardens, grown for its vertical presence and long, red, dreadlock-like seed tassels. 36 to 60 inches.

Antirrhinum majus (Snapdragon)

Diminutive in stature but showy in bloom, snapdragons look best in groups of at least five. Choose old-fashioned varieties that retain the characteristic spicy scent. 24 to 36 inches.

Asclepias currasavica (Red Milkweed)

Showy tropical milkweed grown as an annual in New England. Like all milkweeds, its foliage is food for Monarch butterfly caterpillars. Long blooming period provides valuable late-season nectar. Grow at least three to ensure monarch caterpillars don't bite off blooming stems. 24 inches.

Begonia spp. (Wax Begonia)

Shade- and drought-tolerant flowering nectar plant, ideal for containers or hanging baskets. 12 inches.

Borago officianalis (Borage)

Attracts many bees and beneficial insects. Use the pretty, blue, edible petals to decorate drinks. Planting it in beds makes calcium, potassium, and other minerals available to surrounding plants. Especially useful planted with strawberries. 18 to 30 inches.

Calendula spp. (Pot Marigold)

Nectar-rich cheerful orange or yellow flowers attract many beneficial insects. Easy to grow from seeds pushed into soil in early spring. Drought-tolerant. Excellent for filling gaps in beds. 18 to 24 inches.

Centaurea cyanus (Bachelor's Button or Cornflower)

Cornflower-blue flowers attract ladybugs, lacewings, and predatorial wasps. 24 to 30 inches.

Celosia spp. (Cockscomb)

Pretty plumed flowers for beds and containers. Drought-tolerant. 30 to 40 inches.

171

Cleome hassleriana (Spider Flower)

Exotic flowers, reseeds readily. Drought-tolerant. 36 to 48 inches.

Consolida ambigua (Larkspur)

Pretty nectar plant flowering in purple, pink, and white. 24 to 48 inches.

Cosmos sulphureus (Cosmos)

Rich in accessible nectar, cosmos flower in many colors and grow in poor, dry soils. 3 to 48 inches.

This bumble bee is resting on a cosmos flower, waiting to warm up enough to fly. Once hatched, bumble bees never return to the nest and often spend the night inside nectar-rich flowers.

Cuphea ignea (Cigar Plant)

Grown here as an annual. Tubular red flowers attract hummingbirds. Needs full sun, heat, and consistent moisture. 12 to 24 inches.

Dianthus chinensis (China Pink)

Biennial pink utilized for rock gardens. 6 to 12 inches.

Digitalis purpurea (Foxglove)

Beautiful heirloom biennial. Performs best in soils with consistent moisture. 36 to 48 inches.

Eschscholzia californica (California Poppy)

Native to California, with orange flowers that attract many beneficial insects. Drought-tolerant. Direct sow. 12 to 15 inches.

Fuschia 'Gartenmeister Bonstedt'

Grow this hummingbird plant in pots or baskets. More upright than the common fuchsia sold for hanging baskets, and prefers more sun. Take cuttings and overwinter indoors. 12 to 24 inches.

Gazania spp.

Grown for its large showy flowers that attract butterflies, and its tolerance to drought and poor, dry soils. 8 to 12 inches.

Helianthus annuus (Sunflower)

Native to California, it's one of the easiest annuals to grow for bird seed! Also attracts many beneficial insects. Use tall varieties in wildflower meadows or against a wall, and dwarf varieties in beds or in pots. 12 to 96 nches.

Heliotrope spp.

Fragrant flowers attract many butterflies and moths. Needs consistent moisture. Pinch stems to promote branching. 18 inches.

Iberis umbellata (Candytuft)

Pretty purple, pink, or white flowers. 6 to 16 inches.

Impatiens wallerena (Busy Lizzie, Patience Plant)

Readily available, popular for its profuse flowering in full shade. Needs consistent moisture and shade. 12 to 36 inches.

Ipomoea spp.

Fast-growing annual flowering vines. **Cypress vine** *(I. multifida)* and **cardinal climber** *(I. quamoclit)* have red flowers very attractive to hummingbirds. **Moonflower** *(I. alba)* has fragrant white flowers that open at night, attracting night-flying pollinators. Grow **morning glory** *(I. tricolor)* up a fence or pole where you can admire its pretty flowers early in the day.

Lantana camara (Lantana)

Desert shrub grown as an annual here for its lemon-scented flowers. Needs full sun and very well drained soil. 12 inches.

Lathyrus odoratus (Sweet Pea)

Choose old-fashioned varieties for sweet fragrance. Needs support or other plants to climb up. 60 to 96 inches.

Lobularia maritima (Sweet Alyssum)

Low mounds of tiny white, pale pink, or violet flowers, which attract beneficial insects and shelter spiders and ground beetles right up until frost. One of the best edging plants for flower, herb, or vegetable gardens. Self sows. 3 to 8 inches.

Mirabilis jalapa (Four-O-Clock)

Blooms in early evening, attracting night-flying pollinators. Plant around other plants ravaged by Japanese beetles—the beetles will flock to the four-o-clocks, where you can sweep them into a bucket of soapy water to drown them. Seeds are poisonous to humans. 15 to 24 inches.

Nasturtium spp.

Easy annual with pretty, edible flowers and foliage. Use as a sacrifice plant to attract aphids and leafminers. Provides shelter for ground beetles and spiders. Some varieties are vining. 10 to 16 inches.

Nicotiana spp. (Tobacco flower)

Flowering tobacco (N. alata) will self-sow in moist areas. Grow in a moon garden or somewhere you can enjoy the evening fragrance. Flowers in pink, white, and shades of red attract many pollinators. For best scent, sow seeds rather than buying hybrids. Use as a sacrifice plant for hornworm caterpillars. 24 to 60 inches. Woodland tobacco (N. sylvestris) is taller and has interesting droopy white tubular flowers.

Pennisetum glaucum (Ornamental Millet)

Superb annual grass for a hot, sunny spot. "Purple Majesty" has striking purple foliage. Save a few seeds for next year, before the birds eat them! Purple fountain grass (P. advena "Rubrum") is another dark-stemmed annual grass for containers, but is sterile and produces no seed. 36 to 48 inches.

Penta spp. (Egyptian Star Cluster or Star Flower)

Tropical annual with red, pink, lavender, and white blooms. 10 to 16 inches.

Petunia spp.

Readily available and heavily hybridized. Choose single-flowering petunias for accessible nectar. Needs regular deadheading, although smaller-flowering "supertunia" hybrids are sterile and self-cleaning. 12 to 24 inches.

Phlox drummondii (Annual Phlox)

Pretty annual phlox for draping through plants in containers. Available in wide range of colors, and several dwarf varieties. Excellent for sunny locations, but fades as the season gets warmer. 6 to 20 inches. See also *Phlox* in Perennials (page 187.)

Salvia spp. (Sage)

Annual salvia provides late-season color and nectar. Needs sun and good drainage. For best effect plant in large numbers. **Mealy-cup sage** (*S. farinacea*) blooms with deep purple flowers that butterflies love. **Scarlet sage** (*S. coccinia*) is guaranteed to attract ruby-throated hummingbirds. 20 to 30 inches. See also *Salvia* in Herbs (page 75.)

Scabiosa spp. (Pincushion Flower)

Pretty flowers. Prefers rich, well-drained soil. 24 to 36 inches.

Tagetes spp. (Marigold)

Its rich nectar and pest-controlling properties make this an essential addition to every vegetable garden. Choose single-flowered marigolds for pollinator access and plant densely for best effect. 8 to 36 inches.

Tithonia spp. (Mexican Sunflower)

Butterflies and beneficial insects love the orange blooms! "Torch" grows to 6 feet, and needs lots of room. "Fiesta del Sol" is a shorter cultivar, suitable for containers. 48 to 72 inches.

Verbena bonariensis (Brazilian Verbena)

Excellent for scattering through garden beds. The tall, airy stems take up little room and the violet flowers contrast well. Attracts many butterflies and birds. Usually reseeds. 36 to 48 inches.

Viola tricolor (Johnny-Jump-Up, Hearts-Ease)

Old-fashioned plant with tricolor flowers. Usually reseeds heavily. 5 to 7 inches.

Zinnia elegans (Zinnia)

Showy, in-your-face flowers, in all colors and patterns. Choose single-flowering varieties for best nectar access. Use short varieties, such as "Profusion," in containers or as a groundcover. Blooms more heavily if you regularly cut some flowers for your own use! 12 to 36 inches.

Vegetables and Culinary Herbs

Most culinary herbs are easy plants for full sun and alkaline soil. Good drainage is essential to overwintering perennial herbs. Use leaves in cooking, but always allow a few plants to flower, to attract beneficial predators such as parasitic wasps, hoverflies, bees, lady beetles, and spiders. Herbs with strongly aromatic foliage will repel some pests.

Annual Varieties

Anethum graveolens (Dill)
Host plant for black swallowtail butterfly caterpillars. Grow near carrots to lure caterpillars away from your carrot tops. Pretty yellow flowers work well in any garden, and will reseed.

Brassica nigra, B. juncea, B. hirta (Mustard)
Use as sacrifice plant to attract cabbage moths from your cabbage and other brassicas. Seeds are used for mustard, and plants can be used as a cover crop/green manure.

Coriandrum sativum (Cilantro or Coriander)
The foliage is known as cilantro, while the edible seed is called coriander. Foliage has a strong scent which repels aphids.

Foeniculum vulgare (Leaf Fennel)
Attracts hoverflies, lacewings, parasitic wasps, tachinid flies.

Petroselinum crispum (Parsley)
Foliage deters carrot flies and other pests.

Rosmarinus officinalis (Rosemary)
An annual across most of New England, but you can overwinter it indoors in a sunny location.

Phaseolus coccineus (Scarlet Runner Bean)
Vining bean will climb a trellis. Attracts hummingbirds. Flower color is closer to orange than scarlet.

Zea mays spp. (Corn)
Corn tassels produce large amounts of pollen which attract many beneficial insects and pest predators. Grow corn in a garden as a quick-growing, tall, ornamental grass.

Perennial Varieties

Allium spp. (Onion)
There are many varieties (native and nonnative) of this trouble-free bulb. Most have soft, grassy or straplike foliage. Lovely when planted in large numbers in a border, meadow, rock, or wild garden. **Wild leek** (*A. tricoccum*), also known as ramp, is a short native allium blooming in summer, growing best in moist spring soil. Zone 3+. **Nodding onion** (*A. cernuum*) grows in rocky outcrops and woodlands. Nonnative **Purple chives** (*A. schoenoprasum*) and **garlic chives** (*A. tuberosum)* are both culinary herbs with pretty purple or white flowers. Purple chives spreads quickly into a clump of grasslike foliage even in shallow soils. Chives improves the growth and flavor of tomatoes and carrots, attracts aphids from other plants, and protects apple trees from scab. Also prevents black spots on neighboring roses. **Ornamental onion** is a fall-planted bulb with "lollipop" type flower balls in early summer, and foliage that disappears after blooming.

Mentha spp. (Mint, Spearmint)
All members of the mint family have tiny flowers that attract hoverflies and beneficial wasps. Grow in a pot or a contained area, because mints are aggressive root spreaders.

Origanum spp. (Oregano, Marjoram)
Common oregano (*O. vulgare*) is a culinary herb becoming more popular as an ornamental groundcover due to its drought tolerance and fast-creeping habit. Tiny, white, summer flowers attract beneficial insects. **Marjoram** (*O. majorana*) is similar but not as strong-flavored.

Salvia spp. (Sage)
All salvia species are excellent nectar plants with many varieties readily available from garden centers or from seed. **Common sage** (*S.officinalis*) is a culinary herb with lavender flowers in early summer. Perennial **salvia** (*S.nemerosa*), with blue summer flowers, is readily available. See also *Salvia* in Annuals (page 174.)

Tanacetum vulgare (Tansy) **and** *T. parthenium* (Feverfew)
Prolific self-seeder, good for poor soil. Attracts ladybeetles, lacewings, and parasitic wasps.

Taraxacum officinale (Dandelion)
Early season nectar for many beneficial insects. Seeds feed birds. Fluffy seed coverings provide soft nest materials for many birds. Young leaves are edible and contain more iron than spinach! An indicator of low soil calcium.

Thymus spp. (Thyme)
In early summer, tiny white or purple flowers attract beneficial insects. **Creeping thyme** (*T. serpyllum*) spreads into a large mat of low fragrant foliage, which tolerates some foot traffic. Use for edging herb gardens or as a groundcover between stepping stones.

Herbaceous Perennials and Bulbs

Achillea spp. (Yarrow)

Flowers best in full sun, in a wide variety of colors. Drought-tolerant. Its shallow clusters of tiny flowers attract many pollinators. Spreads quickly by underground runners. 24 to 36 inches. Zone 3+.

Yarrow likes it hot, sunny, and well-drained, and makes a good companion to **butterfly weed** *(Asclepias tuberosa), which likes the same conditions.*

Actaea spp. (Baneberry or Bugbane)

Attracts a diversity of tiny pollinators, and fruits are eaten by many birds, including thrushes and yellow-bellied sapsuckers. **Black cohosh** *(A. racemosa)*, also called **black snakeroot** or **fairy candles**, has stately white spires that strikingly contrast against a darker background—perfect for a woodland edge. Requires consistent moisture (but not standing water) and some shade. Used medicinally by Native Americans as a treatment for rheumatism, it's an endangered plant in Massachusetts. Grows 3 to 5 feet. **Red baneberry** *(A. rubra)* berries are shocking red in the middle of summer and grow well with ferns. 16 to 18 inches. **Doll's eyes** *(A. pachypoda)* berries (pictured below) are chalky white with a dark eye spot. 12 to 16 inches.

Agalinis acuta (Sand-plain Gerardia)

A rare pink-flowering plant that grows in sandy soils along with little bluestem grass, whose roots it uses to mine for soil nutrients. It is on federal and state-listed endangered species lists, so if you see it, please report your sighting to your local wildflower society. 5 to 15 inches.

Agastache spp.

Flower spikes with small tubular flowers attract bees, beneficial insects, and hummingbirds, and provide seed for hungry birds. Highly fragrant foliage with common names such as "bubblegum," "root beer," and "licorice" mint. **Korean mint** *(A. foeniculum)* and **anise hyssop** *(A. rugosa)* bloom the first year from seed, with purple or white flowers. Western US native **sunset hyssop** *(A.rupestris)* and hybrids will overwinter in New England only in a warm spot in very well drained soil—no wet feet. 24 to 36 inches. Zone 4+.

Ageratina altissima (White Snakeroot)

Blooms in fall, with pure white flowers popular with pollinators. Native to moist woods. "Chocolate" is a readily available cultivar with burgundy foliage. Reseeds heavily in moist soils. Formerly known as *Eupatorium rugosum*. 24 to 48 inches. Zone 4+.

Aletris farinosa (Colicroot or Stargrass)

In the lily family, colicroot grows wild in meadows, open woods, and the edges of peat bogs. Very rare. Tall spikes of small white flowers late spring to summer. 12 to 36 inches.

Amsonia (Bluestar)

All bluestars have pretty blue flowers in spring, supplying early-season nectar. **Common bluestar** *(A. tabernaemontana)* has a shrubby habit, grows in moist or dry soil, and tolerates more shade than other bluestars. 36 inches. Zone 3+. **Hubricht's bluestar** *(A. hubrichtii)* has fine threadleaf foliage which turns a striking glowing yellow in fall. Needs moist soil. 36 inches. Zone 5+. **Jones' bluestar** *(A. jonesii)* is native to arid areas of the west but can be grown here in a well-drained spot in full sun. Slow to establish, but drought-tolerant, with showy ice-blue flowers. Zone 5+. 16 to 28 inches.

Anaphalis margaritacea (Pearly Everlasting)

Tiny white and yellow flowers in late summer. Grows wild in dry fields, roadsides. Host plant for many small butterfly species. 12 to 36 inches. Zone 4+.

Anemone spp.

Native anemones are low growers for sun or shade, in moist or dry soil. **Canada anemone** *(A. canadensis)* spreads aggressively in moist soil. White early-summer flowers. 12 to 24 inches. Zone 2+. **Wood anemone** *(A. quinquefolia)* is suitable for any shady garden soil with some moisture. A spring ephemeral, plant it alongside other summer perennials because it goes dormant after blooming. Zone 3+. 3 to 6 inches.

Antennaria spp. (Pussy-toes, Woman's Tobacco)

Tough plant for sunny areas with dry, well-drained soil. **Plaintain-leaved pussytoes** *(A. plantaginifolia)* is the eastern native with basal leaves and fuzzy white flower heads. **Mountain everlasting** *(A. dioica)* is a related evergreen creeper from Europe, suitable for alpine regions. 3 to 16 inches. Zone 3+.

Angelica atropurpurea (Purplestem angelica)

Tall member of wild carrot family native to swampy woodlands. Hollow stems were used by native Americans for pipes, and edible stems taste like celery. 72 inches.

Aquilegia canadense (Red Columbine)

Easy to grow garden plant loved by hummingbirds. Can be short-lived, but abundantly reseeds. Other nonnative columbines also grow well in New England. 10 to 24 inches. Zone 2+.

Arisaema triphyllum (Jack-in-the-pulpit)

Swamp dwellers in the wild, grow as a specimen plant in a moist shady area to watch small pollinating flies crawling down into the unusual green-brown flowers in spring. Bright red fall berries are eaten by wood thrushes. 12 to 28 inches. Zone 3+.

Aruncus dioicus (Goat's Beard)

Native to regions more south than New England, the tall plumes of white early-summer flowers attract a frenzy of tiny pollinators. Grow in moisture-retentive soil or anywhere that is not too dry. Give it some room. Excellent for a woodland edge. 48 to 72 inches. Zone 4+.

Asarum canadense (Wild Ginger)

Native groundcover for shade gardens. Spreads more quickly in moist soil. Spring flowers are sheltered under the large heart-shaped foliage, and visited by ground-level pollinators. 6 to 8 inches. Zone 3+.

Asclepias spp. (Milkweed)

Milkweeds are the exclusive food plants for Monarch butterfly caterpillars and their showy flowers provide nectar for many pollinators. Silky seed casing is used for nestbuilding, and seeds are eaten by many birds. Most bloom their first year from seed. **Swamp milkweed** *(A. incarnata)* grows in moist to wet soils, with pink honey-scented summer flowers. 24 to 48 inches. **Butterfly weed/pleurisyroot** *(A. tuberosa)* is showy and rugged, blooming neon-orange early summer. Best in full sun and with good drainage. Roots used medicinally. 12 to 36 inches. **Common milkweed** *(A. syriaca)* grows in open areas and old fields, and spreads rapidly by underground runners—not for garden use! 24 to 48 inches. **Purple milkweed** *(A. purpurascens)* is a better-behaved alternative for open, dry soils. Zone 3+.

Aster, see *Doellingeria, Eurybia, Symphyotrichum, Sericocarpus*

Baptisia spp. (Indigo)

Indigos are shrublike in habit, growing in acidic, well-drained soils in sun or part sun. the legume family. Pollinated flowers form thick pea-like pods. Important host plants for many butterfly species. **Wild indigo** *(B. tinctoria)* grows well in poor, dry soils. Tiny yellow flowers in summer. Zone 3+. Although native New York southward, **blue false indigo** *(B. australis)* is  long-lived and hardy here. Zone 4+. **White wild indigo** *(B. alba)* has elegant white blooms. Native to Virginia south. Zone 5+. 24 to 48 inches.

Boltonia asteroides (False Aster)

Native to southern New Jersey. Tall, and covered in pretty white or pink aster-like flowers in fall, it grows nearly anywhere. Most cultivars are descended from "Snowbank," which was introduced by the New England Wild Flower Society for its compact habit. 36 to 48 inches. Zone 4+.

Brasenia schreberi (Watershield)

Floating leaf plant of shallow ponds and slow streams. Reddish brown summer flowers, and a clear gelatinous coating on stems and underside of leaves. Stems, leaves, and seeds are eaten by waterfowl. Zone 3+.

Cakile edentula (Sea Rocket)

Native member of the **Mustard** *(Brassicaceae)* family, growing on sand dunes and beaches above the high tide line. Fleshy leaves and pale lavender to white flowers from midsummer to early fall. May be a reseeding annual or biennial. 6 to 20 inches. Zone 5+.

Calla palustris (Water Arum, Wild Calla)

A relative of the tropical **calla lily** and the common houseplant the **Peace Lily**, with similar pure-white spathe flowers. Bold foliage. Grows in standing water, as well as in soil that dries out in summer. Blooms best in sun. 12 inches. Zone 3+ .

Calopogon tuberosus (Grass Pink)

One of our rare native orchids, produces bright lavender flowers. Good for wet meadows or bog gardens that remain moist through the year. 12 to 24 inches Zone 3+.

Caltha palustris (Marsh Marigold)

Cheery yellow flowers light up early spring wetlands. Good early season nectar source. Grows in shallow water up to 4 to 5 inches deep. Leaves provide shelter for amphibians. 12 to 24 inches. Zone 1+.

Camassia spp. (Indian Hyacinth, Wild Hyacinth, Indian Camas)

Autumn-planted bulb native to Western North America. Pretty blue/purple flowers atop slim stems. Once an important food for Native Americans. 12 to 50 inches.

Chamaelirium luteum (Devil's Bit)

Very rare in the wild in New England, but worth growing if you have moist shade. Pretty white early summer flowers. 8 to 14 inches. Zone 4+.

Chelone glabra (Turtlehead)

Common wetland plant with white flowers, attracts bumblebees and hummingbirds. 36 inches. Zone 3+. Host plant for Baltimore checkerspot butterfly. **Pink turtlehead** (*C. lyonii*) is native to the South. Zone 4+

Chrysogonum virginianum (Golden Star)

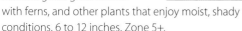

Native to Mid-Atlantic and Southeastern US. Pretty yellow stars in spring will rebloom sporadically through summer. Makes a good groundcover with ferns, and other plants that enjoy moist, shady conditions. 6 to 12 inches. Zone 5+.

Chrysopsis mariana (Maryland Golden Aster)

Yellow, aster-like blooms in early fall. Needs dry, well-drained soil. See also **Pityopsis**. 8 to 16 inches. Zone 5+.

Claytonia spp. (Spring Beauty)

Short but pretty spring ephemeral native to moist, rich woodlands. Plant goes dormant after blooming, and the foliage disappears completely by the summer. *C. caroliniana* blooms in light or strong pink in early spring. *C. virginica* blooms white/pink or yellow in spring. 3 to 6 inches. Zone 3+.

Clintonia borealis (Blue Bead Lily)

Native lily with yellow springtime flowers and large, striking blue berries that stand on tall stalks. Most at home in cool, moist woods and bogs of higher elevations. Forms colonies of glossy basal leaves. Often seen growing with hobblebush and striped maple. Height: 8 to 12 inches. Spread: 12 inches. Zone 2 to 6.

Conoclinium coelistinum (Mist Flower, Wild Ageratum)

Nectar-rich, violet-blue flowers in late summer. Spreads vigorously by runners in moist soil. Late to emerge in spring. Formerly *Eupatorium coelistinum*. 24 to 36 inches. Zone 4+.

Coptis trifolia (Goldthread)

Groundcover of cold forests and bogs, often associated with moss. Shallow-rooted, spreads by rhizomes which are sensitive to disturbance. Pretty, single, white, spring flowers and glossy dark green leaves divided in three parts much like wild strawberries. A long history of medicinal uses by Native Americans. Height: 1 to 2 inches. Spread: 6 to 8 inches. Zones 2 to 7.

Coreopsis spp. Tickseed)

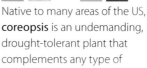

Native to many areas of the US, **coreopsis** is an undemanding, drought-tolerant plant that complements any type of garden from a formal border to a wildflower meadow. Summer flowers are mainly yellow but there are pink varieties. Single flowers attract many beneficial insects, and the seeds feed birds. **Pink coreopsis** *(C. rosea)* is native to wet, sandy pond shores along the coast. **Threadleaf tickseed** "Moonbeam" is a sterile hybrid of *C. verticillata*, so it blooms for an extended period in summer. **Lance-leaved tickseed** *(C. lanceolata)* grows in sandy soils. 12 to 24 inches. Zone 3+.

Cornus canadensis or *Chamaepericlymenum canadense* (Bunchberry)

Also known as the **perennial dogwood**, it flowers in spring with typical dogwood flowers. Use as a groundcover in cool, moist areas, in woodland soil enriched with leaves, pine needles, and other "tree trash." Pollinated by small insects attracted by the white bracts. Fruits (not berries, but drupes) are relished by many large and small mammals, and birds such as the warbling vireo. 3 to 6 inches. Zone 2+.

Cypripedium spp. (Lady's slipper)

Native orchids with unmistakable showy flowers. Not easy to cultivate, so they are expensive to buy. **Pink lady's slipper** *(C. acaule)* is very difficult to transplant because of essential fungal soil partnerships, but may pop up in the dry, acidic soils of upland woods. 12 inches. Zone 3+. **Showy lady's slipper** *(C. reginae)* is native to limestone wetlands and prefers consistent moisture. 14 to 28 inches. Zone 3+. Both **small** *(C. parviflorum)* and **large yellow** *(C. pubescens)* **lady's slippers** grow well in light shade in moist soils. 10 to 18 inches. Zone 4+.

Decodon verticillatus (Swamp Loosestrife or Water-willow)

Pink, mint-like flowers in midsummer. Native to coastal bogs, swamps, and shallows. 2 to 8 feet. Zone 3+.

Dentaria spp. (Toothwort)

Diminutive spring ephemerals with white flowers and toothed foliage. Ideal for moist woodland gardens. In the **Mustard** family. 3 to 6 inches. Zone 3+.

Desmodium canadense (Showy Tick-trefoil)

Flowers in July/August with pink flowers that attract butterflies. Host plant for eastern blue butterfly caterpillars. A nitrogen-fixing legume. 24 to 72 inches. Zone 3+.

Dicentra spp. (Dutchman's Breeches, Bleeding Hearts)

Spring bloomers excellent underneath deciduous trees. Flowers in white or pink are buzz-pollinated by long-tongued bumblebees, which use the tiny "handles" at the flower's bottom to hang onto the flowers. **Dutchman's Breeches** *(D. cucullaria)* is short (3 to 6 inches) perennial. Zone 3+. **Squirrel corn** *(D. canadensis)* is similar, but flowers are fragrant and bloom later. **Fringed bleeding heart** *(D. eximia)* is native to the southern Appalachians, but is long-blooming and hardy, growing 12 to 18 inches in either sun or shade. Zone 4+. Old-fashioned **bleeding heart** *(D. spectabilis)* is not native, but performs well in New England. Zone 2+.

Doellingeria umbellata (Flat-topped White Aster)

Grows in moist, sunny meadows, flowering in fall with white flowers atop tall stems. Sole host plant for Harris' checkerspot butterfly. 36 to 84 inches. Zone 3+.

*Draba arabisans (*Rock whitlow-grass, Rock cress)

Very rare wild member of the **Mustard** family, growing in rock crevices and outcrops in northern New England. White flower clusters in spring. 4 to 8 inches. Zone 6+.

Drosera rotundifolia (Roundleaf Sundew)

Carnivorous bog plant with white or pink flowers and bright red foliage. Hairs with adhesive "glue" trap flies and other insects that are then digested by the plant. Threatened or endangered in some locations outside New England. 6 to 10 inches. While many sundews prefer a more temperate climate, this variety is hardy to Zone 4.

Echinacea purpurea (Purple Coneflower)

Purple coneflower has large pink, white, or yellow summer flowers that butterflies love. Easy to buy anywhere plants are sold, but cultivars and hybrids are not always reliably hardy. Prefers rich, well-drained soil. Goldfinches love the large seeds. 36 to 48 inches. Zone 3+.

Epigaea repens (Mayflower, Trailing Arbutus)

The state flower of Massachusetts. A tiny member of the heath *(Ericaceae)* family, **Mayflower** has small bell-shaped pink or white blooms with an unexpectedly strong fragrance in early spring. Not easy to grow in cultivation, it grows wild in sandy or rocky woods. Plant container-grown plants in spring for best results. 1 to 4 inches. Zone 3+.

Erythronium americanum (Yellow Trout Lily)

Eastern spring ephemeral, growing from corms (bulbs). Grow them where you can view their tiny but exquisite lily-like flowers. So-called because the mottled pattern of the foliage resembles the side of a brook trout. Foliage goes dormant in summer—plant with other perennials that will fill in later in the season. 2 to 6 inches. Zone 3+.

Eupatorium spp.

Large white flower clusters are very attractive to butterflies and other late-season pollinators, and birds love their seeds. **Boneset** *(E. perfoliatum)* blooms for a long period and is ideal for a rain garden. 24 to 48 inches. Zone 3+ **Hyssop-leaved thoroughwort** *(E. hyssopifolium)* prefers dry, sandy soil. 12 to 36 inches. Zone 4+. See also *Eutrochium*.

Euphorbia corollata (Flowering Spurge)

Numerous tiny white flowers in summer makes this the native alternative to baby's breath! Drought-tolerant and suitable for poor, dry soil. 24 to 36 inches. Zone 3+.

Eurybia spp.(Aster)

Native asters are important plants for birds and pollinators and there is an aster for every soil type. **Showy aster** *(E. spectabilis)* is native to dry, sandy woods and pine barrens near the shore. Violet flowers in late summer and early fall. **White wood aster** *(E. divaricata)* grows in sun or shade on woodland edges and clearings. **Big-leaved aster** *(E. macrophylla)*, growing in moist, shady woods in dense colonies, has heart-shaped large lower leaves and light violet flowers. See also *Doellingeria, Seriocarpus, Symphyotrichum*. 12 to 30 inches. Zone 3+.

Euthamia graminifolia (Lance-leaved or Flat-topped Goldenrod)

Native to wet meadows and coastal grasslands. Yellow goldenrod-like flowers from late summer to fall. Spreads by rhizomes. Formerly classified as *Solidago*. 12 to 48 inches. Zone 2+.

Eutrochium spp. (Joe-Pye Weed)

Formerly known as *Eupatorium*, Joe-Pye Weed is a familiar native plant of moist areas. Large dusky-pink summer flowers are a favorite of butterflies and other pollinators. Tall, adaptable plant. Late to emerge in spring. Available varieties are **eastern Joe-Pye weed** (*E. dubium*), **spotted Joe-Pye weed** (*E. maculatus*), **hollow Joe-Pye weed** (*E. fistulosum*) and **sweet Joe-Pye weed** (*E. purpureum*). 24 to 96 inches. Zone 3+.

Filipendula rubra (Queen of the Prairie)

Native to New York, south and westwards. Excellent tall meadow plant for a moist, fertile soil. Plumes of pink summer flowers that look like cotton candy. Spreads with rhizomes, so not suitable for small gardens. 36 to 84 inches. Zone 3+.

Fragaria virginiana (Wild Strawberry)

Low, trailing groundcover. Extensively hybridized to create cultivated strawberries. White spring flowers. Many birds and also wood turtles forage on their fruits. Host plant for gray hairstreak butterflies. 6 inches. Zone 2+.

Gaultheria spp. (Wintergreen)

Gaultheria do best in damp soil with a few hours of sunshine per day. Berries appear in summer. **Wintergreen** (*G. procumbens*) can thrive in dry shade, and its berries provide the familiar flavor found in chewing gum and toothpaste. **Creeping snowberry** (*G. hispidula*) likes it cool and does well wherever moss grows. 1 to 6 inches. Zone 2+.

Gentiana spp. (Gentian)

Our native gentians bloom in a wonderful blue, in fall. **Fringed gentian** (*Gentianopsis crinita*) is biennial, blooming in its second year. Thrives in a sunny spot with neutral to alkaline soil. **Closed bottle gentian** (*G. clausa*) flowers only open enough to allow pollinating bees to enter. Excellent for woodland gardens. 14 to 36 inches. Zone 3+.

Geranium maculatum (Wild Geranium, Cranesbill)

Pretty pink spring flowers perfect for a woodland edge. Grows best with some spring moisture. Nonnative varieties are readily available, including the drought-tolerant **bigroot geranium** (*G. macrorrhizum*). 14 to 18 inches. Zone 3.

Geum spp. (Avens)

Water avens (*G. rivale*) grows in wetlands, with nodding bell-shaped red-purple flowers in late spring. Native to wetlands. 16 to 24 inches. Zone 2+. **Prairie smoke** (*G. triflorum*) has pink spring flowers and grows in dry, gritty soils. Ornamental seed heads persist through summer. Zone 3+.

Helenium autumnale (Sneezeweed)

Native to wet meadows and swamps, Sneezeweed also grows in drier soils. Cheerful yellow and orange flowers bloom from late summer right through fall. 24 to 60 inches. Zone 3+.

Helianthus spp. (Perennial Sunflower)

New England has several native sunflowers with smaller, but much more numerous blooms than the annual sunflower. Excellent source of fall and winter seeds for many birds. All grow very tall, suiting them to restoration areas or screening, but not for small gardens. 48 to 108 inches. Zone 3+. **Swamp sunflower** (*H. angustifolius*) blooms in fall and prefers moist soil. Can grow to 9 feet. **Woodland sunflower** (*H. divaricatus*) is perfect for "wild" roadside and woodland edges where it can spread. Smaller, growing 24 to 48 inches. **Jerusalem artichoke** (*H. tuberosus*) is a very aggressive spreader, so do not grow near other garden plants. Edible roots.

Heliopsis helianthoides (Oxeye, False sunflower)

Showy sunflower-like blooms in summer with persistent petals (unlike *Helianthus*, the true sunflowers). Single-flowering form feeds many pollinators and birds. Grows in any soil. 36 to 60 inches. Zone 3+.

Helonias bullata (Swamp Pink)

Native from New Jersey southwards, but can be used effectively here as a groundcover in mucky or boggy areas. Spring flowers look like pink pussy willows, but have a sweet scent. 10 to16 inches. Zone 5+.

Hepatica spp. (Leafwort or Liverwort)

Spring-blooming woodland natives with violet-blue flowers. **Sharp-lobed hepatica** (*H. acutiloba*) is often found on limestone in early spring. **Round-lobed hepatica** (*H. americana*) blooms a little later. 3 to 6 inches. Zone 3+.

Heracleum maximum (Cow Parsnip, Wild Carrot, Wild Parsley)

Native wild carrot very similar in appearance to the nonnative Queen Anne's lace, with tall stems of white flower clusters in summer. Native to moist thickets and streambanks across North America. 4 to 9 feet. Zone 3+.

Heuchera spp. (Alumroot, Coralbells)

Excellent low-growing groundcovers for cool, partly shaded areas in dry or moist soils. Semi-evergreen foliage. Most Heuchera sold in nurseries are hybrids of **common alumroot** (*H. americana*), which is native to southern New England, and the western US native **coralbells** (*H. sanguinea*). Red-flowering cultivars such as "Firefly" are very popular with hummingbirds. 8 to 20 inches. Zone 4+.

Hibiscus moscheutos, H. palustris (Swamp or Common Rose Mallow)

If you have a moist, sunny area, plant rose mallow for the sheer "wow" factor of its enormous blooms, and its rich nectar for pollinators. Late to emerge in spring but quickly makes up for lost time by growing up to 7 feet by summer's end. Reduce height by pinching back stems in early summer. Can be grown in water gardens with water up to 6 inches over the crown, or in containers. Often hybridized. 48 to 84 inches. Zone 4+.

Houstonia caerulea, H. longifolia (Bluets, Quaker Ladies)

Bluets (*H. caerulea*) are a familiar spring wildflower, growing in disturbed areas or naturalizing into lawns. A tough plant, tolerating foot traffic and blooming in cheerful drifts in spring. **Long-leaf bluets** (*H. longifolia*) are native to gravelly soil and pine barrens. Very drought-tolerant. 1 to 4 inches. Zone 3+.

Hydrastis canadensis (Goldenseal)

Interesting woodland ground cover for shady areas, with white flowers and fruits that look like red raspberries. Slow-growing medicinal herb that spreads by underground rhizomes. 6 to 8 inches. Zone 4+

Native plants that offer useful medicinal qualities face threats from invasive plants and from being overly picked in the wild.

Hylotelephium spectabilis (Stonecrop)

Formerly known as a *Sedum*, stonecrop is an extremely tough, drought-tolerant plant blooming in late summer through fall. Many beneficial insects and butterflies love the large broccoli-shaped flower heads. Easy to propagate by cutting and replanting stems. 24 inches. Zone 3+.

Hypoxis hirsuta (Yellow Star Grass)

Long-blooming yellow spring/summer wildflower with grasslike foliage. Self-sows and spreads by corms to form a thick mat. 3 to 6 inches. Zone 3+.

Iberis sempervirens (Evergreen Candytuft)

Low-growing evergreen plant suitable for rock gardens or as edging or a groundcover, with white flowers in early spring. Grows best in slightly alkaline soil in full hot sun. 6 to 12 inches. Zone 3+.

Iris spp.

Blue flag (*I. versicolor*) is New England's native iris, growing in moist to wet areas, even standing water. For water gardens, plant in a medium container in at least 6 inches of water. Blue/purple late spring flowers. 36 inches. Zone 4+. Slender blueflag (*I. prismatica*) is shorter, 10 to 14 inches, blooming in early summer.

Spreads quickly. Zone 3+. Crested iris (*I. cristata*) is native to Maryland southwards, but makes a cheerful woodland ground cover with violet or white flowers. 4 to 8 inches. Zone 4+.

Liatris spp. (Blazing Star, Gayfeather)

Beautiful and rugged plants essential to every New England garden, blooming in midsummer with thick purple or white flower spikes (or buttons, in some species). Foliage looks ratty after blooming, but place somewhere you can leave the seed heads on the plants for birds to eat. Also attracts butterflies, parasitic wasps, hoverflies, and hummingbird moths. **Northern blazing star** (*L. scariosa*) is New England's only true native blazing star, growing in sandy soils near the coast. In cultivation they can reach 5 feet. **Marsh blazing star** (*L. spicata*) is good for wetlands and is readily available. Other hardy varieties, **Eastern** (*L. scariosa*), **Rocky Mountain** (*L. ligulistylis*), and **prairie** (*L. pycnostachya*) blazing stars grow in drier soils. The bulb-like roots can be divided when plants are still dormant in early spring. 24 to 36 inches. Zone 3+.

Lilium spp.

Our spectacular native lilies with their orange/red/yellow flowers are under great threat from the devastating Asian lily leaf beetle. **Canada lily** (*L. canadense*) blooms in tall trumpets in summer. 36 to 60 inches. Zone 3+. **Turk's cap** (*L. superbum*) needs moist soil and sun.

Zone 4+. Grow the smaller **wood lily** (*L. philadelphicum*) in moist, dry, or sandy soils. 6 to 24 inches. Zone 3+.

Limonium carolinianum (Sea Lavender, Marsh Rosemary)

Native to salt marshes, flowers in a haze of purple flowers in August. 12 to 24 inches. Zone 5+.

Linnaea borealis (Twinflower)

Small white-pink bell-shaped flowers in spring. At home in cool woods and bogs, it burns in full sun and is often found growing in and around moss and old logs. Height: 1 to 3 inches. Spread 12 inches. Zone 2 to 6.

Lobelia spp.

Cardinal flower (*L. cardinalis*) flowers are a stunning and pure red that attracts hummingbirds. Tolerates shade as long as soil is moist. Sometimes a short lived perennial, in favorable conditions it self sows. For water garden use, plant in a medium or large container in 1 to 2 inches of water. Great blue lobelia (*L. siphilitica*) is shorter, with beautiful violet-blue flowers on tight vertical stalks in late summer. Plant in a medium container in up to 2 inches of water. 24 to 48 inches . Zone 3+.

Lupinus perennis (Wild Blue or Sundial Lupine)

This is the native species, not the hybrid lupines you generally see on northern New England roadsides. Essential food plant to the nearly extinct Karner blue butterfly's larvae. Best grown in gritty, well-drained soil. As a legume, lupine is a nitrogen fixer. 24 to 48 inches. Zone 3+.

Lysimachia terrestris (Yellow Loosestrife, Swamp Candles)

Not related to the invasive nonnative purple loosestrife (*Lythrum salicaria*), yellow loosestrife is native to wetlands. Short-tongued bees (*Adrenidae*) collect its oil and pollen to form balls to feed their larvae. Fringed loosestrife (*L. ciliata*) has pretty, small, yellow flowers with toothed petals. There is also a cultivar, with maroon-colored leaves. 12 to 48 inches. Zone 3+.

Maianthemum spp.

Canada mayflower (*M. canadense*) is a familiar native woodland wildflower that often consists of only a single leaf and flower stalk. Can be used as an effective groundcover for shady locations. 2 to 4 inches. False

Solomon's seal (*M. racemosa*) is very attractive to pollinators, and its berries are eaten by birds and small mammals. Blooms in late spring with charming white racemes. Grows anywhere. 24 to 36 inches. Zone 3+.

Mertensia spp. (Bluebells)

Seaside bluebell (*M. maritima*) is a native to cold, northern beaches (above the tide line) and is endangered in New England. 14 to 20 inches. Zones 3 to 6. Virginia bluebells (*M. virginica*) is a spring-blooming bulb native to New York south. Grows anywhere with spring moisture and sun, such as under deciduous trees or in a woodland garden. Quickly goes dormant after blooming, so interplant with later-blooming species. Flowers emerge a deep purple, gradually change to soft pink, and finally blue. Up to 24 inches. Zone 3+.

Mitchella repens (Partridgeberry)

Slow growing evergreen groundcover that grows best in a shaded area with few other plants to compete with. Tolerates dry soil. 1 to 2 inches. Zone 3+ .

Monarda spp. (Bee Balm, Oswego Tea, Wild Bergamot)

Bee balm (*M. didyma*) and wild bergamot (*M. fistulosa*) sport midsummer scarlet or violet blooms, attracting hordes of beneficial insects and hummingbirds. Spreads vigorously in moist soil but easy to divide and share with friends. Choose modern cultivars which are labeled as resistant to mildew (cultivars still provide plenty of nectar). When planted near tomatoes, bee balm improves their growth and flavor. Horsemint, or spotted bee-balm, (*M. punctata*) has unusual flowering bracts and grows well in sandy coastal soils. (Zone 5a+). 36 to 60 inches. Zone 3+.

Nelumbo lutea (Yellow Lotus)

Native water lily widely crossed with Asian species to create hybrids for water gardens. Light yellow flowers bloom in late spring and summer. Very aggressive spreader, keep contained in small ponds. Roots, foliage, and seeds are edible. 36 to 72 inches. Zone 4+.

Nuphar lutea (Yellow Pond Lily, Spatterdock)

Native pond lily providing cover and nesting places for many fish, insects, reptiles and amphibians. Ducks and other waterfowl eat the seeds. Beaver and muskrats eat roots and leaves. Large yellow flowers, and thick heart-shaped leaves which are attached to a stalk anchored in the mud below. Colonizes, so keep contained in water gardens. You can pop the seeds like popcorn. Grows best in 1 to 3 feet of water. Zone 4+.

Nuttallanthus canadensis (Blue Toadflax)

Tiny blue snapdragon-like flowers on top of slender stalks. Often found in old fields or roadsides in dry, sandy, or rocky soil. 6 to 24 inches. Zone 4+.

Nymphaea odorata (Fragrant Water Lily)

Essential to every water garden for its floating "lily pads" and fragrant white flowers that open during the day. Important food for ducks and aquatic mammals. Site in shallow (less than 6 foot depth), slow-moving water. Zone 4+.

Oenothera spp. (Sundrops, Evening Primrose)

Sundrops *(O. fruticosa* and *O. tetragona)* have bright yellow early summer flowers and a spreading habit. Grows in any well-drained soil, including sandy soil. **Showy evening primrose** *(O. speciosa)* has pretty white or pink flowers in summer, pollinated by night-flying sphinx moths. Aggressive spreader in moist soils. 10 to 30 inches. Zone 4+.

Orontium aquaticum (Golden Club)

Native to Southern New England but now nearly extinct in the wild. Unusual yellow-tipped flower spikes in spring. Its large leaves shelter fish and aquatic wildlife. Trouble-free water garden plant with foliage floating on or just below the surface. Plant in mucky or shallow water, or sink container 12 inches in a water garden. 8 to 12 inches. Zone 5+.

Oxalis montana (Mountain Wood Sorrel)

Evergreen groundcover of moist, shady high-elevation woodlands and partially exposed bedrock. Pretty white/pink summer flowers and three cloverlike leaflets look like shamrocks. Spreads with scaly, clonal rhizomes that can creep up steep rocky slopes. 1 to 12 inches. Zone 3+.

Pachysandra procumbens (Allegheny Spurge)

Native to Kentucky south, **Allegheny spurge** is an excellent woodland groundcover. Does not spread as aggressively as Japanese pachysandra. 6 to 10 inches. Zone 4+.

Panax quinquefolius (American Ginseng)

Grown usually for its medicinal qualities, ginseng also feeds birds with its red berries. Requires neutral to alkaline, moist but well-drained soil. 8 to 16 inches. Zone 3+.

Peltandra virginica (Arrow Arum)

Aquatic native that forms colonies, not for small ponds. Arrow-shaped leaves and foliage invokes a tropical feel, and berries feed wood ducks. Grows in a water with depth of up to 12 inches. 36 to 48 inches. Zone 5+.

Penstemon spp. (Beardtongue)

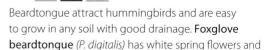

Beardtongue attract hummingbirds and are easy to grow in any soil with good drainage. **Foxglove beardtongue** *(P. digitalis)* has white spring flowers and grows best with some moisture. 24 to 48 inches. **Hairy beardtongue** *(P. hirsutus)* self-seeds in dry and sandy meadows, blooming in pale violet or rose flowers in early summer. 12 to 18 inches. Zone 3+. Other (nonnative) beardtongues are readily available, most of them preferring dry, alkaline soil.

Phlox spp.

Although not all species are native to New England, phlox belongs in every garden, for its wonderfully fragrant flowers and its appeal to pollinators. **Wild blue phlox** *(P. divaricata)* and **creeping phlox** *(P. stolonifera)* are short spring ephemerals for shady eastern woods, with pretty lavender blue or white flowers. **Moss phlox** *(P. subulata)* spreads quickly in a sunny areas with sandy or shallow soils and some alkalinity. Evergreen, needle-like foliage and traffic-stopping pink, lavender, or white flowers in spring. 2 to 6 inches. **Wild sweet William** *(P. maculata)* blooms in bright pink and lavender in summer. 24 to 36 inches. **Summer** or **border phlox** *(P. paniculata)* blooms in large showy clusters in midsummer. Needs sun, fertile soil, and good air circulation to prevent mildew. Some cultivars are mildew-resistant. Attracts night-flying sphinx moths. 36 to 60 inches. Zone 3+.

Physostegia virginiana (Obedient Plant or False Dragonhead)

So-named for the way its flower stems stay in whatever position they're bent. Spreads aggressively by rhizomes, in moist soils. Attracts pollinators and moths with its late summer pink or white blooms. 24 to 60 inches. Zone 3+.

Phytolacca americana (American Pokeweed)

Inconspicuous self-pollinating white flowers in summer, but the late summer and fall berries are large, and very popular with birds, which sometimes become intoxicated from ingesting them! Seeded by birds, often seen in waste places. So-named because each berry has a small dimple in it, as though it had been poked. Young stems and leaves are edible, but once flowers begin, all other parts of the plant are poisonous to humans. Eaten by many birds, including bluebirds, crested flycatcher,

rose-breasted grosbeak, eastern kingbird, mockingbird, phoebe, yellow-bellied sapsucker, thrush, vireo, cedar waxwing, and hairy woodpecker. Used by Native Americans medically, as well as for a dye. According to folklore, the Declaration of Independence was written using the fermented juice from pokeweed berries. 96 inches. Zone 6+.

Pinguicula vulgaris (Common Butterwort)

Hardy carnivorous plant native to northern New England bogs and limestone fens. Very rare. 2 to 8 inches. Zones 3 to 4.

Pityopsis falcata (Sickle-leaved Golden Aster)

One of the few plants that will grow in sand dunes. Attracts a wide range of beneficial insects with its yellow aster-like blooms in mid to late summer. Formerly *Chrysopsis*. 4 to 8 inches. Zone 5+.

Podophyllum peltatum (Mayapple)

Easy to grow in shade or some sun. Makes a quickly spreading ground cover for tough places. Tall stems and large wide leaves. Best in rich, fertile soils with some moisture. Produces large fruit in late summer that's a favorite with eastern box turtles. 8 to 16 inches. Zone 3+.

Mayapple has recently been found to contain chemical compounds that show promise as a cancer treatment. Consider it worth protecting?

Pogonia ophioglossoides (Rose Pogonia or Snakemouth Orchid)

Probably the easiest native orchid to cultivate in boggy soil. Pretty pink to yellow flowers. 5 to 12 inches. Zone 3+.

Polemonium spp. (Jacob's Ladder)

Appalachian Jacob's ladder *(P. vanbruntiae)* is native to New England, but rare, growing in bogs and swampy areas. 24 to 36 inches. **Spreading Jacob's ladder** *(P. reptans)* is widely available and has bell-shaped blue spring flowers. Native from New York south. 10 to 16 inches. Zone 3+.

Polygonatum spp. (Solomon's Seal)

Essential to every woodland garden, with its arching stems and white, bell-shaped, spring flowers, pollinated by bumblebees. **Giant Solomon's seal** *(P. commutatum)* (pictured on page 216) is a much taller and commanding cultivar than the species. 12 to 36 inches. Zone 3+

Polygonum amphibium (Water Smartweed)

Shoreline plant with hot-pink summer spires, attracting many beneficial insects as well as damselflies and dragonflies, which use the flowers as a perch. When grown in water, the leaves float on the surface. 4 to 30 inches. Zone 3+.

Pontederia cordata (Pickerelweed or Pickerel Rush)

Heart-shaped foliage, spikes of deep blue or white flowers for mud or shallow ponds. Confine its vigorous root growth by planting in a bucket or tub. Grow in water up to 8 inches deep. 24 to 30 inches. Zone 3+.

Pycnanthemum spp. (Mountain-mint)

All species of mountain-mint are a big hit with pollinators, with pale purple to white nectar-rich flowers in mid- to late summer. Tough plant adaptable to most soils. Spreads by clumps rather than the runners of many mints. Attractive silvery foliage with typical minty fragrance. 12 to 36 inches. Zone 4+.

Pyrola americana (Round-leaved Pyrola)

Small plant with fleshy green leaves in the wintergreen family. Interesting white summer flowers on tall stalks. Underground rhizomes spread slowly. 6 to 15 inches. Zone 3+.

Rhexia virginia (Meadow Beauty)

Very pretty small tropical-looking rose-pink flowers in late summer, for wet sandy soils. 8 to 12 inches. Zone 3+. **Dull meadow-pitcher** *(R. mariana)* is native from Massachusetts south. 12 to 36 inches. Zone 6+.

Rudbeckia spp. (Black-eyed Susan)

All Rudbeckia species are superb ornamental nectar plants for many pollinators, and seed plants for birds. Mostly native to grassy/prairie regions of the US, some species have crept east into New England. **Black-eyed Susan** *(R. hirta)* is familiar, readily available, and does well in most soils. Some cultivars are marginally hardy in New England, but can be grown as annuals. **Cutleaf coneflower** *(R. laciniata)* grows in open, moist areas, spreading quickly by underground stems. 20 to 36 inches. Zone 3+.

Sabatia spp. (Sea-Pink)

Freshwater shoreline plants worth growing in any moist garden soil, for their rose-pink and white summer flowers. **Plymouth gentian** *(S. kennedyana)* is very showy, and rare in the wild. **Rose pink** *(S. angularis)* and **sea-pink** *(S. dodecandra)* are native to Connecticut coastal marshes. 16 to 26 inches. Zone 4+.

Sagittaria latifolia (Arrowhead, Duck Potato)

Shiny arrow-shaped foliage and showy white flowers with yellow anthers on long, arching stems. Tubers are eaten by waterfowl and muskrats. Requires water depth of 1 to 6 inches. 36 to 48 inches. Zone 3+.

Sanguinaria canadensis (Bloodroot)

One of the earliest spring wildflowers to bloom, its attractive leaves fill in after blooming to make a nice woodland groundcover. Foliage and rhizomes contain a toxic, acrid juice which deer dislike. 5 to 12 inches. Zone 3+.

Sarracenia purpurea (Northern Pitcher Plant)

In the "strange and beautiful" category. Leaves shaped like pitchers, this bog plant is insectivorous! The inner leaf surface has downward-pointing hairs which trap and digest unfortunate insects. Flowers in spring, with unmistakable dark red blooms. Easy to grow. Never fertilize, and use rainwater if you need to water it. 6 to 12 inches. Zone 2+.

Saururus cernuus (Lizard's Tail)

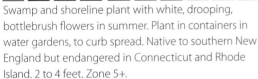

Swamp and shoreline plant with white, drooping, bottlebrush flowers in summer. Plant in containers in water gardens, to curb spread. Native to southern New England but endangered in Connecticut and Rhode Island. 2 to 4 feet. Zone 5+.

Sedum spp. (Stonecrop)

All sedums are low, shallow rooted perennials with pollinator-friendly flowers and a preference for well-drained soil, but most varieties are native to sandy, arid regions of the west. Shallow-rooted, easy to propagate by cutting stems and rooting them in moist soil. New England's native **wild stonecrop** (S. ternatum) grows in moist soils and ledges. See also *Hylotelephium spectabilis*, formerly known as *Sedum* "Autumn Joy." 4 to 8 inches. Zone 4+.

Senecio aurea (Golden Ragwort)

Yellow late-spring flowers are a magnet to bees and other pollinators. Good for moist to dry woodland gardens. 12 to 36 inches. Zone 3+.

Sericocarpus asteroides (Narrow-leaved White-topped Aster)

Rare aster-like plant growing in dry, sandy woods and openings. Flat-topped clusters of white summer flowers with only four to eight rays—most asters have many more. Endangered in Maine. Formerly in the *Aster* genus. 6 to 24 inches. Zone 5+.

Silene spp. (Campion)

Starry campion (S. stellata) is native from Connecticut south with nodding, white, fringed flowers. Grows even in dry woods. 12 to 24 inches. **Fire pink** (S. virginica) is native to New Jersey south, but is an excellent hummingbird plant for any moist, well drained area. Remove some spent blossoms to promote new crown growth, which helps it survive the winter. 8 to 14 inches. **Moss campion** (S. acaulis) is a Colorado wildflower growing at high elevations in soil with sharp drainage. As a groundcover, it tolerates moderate foot traffic. Pretty hot pink flowers.1 to 6 inches. Zone 4+.

Sisyrinchium (Blue-eyed Grass)

In the Iris family and not a true grass, blooming in late spring and early summer with pretty blue flowers. **Eastern blue-eyed grass** (S. atlanticum) grows on sandy edges of salt marshes, flowering in late spring and early summer. **Common blue-eyed grass** (S. angustifolium) grows in damp openings and meadows. 6 to 20 inches. Zone 3+.

Solidago spp. (Goldenrod)

Important late-season nectar plant for many bees and beneficial insects, and seeds for winter birds. Goldenrod spiders hide in plants, devouring the numerous insect visitors. **Canada goldenrod** (S. canadensis) and **rough-**

stemmed goldenrod *(S. rugosa)* both spread aggressively and are not for small gardens, although some cultivars and hybrids are better behaved than the species. **Seaside goldenrod** *(S. sempervirens)* grows wild in sand dunes. See also ***Euthamia***. 24 to 72 inches. Zone 2+.

Sparganium americanum (American bur-reed)

Reed-type plant that spreads aggressively in muddy, shallow ponds. Tuberous roots were used as food by Native Americans, and the seeds are popular with muskrats and aquatic birds. 24 to 36 inches. Zone 3+.

Spigelia marilandica (Indian Pink)

Slow growing Southern native, worth growing in moist soil for the crimson flowers pollinated by hummingbirds and long-tongued bees. 12 to 18 inches. Zone 4+.

Spiranthes odorata (Lady's Tresses)

Fragrant white flowers in late fall. Native to moist or wet acid soils from Pennsylvania south. Slowly forms small colonies. 12 to 24 inches. Zone 5+.

Stokesia laevis (Stoke's Aster)

Beautiful violet flowers in early summer. Native to the southeastern US, well-drained soil improves its winter hardiness in New England. 12 to 15 inches. Zone 5+.

Stylophorum diphyllum (Celandine or Wood Poppy)

Spring ephemeral plant for woodland gardens, with bright yellow flowers. 12 to 20 inches. Zone 4+.

***Symphyotrichum* spp.** (Aster)

Native asters are some of New England's most important nectar and seed plants, blooming in mid to late summer. **Eastern silvery aster** *(S. concolor)* grows in dry, sandy soils on coastal grasslands from Cape Cod southwards, in flowers of purple, blue, and yellow. Zone 5+. **Blue** *(S. cordifolius) and* **white** *(S. divaricatus)* wood asters grow in sun or shade, moist or dry soil. Zone 3+. **Heath aster** *(S. ericoides)* grows in open, dry sites. Good container plant with white ray flowers. Zone 4+. **New England aster** *(S. novae-angliae)* blooms in gorgeous shades of purple and pink in moist, mostly sunny areas. Pinch stems in late spring to prevent flopping. **New York aster** *(S. novae-belgii)* is shorter, and tolerates salinity. Zone 4+. **Perennial salt-marsh aster** *(S. tenuifolius)* is native to salt marshes. **Swamp aster** *(S. puniceus)* is tall (96 inches) for wet soils. See also ***Doellingeria, Eurybium, Sericocarpus***. *12 to 36 inches.*

Symplocarpus foetidus (Skunk Cabbage)

Emerging flowers are a harbinger of the New England spring, attracting early pollinating flies with its skunky scent. Foliage adds a bold and tropical texture to a water garden and its flowers and leaves provide safe cover for amphibians that migrate to marshes and watersides to breed in early spring. Ducks and other birds eat the seeds. 18 to 30 inches. Zone 3+.

Tephrosia virginiana (Goat's-rue*)*

Legume native to sandy, dry soils. Pretty pink and pale yellow pea-like flowers in early summer. 12 to 36 inches. Zone 3+.

***Thalictrum* spp.** (Meadow Rue)

All rues are ideal for naturalized gardens or woodland edges with some moisture. **King of the meadow** *(T. pubescens)* blooms in summer with interesting white flower plumes on tall stems. **Purple meadow rue** *(T. dasycarpum)* has showy pink-purple flowers in early summer. 36 to 120 inches. Zone 3+.

Tiarella cordifolia
(Running Foamflower)

One of our best native plants for use as a groundcover in woodland gardens. Blooms of frothy white spikes are a valuable spring nectar source. Semi-evergreen foliage spreads quickly by stolons (runners) in moist soil. 3 to 10 inches. Zone 3+.

Tradescantia virginiana (Virginia Spiderwort)

Purple spring flowers on a vigorous spreading plant in moist soil. Foliage goes dormant after blooming. Hybrids are readily available. 12 to 24 inches. Zone 3+.

Trientalis borealis (Starflower)

Native to cool woods, blooming in spring with dainty, single, white flowers. Thin rhizomes spread through moist, humus-rich soil until plants go dormant in midsummer. Easily identified because starflower forms whorls of seven leaves and its flowers contain seven petals, seven sepals, and seven anthers. Often grows with moss and partridgeberry in the wild. Zones 2 to 8. 4 to 6 inches.

Trilliums are one of our most beautiful and cherished wild flowers, but they are slow to establish, making them expensive in the trade. Always buy nursery-propagated trilliums—such as these growing in New England Wild Flower Society's raised nursery beds—and confirm with your supplier that plants offered are not harvested from the wild. You can easily propagate trilliums by digging established plants, breaking rhizomes into pieces and replanting in moisture-retentive soil heavily amended with leaves, in an area with dappled shade or protection from the hot summer sun.

Trillium spp.

All trilliums do best in moist, woodland soil. **White trillium** *(T. grandiflorum)* is a showy spring ephemeral, but takes time to get established. **Stinking Benjamin** *(T. erectum)* is common to moist woodlands, with maroon-red flowers pollinated by flies. 8 to 20 inches. Zone 3+.

Trollius laxus (Globeflower)

Thrives in wet, alkaline soils. Pretty buttercup-like flowers in spring. 12 to 20 inches. Zone 4+.

Urtica spp. (Nettle)

The foliage of **stinging nettle** *(U. dioica)* is painful to the touch, so never plant it in your flower beds—however, nettles attract beneficial insects, deter pests, and are food plants for many small butterfly caterpillars. Related **wood nettle** *(Aportea canadensis)* lacks the sting. 30 to 60 inches. Zone 3+.

Utricularia spp. (Bladderwort)

Carnivorous floating plant with snapdragon-like flowers that attract and trap mosquitoes and other insects. Foliage is submerged.

Uvularia spp. (Bellwort, Large Merrybells, Wild Oats)

Lovely spring-flowering woodland lilies. Excellent in a small woodland garden where their tiny graceful flowers invite close inspection by garden visitors, including early-spring pollinators. **Large merrybells** *(U. grandiflora)* has a serene presence and soft yellow weeping lily flowers, and thrives in limestone soil. Keeps its tall stems and foliage until fall unlike some native spring wildflowers who go dormant in the heat of summer. 12 to 16 inches. **Wild oats** *(U. sessifolia)* is fairly drought-tolerant and can be used as a groundcover. 4 to 12 inches. Zone 3+.

Veratrum viride (False Hellebore, Indian Poke)

Wetland plant with clusters of star-shaped flowers in early summer. Wide ribbed leaves are attractive as a foliage plant. 24 to 96 inches. Zone 3+.

Verbena hastata (Blue Vervain)

New England's native verbena is a tall perennial growing in sunny, moist areas. Best in an informal garden setting mixed with other wildflowers. Blue-violet flowers open a few at a time, from summer to early fall. 24 to 48 inches. Zone 3+.

Vernonia noveboracensis (New York Ironweed)

Clumping, tall, native with late-summer clusters of red-purple flower disks, which contrast well with asters and goldenrods. Prefers moist soil but adaptable to drier soils. Statuesque plant that never needs staking. Cut back stems in early summer to stagger its height. 36 to 60 inches. Zone 4+.

Veronicastrum virginicum (Culver's Root)

Tall upright stems loaded with candelabras of white midsummer flowers. Effective for a moist meadow or massed in cottage garden plantings. 36 to 72 inches. Zone 3+ .

Viola spp. (Violet)

New England has many native violets that naturally grow in shady or sunny, moist or dry areas across the region. Important spring nectar source for pollinators, and the sole food plant for fritillary butterfly caterpillars. **Common blue violet** *(V. sororia)* blooms the earliest, and is the state flower of Rhode Island. Readily self-seeds. 3 to 18 inches. Zone 2+.

Waldsteinia fragarioides (Barren Strawberry)

Yellow spring flowers. Forms a thick, evergreen mat that deters weeds even in dry soil. Does not form edible fruits like true strawberries, but its seeds are eaten by birds. 3 to 6 inches. Zone 3+.

Yucca filamentosa (Adam's Needle, Needle Palm)

Interesting white flowers in early summer are pollinated by night-flying moths. Evergreen foliage. Native to sandy areas along the southeastern US coast. 12 to 48 inches. Zone 4+.

Zizia spp. (Alexanders)

In the **Carrot** *(Apiaceae)* family, *Zizia* is a native food plant for black swallowtail butterfly caterpillars. **Golden Alexanders** *(Z. aurea)* is the more common species in New England, growing in open wet areas with late-spring, yellow flowers. **Heart-leaved Alexanders** *(Z. aptera)* is rare in New England, found occasionally in Connecticut and Rhode Island, but adapts to drier summer soils than its cousin. 12 to 36 inches. Zone 4+.

A chipmunk named Nutmeg. If you have stone walls, chipmunks will use their nooks and crannies to store their winter stashes.

Native Grasses, Sedges, Rushes, and other Grasslike Plants

Ornamental grasses belong in every garden for their vertical presence, their plumes of chaff-covered seeds that sway with the breeze, and their late-season and winter value to wildlife. Beware many of the ornamental grasses from Asia available from garden centers, including certain species of *Miscanthus*—their rootballs become very large and thick over time, making them difficult to remove or divide, once established, and they can become invasive in moist soils.

Acorus americanus (Sweetflag)

Fine-bladed rush-like plant for shallow water or any moist soil. Low maintenance. Suitable for erosion control on streambanks. Tiny flowers on a 2 to 4 inches spadix in spring and summer are followed by dark berries. *A. calamus* is very similar but native to Europe and widely naturalized here. 12 to 48 inches . Zone 5+.

Ammophila breviligulata (American Beach Grass)

The classic grass of eastern sand dunes. Spreads quickly, good for erosion control and stabilization of sandy soil in an exposed location. Best planted in fall or early to mid-spring. **Lake Champlain beach grass** (*A. champlainensis*) is a rare subspecies.

Andropogon spp. (Big Bluestem, Broom Sedge)

Native slow-spreading prairie grasses suitable for soil stabilization. **Big bluestem** (*A. gerardii*) grows 3 to 9 feet in moist or dry soils. **Broom sedge** (*A. virginicus*) grows in dry, sandy soils, useful for coastal buffers. 12 to 36 inches. Zone 4+.

Bouteloua curtipendula (Side oats Grama)

Warm-season clumping (bunch) grass suitable for a meadow or a low-mow lawn. One of the few grasses with colorful flowers, which emerge as bright orange/

red anthers dangling from attractive green stems. Delicate feathery seed stems in fall. Actually a Midwestern prairiegrass with small populations in New England. Height: 12 to 24 inches. Spread: 12 to 24 feet. Zone 3+.

Calamagrostis spp.

Calamagrostis is mostly a western prairiegrass, but eastern species include **blue joint** (*C. canadensis*), growing 2 to 5 feet in zones 1 to 7. and **Pickering's reed grass** (*C. pickeringii*) is shorter (8 to 24 inches) and hardy only to Zone 5. Both are wetland species.

Carex spp. (Sedge)

Sedges are low clumping grass-like plants that grow in or near water but will grow in almost any soil with some moisture. They are excellent filler for any habitat garden, providing excellent cover for breeding amphibians, as well as nesting sites for birds and the endangered bog turtle. Leaves and stems are used for nest building and seeds are eaten by many birds. **Tussock sedge** (*C. stricta*) is a graceful specimen that thrives in shallow standing water, but does well in any consistently moist soil. 2 to 3 feet. Zone 5+. **Appalachian sedge** (*C. appalachica*) needs better drainage than other sedges. **Pennsylvania sedge** (*C. pensylvanica*) grows in moist or dry, infertile soils, including sand. Suitable as a lawn substitute, it requires no mowing but can be trimmed to 3 to 4 inches. **Black sedge** (*C. nigra*) is suitable for wet, salty coastal soils. **Plantain sedge** (*C. plantaginea*) is a shorter sedge with evergreen foliage. **Broad-leaf sedge** (*C. platyphylla*).

Zone 4+. Use **Bristle-leaf sedge** (*C. eburnea*) for alkaline soils. **Fernald's sedge** (*C. merritt-fernaldii*) grows in dry, sandy areas. **Sallow sedge** (*C. lurida*), with fresh evergreen foliage and interesting bristly flowers, adapts to most soils. **Beach sedge** (*C. silicea*) is native to New England's beaches and dunes. **Wooly-fruited sedge** (*C. lasiocarpa*) is a beautiful, wispy, extra-cold-hardy native of bogs and lakeshores. **Limestone meadow sedge** (*C. granularis*) grows in limestone fens. Vary in height from 6 to 40 inches. Zone 3+.

Chasmanthium latifolium (Northern Sea Oats)

Interesting grass native to mid-Atlantic and southern stream- and river banks. Bamboo-like foliage produces droopy oat-like flowers that fade from pink to gold in fall. Height: 36 to 48 inches. Zone 4+.

Danthonia spicata (Poverty Oatgrass)

So called because it grows in the poorest and driest of soils. Useful as a no-mow lawn substitute along with other grasses. 4 to 24 inches. Zone 2+.

Deschampsia spp. (Hairgrass)

Hairgrasses are fine-textured, long-lived clumping grasses that are magical in a meadow setting, or used to evoke aspects of a larger space in a small garden. **Tufted hair grass** (*D. cespitosa*) grows in poorly drained areas and bogs. **Wavy hair grass** (*D. flexuosa*) grows in dry, open, sandy places. 36 to 48 inches. Zone 2.

Elymus spp. and *Leymus* spp.

Wild rye (*E. canadensis*) grows in any well-drained soil. Oat-like seeds on arching stems. Quickly establishes good wildlife cover and food and can be used as a

"nurse crop" for perennial seedlings or newly established meadows. 2 to 5 feet. Zone 1+. **Blue lyme grass** (*E. arenarius*) is a small spreading ornamental grass with flat steel-blue foliage. Native to northern Atlantic shores, it is one of the few grasses able to colonize in sand dunes. 2 to 5 feet. Zone 4+. **American dunegrass** (*Leymus mollis*) Common northern beach grass growing in sand dunes from Cape Cod north. Soil-anchoring qualities help prevent coastal erosion. Spreads quickly from rhizomes. Use as a groundcover in coastal gardens. 2 to 6 feet. Zone 2+.

Eragrostis spectabilis (Purple Lovegrass)

Grows well on dry, sandy soils. Looks great planted in sweeps in front of other plants. Blooms in clouds of tiny pink summer flowers that glow and shimmer when hit by the rising or setting sun. 8 to 14 inches. Zone 4+.

Festuca spp. (Fescue)

Fine-textured grasses, often a component of "eco-lawn" seed mixes. **Short-leaf fescue** (*F. brachyphylla*) is a tiny alpine plant perfect for rock gardens. 2 to 16 inches. Nonnative fescues include **blue fescue** (*F. glauca*), with blue stems, and **red fescue** (*F. Rubra*), a naturalized European variety. 1 to 3 feet. Zones 1 to 7.

Juncus spp. (Rush)

Rushes are grass-like wetland plants with cylindrical, upright stems. **Softrush** (*J. effusus*) grows in stiff clumps of wiry evergreen stems. Cultivars with contorted corkscrew-like stems are particularly striking in a water garden. **Saltmeadow rush** (*J. gerardii*) is native to tide lines and salt marshes. 2 to 4 feet. Zone 3+.

Muhlenbergia capillaris (Pink Muhly Grass)

Grow for its stunning explosion of pink (its seed inflorescences) in fall. Grows in any soil with decent drainage. 12 to 40 inches. Zone 5+.

Panicum virgatum (Panic or Switch grass)

Beautiful and adaptable ornamental grass, especially where backlit. Grows in shallow, dry soils as well as areas with poor drainage or salinity. Clump-forming, use in rain gardens, meadows, or coastal buffers. Many cultivars are available. 3 to 6 feet. Zone 3+.

Plantago maritima (Seaside Plantain)

Short, grasslike plant of salty shorelines and exposed rocky outcrops. Seeds are eaten by many birds and mammals. Similar foliage to the **English plantain weed** (*P. major*) naturalized through New England. 2 to 8 inches. Zone 3+.

Schizachyrium scoparium (Little Bluestem)

Low and versatile bunchgrass that grows in most soils. Excellent in containers, with Intense fall color of russet orange/red. 1 to 4 feet. Zone 3+

Schoenoplectus pungens (Chair-maker's Rush, Bulrush)

Tall rush native to coastal marshes. Spreads quickly through rhizomes, not for small gardens. 1 to 7 feet. Zone 3+.

Scirpus cyperinus (Bulrush, Wool Rush)

Bulrush forms dense stands in wetlands. Provides food for ducks and fish and aquatic cover. Upright stems somewhat resemble cattails. 3 to 5 feet. Zone 3+

Sorghastrum nutans (Indian Grass)

Think of prairie grass and you are thinking of **indian grass**. Grows in any soil except waterlogged. Good for meadows and on slopes for erosion control. Beautiful chestnut-brown/golden plume-like flowers in fall. Clumping. 3 to 5 feet. Zone 3+.

Spartina spp. (Cordgrass)

Familiar native of coastal marshes and mudflats. Attractive arching foliage and winter structure/effect. Aggressive spreader. 2 to 5 feet. Zone 3+.

Sporobolus spp. (Dropseed)

Grow dropseed in dry soil as an ornamental grass for its elegant arching clumps of thin, dense leaves and its fall color. **Sand dropseed** (*S. cryptandrus*) and **prairie dropseed** (*S. heterolepsis*) are prairie plants occasionally seen growing in open areas of New England. 1 to 3 feet. Zone 3+.

Tridens flavus (Purpletop)

Upright clumping grass native to most New England states except for Maine. Short-lived, use to quickly naturalize an open area. Often grows on roadsides. 2 to 5 feet. Zone 4+.

Typha spp. (Cattail)

Cattails are the familiar brown, fluffy, sausage-shaped spikes seen in wetlands across New England. Spreads aggressively, so use only for restoring large wetlands. Provides shelter and nesting for red-winged blackbirds and marsh wrens. Roots and shoots are eaten by moose, geese, and muskrats. **Broad-leaved cattail** (*T. latifolia*) grows in any wet soil including alkaline fens, and spreads a little less strongly than **narrow-leaved cattail** (*T. angustifolia*), which will invade even undisturbed wetlands. 3 to 8 feet. Zone 2+.

Native New England Ferns

Ferns make an excellent groundcover for shady areas. As a "living mulch," they help shade the forest floor and provide cover and nesting sites for smaller woodland wildlife, including amphibians and turtles.

Adiantum pedatum (Maidenhair Fern)

Daintier leaves than most native ferns. Best in rich, moist soil, in filtered light. Height: 12 to 24 inches. Spread: 24 inches. Zone 2+.

Asplenium platyneuron (Ebony Spleenwort)

Adaptable, narrow growing fern for rocky outcrops. Height: 10 to 20 inches. Spread: 6 inches. Zone 4+.

Dennstaedtia punctilobula (Hayscented Fern)

Spreads rapidly through dense roots and fronds. Roots outcompete other herbaceous plants, so not suited to in a garden situation. So-named because it smells like newly cut hay when fronds are bruised. Height: 16 to 24 inches. Spread: 36 to 48 inches. Zone 3 to 8.

Diplazium pycnocarpon (Glade Fern)

Elegant, well-behaved fern for moist, rocky woodlands. 24 to 40 inches. Zone 4+.

Dryopteris spp. (Wood Fern)

Many varieties extant, most are native to moist shade. *D. intermedia* and *D. marginalis* grow in dry shade. **Male fern** *(D. filix-mas)* grows in rocky, alkaline soils. Zone 3+.

Equisetum spp. (Scouring Rush and Horsetail)

Grass-like wetland ferns for sun or shade. **Tall scouring rush** *(E. hymale)* spreads aggressively by rhizomes. 1 to 6 feet. Zone 3+. **Dwarf scouring rush** *(E. scirpoides)* is slower growing and shorter. 3 to 10 inches. Zones 1 to 6. **Woodland horsetail** *(E. sylvaticum)* looks like a bonsai fir tree, spreads quickly. 6 to 18 inches. Zones 2 to 7.

Gymnocarpium dryopteris (Common Oak Fern)

Excellent fern for colder areas of New England. Native to coniferous or mixed hardwood forests. Height: 6 to 8 inches. Spread: 12 inches. Zone 2 to 6.

Lycopodium clavatum (Clubmoss)

Clubmosses are ferns that look like miniature pine trees. Cultivate as a groundcover in areas high in surface moisture to encourage natural mycorrhizae to develop on brittle root systems. A similar species found in New England woods is **princess pine** (*Dendrolycopodium obscurum*). Height: 1 to 6 inches. Spread: 12 to 36 inches. Zones 3 to 7.

Lygodium palmatum (Climbing Fern, Hartford Fern)

New England's only vining fern, rare in the wild and can be difficult to propagate. Thoreau described it as a "... *most beautiful slender and delicate fern, twining like (a) vine about the meadow-sweet, panicled andromeda, goldenrods, etc., to the height of three feet or more, and difficult to detach from them.... Our most beautiful fern, and most suitable for wreaths or garlands. It is rare.*" Height: 3 to 4 feet. Spread 2 to 3 feet.Zone 3+.

Matteuccia struthiopteris (Ostrich Fern)

Graceful arching fronds and creeping rootstock. Remove half of each year's new shoots to control growth. The tightly coiled young sprouts (called fiddleheads) are edible and can be boiled, steamed or sautéed. Height: 2 to 4 feet. Spread: 3 to 6 feet. Zone 2+.

Onoclea sensibilis (Sensitive Fern)

Often pops up in rich moist soils. Fresh foliage in late summer. So-called because of its sensitivity to frost. Height: 10 to 24 inches. Spread: 2 to 3 feet. Zone 3+.

Osmunda spp.

Cinnamon Fern (*O. cinnamomea*) has fuzzy brown cattail-like fronds in early summer, used by hummingbirds as nesting material. **Royal fern** (*O. regalis*) grows even in shallow water and is perfect for a pond garden. **Interrupted fern** (*O. claytoniana*) is tolerant of drier soils. Height: 2 to 5 feet. Spread: 2 to 4 feet. Zone 3+.

Parathelypteris spp.

Not as aggressive as other ferns, **New York fern** (*P. noveboracensis*) grows in wet or somewhat dry soils. **Massachusetts fern** (*P. simulata*) is native to bogs and seeps. Height: 16 to 30 inches. Spread: 2 to 3 feet. Zones 4 to 7.

Phegopteris spp. (Beech Fern)

Good all-around groundcover for moist shade, spreading by rhizomes to form a mat. Height: 12 to 26 inches. Spread: 3 feet. Zone 4+.

Polypodium virginianum (Rock Polypody)

Grows wild in pockets of mossy soils, in rocks, making this a great tiny fern for thin soils and shaded rock gardens. Height: 3 to 10 inches. Spread: 8 to 16 inches. Zone 2 to 8.

Polystichum acrostichoides (Christmas Fern)

One of the few evergreen ferns of New England. Not fussy, easily incorporated into any shady garden. Height: 8 to 16 inches. Spread: 14 to 24 inches. Zone 3+.

Thelypteris palustris (Marsh Fern)

Easy fern for wet soils. Height: 1 to 3 feet. Spread: 2 to 3 feet. Zone 3+.

Perennial Vines

Apios americana (Groundnut, Indian Potato)

Fragrant, burgundy summer flowers produce peapods with seeds eaten by wildlife. Tubers were eaten by native Americans and colonists. Aggressively spreads by underground stems, not for small gardens. Zone 4+.

Aristolochia macrophylla (Pipevine, Dutchman's Pipe)

Native to southern Appalachian forests, once popular for keeping front porches cool and shaded. Heart-shaped leaves are a food plant of the pipevine swallowtail butterfly caterpillar. Inconspicuous flowers in spring and early summer. Zone 4+.

Campsis radicans (Trumpet Creeper)

Shrubby perennial vine with spectacular blooms, native to areas south of New England. Can be grown on a porch rail or over a fence, but site carefully—it grows vigorously up to 10 feet in a season, and can damage wood or brick. Zone 4+.

Celastrus scandens (American Bittersweet)

Deciduous native vine with red and orange berries that bluebirds and other songbirds love. Scrambles over the ground or up trees. Don't confuse it with its Asian cousin, Oriental bittersweet (C. orbiculatus), which is highly invasive, strangling groves of native trees and anything else in its way. Birds have spread them across New England by eating their berries, so even if you have never planted it, be sure you don't have this variety growing. They're not easy to tell apart, but on the Oriental variety, the flowers and fruits are found between the leaf and stem, whereas on the natives they're located at the end of each branch. Fruits from late summer to late winter. Zone 3+.

Clematis virginiana (Virgin's Bower, Devil's Darning Needles)

Sprawling vine that reseeds heavily in moist soils. White, late-summer flowers provide a good nectar and seed supply. Twine up an arbor or pergola. Cut stems to ground before spring growth begins to encourage bushiness. Zone 3+.

Lathyrus japonicus (Beach Pea)

Sprawling vine growing on beaches and sand dunes with pretty purple or pink flowers. Circumboreal (native to most northern continents).

Lonicera spp. (Honeysuckle)

Vining honeysuckles are hummingbird favorites and produce small fall berries. **Trumpet honeysuckle** (L. sempervirens) blooms for a long time and is ideal for twining along a fence. Thrives in moist soil with at least a half day of sunshine. Tubular red flowers. **Limber honeysuckle** (L. dioica) grows 4 to 10 feet with multi-toned pinkish yellow flowers in late spring. Grows in moist to dry soils. Zone 3+. **Hairy honeysuckle** (L. hirsuta) clambers through surrounding plants and increases its spread through root suckers. Yellow flowers. Grows in alkaline soil. Zones 4 to 7. See also **Lonicera** under Shrubs.

Parthenocissus quinquefolia (Virginia Creeper)

Twining native vine growing in any soil, with spectacular red fall foliage and fall and winter berries adored by bluebirds, great-crested flycatchers, pileated woodpeckers, and red-eyed vireos. Food plant for many spectacular moth species. Use it to climb up trees, cover stone walls, or as a no-maintenance groundcover in difficult areas. Zone 4+.

Vitis spp. (Wild Grape)

Native grapes are the favorite summer foods of many birds and mammals. Dense foliage provides good nesting and cover for songbirds, and the thin, peeling bark is used for nest-building. Food plant for many moth larvae. Not for the small garden, wild grape needs lots of sunlight and will climb up trees to find it. **Fox grape** *(V. labrusca)* is suitable for any soil, and is the primary ancestor of the Concord grape. **Riverbank grape** *(V. riparia)* is good for streambanks and wet alkaline areas. Zone 4+.

Wisteria frutescens (American Wisteria)

Native to moist soils from Virginia south. The less-aggressive cousin to the commonly grown Asian wisteria, its late spring/early summer flowers are shorter and lacking the intense fragrance, but just as beautiful as the Asian blooms. Host plant for many butterfly and moth caterpillars. The coiling stems grow very thickly, so situate it carefully where it cannot eat through supports. Remove shoots from the base to concentrate foliage higher up on support. Zone 4+.

Poison ivy is not something you want growing in your home gardens because of the awful rash it causes to anyone unfortunate enough to touch it. But its berries are tailor-made for birds to eat, and brilliant yellow-turning-to-red foliage in fall add color. If you have trees in an out of the way area of your property, and no animals or children running through that area, consider allowing some poison ivy vines to climb up trees as a fall and winter food source for birds.

Shrubs and Small Trees

Aesculus spp. (Buckeye)

Bottlebrush buckeye *(A. parviflora)* grows 4 to 8 feet, blooming feathery white in summer. Z4+. **Red buckeye** *(A. pavia)* is a hummingbird magnet with its red tubular spring flowers. In open areas, it grows 10 to 25' with a 10 to 20' spread. Zone 5+.

Alnus spp. (Alder)

Not a tree for the immaculate garden, but an excellent thicket-forming wildlife tree for moist or wet areas, providing good twiggy cover and shelter, plus seeds for overwintering birds and early spring nectar for pollinators. Beavers enjoy their twigs, and its foliage is host to swallowtail, white admiral and mourning cloak butterfly caterpillars. Alder also hosts a type of aphid eaten by harvester butterfly larvae, New England's only carnivorous butterfly. Good for erosion control. **Speckled alder** *(A. incana)* and **smooth alder** *(A. serrulata)* grow 8 to 15 feet in moist or wet soils. **Green alder** *(A. viridis)* is a shorter northern species, growing 4 to 10 feet in full sun. Zone 2 to 7.

Amelanchier spp. (Serviceberry, Shadbush)

One of the best wildlife shrubs, blooming in early spring (before leaves appear), providing nectar for orioles and

pollinating insects when little else is blooming. Birds such as bluebird, robin, cedar waxwings, gray catbirds, scarlet tanagers, and veeries devour the berries almost as soon as they develop in June. **Shadbush** *(A. canadensis)* is good for wet soils and can be pruned into a single trunk tree, or allowed to grow into a naturally multi-stemmed shrub shape. **Downy serviceberry** *(A. arborea)* and **Allegheny serviceberry** *(A. laevis)* both tolerate drier soils. **Apple serviceberry** *(A. x grandiflora)* is a natural hybrid between downy and Allegheny. **Running serviceberry** *(A. stolonifera)* is a low-growing (12 to 72 inches), sun-loving spreader for sandy or rocky soils. Zone 4+.

Andromeda polifolia (Bog Rosemary)

Light-pink spring flowers and lavender-like foliage suitable for acidic bogs. Height: 12 to 20 inches. Spread: 16 to 28 inches. Zones 2 to 6.

Arctostaphylos uva-ursi (Bearberry, Kinnikinnick)

Native groundcover becoming popular in New England gardens. Blueberry-like pink spring blooms and bright red fall berries. Drought-tolerant, it needs good drainage and sun. Useful for stabilizing steep slopes in exposed areas. Height: 3 to 8 inches. Spread: 24 to 48 inches. Zone 3+.

Aronia, see *Photinia.*

Baccharis halimifolia (Groundsel Bush, Sea-myrtle)

Semi-evergreen shrub of salt marshes with showy silvery plumes in fall. 6 feet. Zone 5+.

Calycanthus floridus (Sweetshrub, Allspice)

Small shrub for most soil types except sand. Maroon early summer flowers have the sweetest of fragrance. 4 to 8 feet. Zone 4+.

Ceanothus americanus **(New Jersey Tea)**

Small native shrub requiring well-drained soil and sun. Outstanding nectar plant attracting many beneficial insects, with its billowy white summer flowers. Leaves were used as a tea substitute during the Revolutionary War. Height: 24 to 36 inches. Spread: 24 to 36 inches. Zone 4+.

Cephalanthus occidentalis **(Buttonbush)**

Moisture-loving native wetland shrub with distinctive white pincushion flowerballs. For small gardens, treat as a perennial and cut stems down to 6 to 12 inches in winter. Tubular flowers attract showy butterflies such as swallowtails and fritillaries, and the seeds are eaten by ducks. Height: 3 to 8 feet. Spread: 3 to 6 feet. Zone 4+.

Cercis canadensis **(Eastern Redbud)**

Beautiful small tree that lights up the landscape with bright pink flowers in mid-spring before other trees have leafed out. For winter hardiness, choose cultivars originating from northern genotypes. Redbuds do best in a sunny, sheltered location. Looks good either as single specimen or en masse. Grows taller in a woodland garden, searching for light. Height: 12 to 20 feet. Spread: 10 to 20 feet. Zone 4+.

Chamaedaphne calyculata **(Leatherleaf)**

A true bog shrub, requiring moist but not waterlogged soil. Early-season nectar source, blooming in early spring with white flowers held upside-down in neat rows like bleeding heart. Height: 24 to 36 inches. Spread: 24 to 36 inches. Zones 2 to 7.

Chionanthus virginicus **(Fringetree, Old Man's Beard)**

Caution: The view of a fringetree in full bloom may cause you to drive your car off the road. Its fringed clusters of late spring blossoms look like white clouds, but in fall this shrub is also attractive, forming hard dark blue berries enjoyed by birds. Does best in a moist, fertile soil with at least 3 to 4 hours of sun. Height: 10 to 20 feet. Spread: 10 to 20 feet. Zone 4+.

Clethra altinifolia **(Summersweet, Sweet Pepperbush)**

Easy to grow shrub that does well anywhere but a very dry location. Heavily-scented white or pink summer flowers attract all kinds of enthusiastic pollinators. Blooms best in full sun. Use for wetland restoration or woodland edges. Height: 4 to 9 feet. Spread: 4 to 12 feet. Zone 4+.

Comptonia peregrina **(Sweetfern)**

Not a fern but a small shrub with aromatic foliage for poor, dry soils. Difficult to transplant, use nursery-grown plants. Important food plant for many butterfly and moth caterpillars. 3 feet. Zone 3+.

Corema conradii **(Broom Crowberry)**

Mounding evergreen growing in peaty but well-drained sand dunes and pine barrens near the coast. Dark-red, petal-less blooms in early spring. Good for windswept heathland or rock gardens along with bearberry and broadleaf rhododendron. Threatened on Cape Cod, Nantucket, and Martha's Vineyard because of the potentially invasive Scotch broom. Looks similar to the introduced nonnative heather *Calluna vulgaris*. Height: 10 to 20 inches. Spread: 12 to 36 inches. Zones 4 to 7.

Cornus spp. (Dogwood)

Important bird plants, providing good cover and nesting. Berries and twigs feed many birds including northern flicker, pileated woodpecker, yellow-bellied sapsucker, hairy woodpecker, mockingbird, brown thrasher, robin, bluebird, cedar waxwing, yellow-rumped warbler, thrushes, catbird, vireos, evening and pine grosbeaks, eastern kingbird, wood duck, and cardinal. Many consider **flowering dogwood** (*C. florida*) our most beautiful native tree. **Pagoda dogwood** (*C. alternifolia*) is not as showy, but has an attractive architecture providing winter interest. Shrubby natives are **gray dogwood** (*C. racemosa*) with white fruit, **red osier** (*C. stolonifera* or *sericea*) with red twigs which offer striking contrast against winter snow, and **silky dogwood** (*C. amomum*) which grows in moist thickets. Except for *C. racemosa*, most dogwoods do best with some sun and moisture. Zone 3+.

Corylus americana (American Hazelnut)

Grow hazelnut knowing that you'll be sharing the nuts with squirrels and chipmunks plus large birds such as hairy woodpecker, blue jay, wood duck, wild turkey, ruffed grouse and ring-necked pheasant. Catkins and buds browsed by deer and rabbits. Early spring flowers provide nectar to pollinators. Good understory tree for woodland gardens but dislikes wet feet. Fruits from July through October. Height: 5 to 12 feet. Spread: 4 to 8 feet. Zone 4+.

Crataegus spp. (Hawthorn)

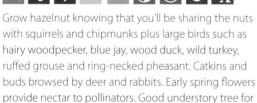

Thorny foliage and large fruits make hawthorn an excellent and tough wildlife shrub for any sunny area. Needs good air circulation to fend off disease. White spring apple-like blooms form abundant fruits that feed birds into winter. Safe cover and nesting for many birds,

hawthorn can be used to form an impenetrable wildlife hedge. For landscaping purposes, look for cultivars that are more disease-resistant than the wild species. **Downy hawthorn** (*C. mollis*) and **Cockspur hawthorn** (*C. crus-galli*) are New England's native hawthorns, growing on roadsides and in old fields. **Bigfruit hawthorn** (*C. macrosperma*) is common throughout New England. Height: 20 to 40 feet. Spread: 20 to 35 feet. Zone 4+.

Diervilla lonicera (Bush-honeysuckle)

Shrubby plant with yellow summer blooms fading to red. Grows in any soil, spreads quickly by suckering roots, to form a low thicket. 2 to 4 feet. Zones 3 to 7.

Dirca palustris (Leatherwood, Ropebark)

Attractive shrub with a tidy form, clean foliage. Adapts to any deep, moist soil with protection from midday sun. Inconspicuous early spring, yellow-green flowers. Bendy but elastic stems were used by Native Americans for rope and bowstrings. Height: 3 to 6 feet. Spread: 4 to 6 feet. Zones 3 to 8.

Elaeagnus commutatus (Silverberry)

Native cousin to invasive Russian and autumn olives, which colonize roadsides. Very hardy and tolerant of poor soils or wind. Attractive silvery foliage. Fragrant blooms in late spring/early summer produce berries quickly eaten by birds. Spreads quickly with runners, so use in naturalized areas or contained areas such as driveway edges. Height: 1 to 7 feet. Spread: 3 to 8 feet. Zone 2+.

Empetrum nigrum (Black Crowberry)

Low shrub native to open, rocky, high-elevations and northern New England coastal bogs. Needle-like foliage, it looks like heather but has red-orange spring flowers which form jet-black berries. Similar to **broom crowberry** (*Corema conradii*) but hardier. 6 inches. Zone 2 to 7.

Eubotrys racemosa (Sweetbells, Swamp Dog-laurel)

Native to coastal swamp edges and sandy woods from Massachusetts south, with white blueberry-like flowers in spring. Formerly *Leucothoe*. 3 to 5 feet. Zone 5+.

Fothergilla spp. (Witch-alder)

Attractive fuzzy brush-like flowers in spring and beautiful glowing fall color. Native to the Appalachians southward, but an excellent plant for New England gardens. **Dwarf witch-alder** *(F. gardenii)* cultivars and hybrids are readily available. 3 to 6 feet. Zone 5+. **Large witch-alder** *(F. major)* is taller, 4 to 15 feet and hardier (Zone 4+).

Gaylussacia spp. (Huckleberry, Dangleberry)

Huckleberry looks similar to blueberry, and they share the same soil preferences. Pink late-spring flowers are pollinated by bumblebees. **Black huckleberry** *(G. baccata)* has black berries and red fall foliage. Grows up to 3 feet in sandy, open areas. Zone 4+. **Dangleberry** *(G. frondosa)* is suitable for moist shady areas. 3 to 6 feet. Zone 5+. **Box huckleberry** *(G. brachycera)* is native to southern areas. Difficult to establish, but a nice groundcover. 8 to 12 inches. Zones 5 to 7.

Halesia tetraptera (Carolina Silverbell)

Native to the Carolinas south grown for its beautiful white bell-shaped spring flowers and interesting winter bark and fruits. Grows into a large tree in full sun. Host plant for promethea moth caterpillars. 20 to 40 feet. Zone 4+.

Hamamelis virginiana (Witchhazel)

Yellow flowers produced in late fall, a rare late-season nectar source. Grows quickly when young, and works well planted under larger trees. Woody seeds, buds, twigs, and bark are all eaten by many birds and mammals. **Spring witchhazel** *(H. vernalis)*, native to the South, blooms in late winter. 8 to 20 feet. Zone 3+.

Hudsonia ericoides , H. tomentosa (Golden Heather, Beach Heather)

Beach heather *(H. tomentosa)* is one of the few plants that grows on outer sand dunes. Yellow heather-like flowers in spring and early summer, and dried foliage remains on stems through winter. In decline, it is rarely found in the wild in New England. 3 to 12 inches. Zones 2 to 8. **Golden heather** *(H. ericoides)* is less hardy (Zones 4 to 8), growing in sand barrens, tolerates slightly more shade than beach heather.

Hydrangea arborescens (Wild Hydrangea)

Native to southern New England southward, wild hydrangea has nectar-rich flowers and grows more like a loose perennial than a shrub. Large-flowering cultivars such as "Annabelle" have sterile blooms, so choose species cultivars such as "White Dome." 2 to 4 feet. Zone 4+. **Oakleaf hydrangea** *(H. quercifolia)* is native to the South, with beautiful white summer blooms. Hardy in warmer zones of New England. Zone 5+.

Hypericum prolificum (Shrubby St. John's Wort)

Small, bee-friendly shrub for any well-drained soil. Golden yellow flowers in summer. 3 to 6 feet. Zones 4 to 8.

Ilex spp. (Holly)

Hollies are berrying shrubs important for overwintering songbirds such as robins, cardinals, and chickadees. **Inkberry** (*I. glabra*) has black berries and is a good substitute for boxwood, because it can be sheared to form a hedge. Tolerates wind better

than other evergreen hollies. Tolerates sandy, drier soils. Prefers sun but tolerates some shade. Less palatable to deer than other hollies. 4 feet. Zone 5+. **American holly** (*I. opaca*) needs protection from drying winter winds and grows in sandy soil. Height: 20 feet . Spread: 8 feet. Zone 4+. **Winterberry** (*I. verticillata*) is deciduous, forming beautiful red berries unmistakable from a distance in winter. Requires moist soil. Zone 3+. **Mountain holly** (*I. mucronata*) is native to bogs and swamps and forms summer berries immediately devoured by birds. Blue-green foliage. 4 to 8 feet. Zone 3+.

Itea virginica (Virginia Sweetspire)

Native from New Jersey south, but excellent for New England gardens, in moist soil and sun. Brilliant fiery red fall foliage and pretty white early-summer flower spires. A short cultivar, "Little Henry" grows to about 3 feet. Foliage is very late to appear in spring. 36 to 72 inches. Zone 5+.

Juniperus spp. (Juniper, Cedar)

Juniper is essential to every wildlife garden, its dense evergreen foliage providing protection as well as food for birds, mammals, and butterfly caterpillars. Only females produce cones, but plants are rarely labeled as male or female. Fruits September through March. Tiny

yellow flowers bloom in spring. Perfect for dry slopes where nothing else will grow. Available in many forms. **Common juniper** (*J. communis*) grows in the toughest soils, including gravel and alkaline soil. Zone 2+. **Eastern redcedar** (*J. virginiana*) is a small tree that becomes rounder with age. 10 to 40 feet. Zone 4+. **Creeping juniper** (*J. horizontalis*) is a low groundcover growing 2 to 12 inches in any soil, including sand dunes and alkaline soil. Zone 2+.

Kalmia spp. (Laurel)

Evergreen shrub blooms from late spring into early summer. Connecticut's state flower, **mountain laurel** (*K. latifolia*) is a familiar native of cool, moist forest slopes, with beautiful white or pinkish flowers. Perfect singly or en masse, for any scale of naturalistic landscaping. Blooms best in full sun but tolerates quite a bit of shade. **Bog laurel** (*K. polifolia*) is a short (12 to 24 inches) bog plant. **Sheep laurel** (*K. angustifolia*) grows 16 to 38 inches in sandy or infertile soils.

Ledum groenlandicum (Labrador Tea)

Evergreen shrub that looks like a small rhododendron, with pretty clusters of aromatic white spring flowers. Well-suited for cold bogs and peaty soils in northern New England. 16 to 30 inches. Zone 2 to 6.

Leucothoe. See *Eubotrys.*

Lindera benzoin (Spicebush)

An underused native shrub, spicebush lights up low woods in early spring with tiny yellow flowers. Tiny red fruits (high in lipids) are eaten by many birds including eastern kingbird, great crested flycatcher, and mockingbird. Preferred host plant for spicebush swallowtail butterfly larvae. Okay in shade as long as it gets a few hours of sun per day. 8 to 15 feet. Zones 4+.

Lonicera canadensis (American Fly Honeysuckle)

Straggly understory swamp honeysuckle with pairs of 3/4 to 1 inch, pale yellow flowers in spring, followed by berries eaten by birds. 2 to 6 feet. Zones 3 to 7. See also *Lonicera* under Vines.

Magnolia virginiana (Sweetbay Magnolia)

Beautiful tree native to coastal swamps and low woods. A multi-stemmed deciduous shrub with 1 to 3 inch, fragrant, cupped flowers in late spring. Branching structure provides good shelter for birds, and fall berries are eaten by many species including brown thrashers, catbirds, kingbirds, mockingbirds, vireos, towhees, and woodpeckers. Height: 20 to 50 feet. Spread 8 to 20 feet. Zone 5+.

Malus spp. (Apple, Crabapple)

All members of the apple family have fruits, twigs, buds, bark, and foliage that are valuable to wildlife. Good nesting for birds. A naturalized nonnative, many Asian species and hybrids are readily available. Scented flowers in spring attract many pollinators, and the foliage feeds many insects. Fruits September to March.

Morella pensylvanica (Bayberry)

Familiar to visitors of Cape Cod where it grows wild on dunes. Adaptable to most conditions, but spreads best in dry, sandy soils. Semi-evergreen foliage, with waxy gray/blue fruits eaten by many birds. Orioles drink nectar from the small green blooms in spring. Berry wax was used by early settlers to create scented candles. Can be pruned as a hedge. Formerly *Myrica*. Height: 2 to 6 feet. Spread: 3 to 10 feet. Zones 4 to 7.

Morus rubra (Red Mulberry)

Grown for its blackberry-like sweet fruits and excellent bird nesting habitat. Fast-growing, with messy fruits and tangles of branches, but suitable for wild areas. Endangered in New England due to hybridizing with Asian white mulberry. Height: 40 feet. Spread 20 to 30 feet. Zone 3+.

Myrica gale (Sweetgale)

Suckering shrub for wet, sunny northern New England gardens. Height: 2 to 5 feet. Spread: 3 to 6 feet. Zone 2 to 6.

Oxydendrum arboreum (Sourwood)

Small tree native to Pennsylvania south. Good tree for urban areas because of its narrow, conical shape. Excellent midseason nectar source. Does best in sun, but tolerates light shade. Height: 15 to 30 feet. Spread: 6 to 12 feet. Zone 5+.

Physocarpus opulifolius (Atlantic Ninebark)

Beautiful, white, snowball flowers in late spring provide a nectar feast. Good bird nesting. Multi-stemmed, with exfoliating bark. Many cultivars available with attractive, colorful foliage. Tolerates dry soil, best with moisture. Height: 6 to 12 feet. Spread: 6 to 20 feet. Zone 4+.

Potentilla fruticosa (Shrubby Cinquefoil)

Adaptable shrub grows in the coldest areas. Yellow summer flowers. Choose local species that self-pollinate rather than European cultivars that require both male and female plants to set seed. 1 to 3 feet. Zone 1 to 6.

Prunus spp. (Wild Plum, Wild Cherry)

All wild cherries and plums are a wildlife favorite, with the flowers, fruits, buds, foliage all providing resources. Shrubby species form dense thickets for nesting and cover, and thorny plum stems provide good safety from predators. Preferred food for ruffed grouse, northern flicker, yellow-bellied sapsucker, eastern kingbird, blue jay, common crow, mockingbird, catbird, brown thrasher, robin, thrush, veery, bluebird, cedar waxwing, vireo, orchard and northern orioles, tanager, cardinal, grosbeak, purple finch, and white-throated sparrow. Good for erosion control on sunny slopes and dry, sandy soils. **Black cherry** *(P. serotina)* can become a large tree, if not taken down when young by fungal disease. Zone 3+. **Pin cherry** *(P. pensylvanica)* fruits last into early winter, browsed by fox, raccoon, black bear, and red squirrel. Zone 3+. **Chokecherry** *(P. virginiana)* is weedy looking but grows in any soil. Zone 3+. **Beach plum** *(P. maritima)* is the shrub Plum Island was named for, growing 4 to 7 feet in sand. Zone 4+. **Sand cherry** *(P. pumila)* is a low (1 to 3 feet) sprawling cherry for sandy soils. Zone 3 to 6.

Rhododendron spp. (Azalea, Rhododendron)

Most nursery azaleas are Asian hybrids, and rhododendrons mostly crossed with the Southern native catawba, but natives are increasingly available. All thrive in

damp, acidic organic soil in shade or sun but bloom best with some sun. The **evergreen rosebay**, or **great laurel**, *(R. maximum)* is native to mountain forests and swamps from eastern Maine south. Wild populations of rosebay are at risk due to deer foraging. **Pinxterbloom azalea** *(R. periclymenoides)* grows 7 feet, with pink spring flowers. Zones 4 to 8. **Swamp azalea** *(R. viscosum)* has white flowers with a wonderful fragrance similar to honeysuckle. 3 to 10 feet. **Rhodora** *(R. canadense)* is low (1 to 3 feet), growing in cold bogs. Pink/purple spring flowers. Zones 3 to 6. **Flame azalea** *(R. calendulaceum)* is native from the Pennsylvania Appalachians south, and worth growing for its striking orange June flowers. Zone 4+.

Rhus spp. *(Sumac)*

Colonizing shrubs often seen growing in old fields and clearings. Will grow in virtually any soil (although they do need summer sun). Fiery red or orange fall foliage, nectar-rich flowers, and large fuzzy fruit clusters (rich in Vitamin A) that are an important winter food source for many species. **Staghorn** *(R. typhina)* and **smooth sumacs** *(R. glabra)* grow to 8 to 18 feet. Cultivars, such as "Tiger Eyes," are not as vigorous as the species. **Winged sumac** *(R. copallina)* grows to 8 feet and does well in dry, sandy or rocky areas. **Fragrant sumac** *(R. aromatica)* is named for the skunkish smell of the crushed leaves. Blooms earlier than other sumacs, and grows in dunes and open, dry areas. 3 to 6 feet, with a 4 to 10 feet spread. "Grow-Lo" is a short cultivar effective as a ground cover. Zone 4+.Ht: 3-6' with a 4-10' spread.

Ribes spp. (Currant, Gooseberry)

Short berrying shrub providing good cover for birds. Foliage hosts many butterfly caterpillars. Highly susceptible to an imported blister rust that kills white pines—if you see leaves developing orange blisters in summer, pull all infected plants and burn them. **Eastern black currant** *(R. americanum)* is a multi-stemmed native substitute for the European variety. White blooms in spring. **Common gooseberry** *(R. hirtellum)* is a twiggy, thorny shrub with late spring blooms that form translucent green fruits. 2 to 5 feet. Zones 3 to 7.

Rosa spp. (Rose)

All varieties of our native roses bloom in fragrant pink or white in summer. Many are parents to hybrid roses in the trade. Rose hips (the fruits of rose flowers) supply valuable late-winter food for birds and mammals. Great cover and nesting due to its thorny stems. **Virginia rose** (*R. virginiana*) spreads strongly from runners to form a thicket in any well-drained soil. Tolerates some salt. 2 to 4 feet. Zones 3 to 8. **Smooth rose** (*R.blanda*) is similar but with taller stems, to 6 feet. Zones 3 to 7. **Pasture** or **Carolina rose** (*R. carolina*) is similar to Virginia Rose but its mounding habit makes it suitable for smaller gardens. 2 to 3 feet. Zones 4+. **Swamp rose** (*R. palustris*) and **shining rose** (*R. nitida*) are both suitable for bogs and wetlands. 1 to 5 feet. Zone 4+.

Rubus spp. *(*Blackberry, Raspberry, Bramble, Dewberry)

Native shrubs that berry best with some moisture, but will also thrive in a drier location. Summer and fall fruits and canes are eaten by many birds and mammals. Excellent wildlife cover and nesting because of its prickly foliage. Forms thickets of canes. **Common blackberry** (*R. allegheniensis*), **red raspberry** (*R. idaeus*), **blackcap** (*R. occidentalis*), and purple-flowering raspberry (*R. odoratus*) are all native, blooming in summer. **Dewberry** (*R. pubescens*) is a short, trailing, bramble-like species that grows in moist shade. 2 to 6 feet. Zone 3+.

Salix spp. (Willow)

Important wildlife tree. Buds, catkins, twigs, and bark feed many birds and small mammals. Acts as host plant for many distinctive moth and butterfly caterpillars. Willow flowers bloom yellow in spring, attracting many pollinators. With the disappearance of American elm as a preferred nesting tree, northern orioles now use willow instead. **Pussy willow** (*S. discolor*) blooms in late winter and early spring, making it one of the earliest-available natural nectar sources. Grows in swamps and other wet areas, to 15 feet. Zone 2 to 7. **Sage willow** (*S. candida*) is smaller, growing in alkaline wetlands, in colder regions. 3 to 5 feet. Zones 2 to 6.

Sambucus spp. (Elderberry)

Common elderberry (*S. canadensis*) blooms in creamy white in early summer, and is later on loaded with sugary fruits enjoyed by summertime birds. Fruits, twigs, and bark all feed wild turkey, ring-necked pheasant, robin, catbird, bluebird, cardinal, indigo bunting, and brown thrasher, as well as small mammals. Will grow in most soils as long as it receives a few hours of sunlight and some moisture. Prune out older, weaker stems in late winter, to encourage new sprouting canes, which will flower more heavily. 5 to 10 feet. **Scarlet elder** (*S. racemosa*) blooms in spring, fruits earlier than elderberry. 4 to 10 feet. Zone 3+.

Sorbus spp. (Mountain Ash)

American mountain ash (*S. americana*) is worth planting for its conspicuous clusters of berries eaten by cedar waxwings, pine grosbeaks, and other fall and winter birds. Showy white spring flowers. Good for lawns, casting only light shade. A short-season tree, it tends to lose leaves earlier than other species. Needs good drainage and fruits best with some sun. **Showy mountain ash** (*S. decora*) is endangered, and found in high-elevation balsam fir forests of northern New England. 15 to 35 feet. Zones 2 to 6.

Spiraea spp. (Meadowsweet)

Excellent nectar plants with white or pinkish-white mid to late summer flower clusters. Foliage of native spiraea feeds sphinx moth larvae. **Meadowsweet** (*S. alba*) is a fast-growing, tough native shrub for meadows, near water, and in mixed borders. **Steeplebush** (*S. tomentosa*) grows in moist to fairly dry soils. Note that the popular Japanese Spiraea has potentially invasive attributes due to heavy reseeding. 2 to 5 feet. Zone 3+.

Symphoricarpos spp. (Snowberry, Coralberry)

Short, suckering shrubs that grow even in tough, dry, exposed conditions, in sun or medium shade. Good nesting and cover, and loaded with fall berries that feed many birds. Cut stems back occasionally to 6 inches, to encourage heavier berry production. 2 to 4 feet. Zone 3+.

Common snowberry *(S. albus)* has very ornamental white berries. Zones 3 to 7. **Coralberry** *(S. orbiculatus),* with coral-red fruits, is native to southern New England south. Zones 3 to 8.

Taxus canadensis (Canada Yew)

Thrives in shade in any soil except waterlogged. Dense needled branches provide excellent winter cover for birds. All yew berries are poisonous, but several birds including ruffed grouse are able to eat the summer berries by excreting the entire, undigested seeds. Canada yew is a favorite winter food for deer. 2 to 3 feet. Zones 2 to 6.

Vaccinium **spp.** (Blueberry, Cranberry, Lingonberry)

Important native shrub for its abundant twigs, buds, nectar, and fruits eaten by many birds, mammals, and humans alike! Delicious fruits from July through early fall. Food plant for hundreds of butterfly and moth species. **Lowbush blueberry** *(V. augustifolium)* and **velvetleaf blueberry** *(V. myrtilloides)* are the familiar Maine blueberries, growing best in a moist, well-drained soil, but will grow anywhere sun is available, even under pine trees. Effective as groundcover. 8 to 24 inches. **Highbush blueberry** *(V. corymbosum)* is the shrub blueberry, preferring a wet to moderately dry soil (including sand) and full sun. 3 to 10 feet. Beautiful flaming-red fall foliage. **Cranberry** *(V. macrocarpon)* remains an economically and ecologically important crop of New England's coastal bogs. Good groundcover for any moist soil. 1 to 3 inches. **Mountain cranberry** *(V. vitis-idaea)* is a small evergreen lingonberry which grows in cool, damp regions. Good for high-elevation moss and bog gardens. 4 to 8 inches. Zones 3 to 6.

Viburnum **spp.**

All native viburnums produce late summer and fall berries important to many bird species, including catbirds, thrushes, brown thrashers, cedar waxwings, and robins. White flowers are excellent spring and early summer nectar source for many pollinators. Bark, twigs and buds also feed wildlife, and twiggy structure

provides safe shelter and nesting for birds. All are tolerant of most soils but do best with some moisture and sun. Zone 2+. **Mapleleaf viburnum** *(V. acerifolium)* blooms in late spring and tolerates dry shade better than other viburnums. 3 to 6 feet. Zone 3+. **Witherod** *(V. nudum var. cassinoides)* blooms in late spring, has striking blue berries and fall foliage. 6 to 8 feet. Zone 3+. **Arrowwood** *(V. dentatum)* blooms in late spring in moist or dry soil. 6 to 12 feet. Zone 4+. **Hobblebush** *(V. lantanoides)* has fragrant hydrangea-like late spring/early summer blooms. **Nannyberry** *(V. lentago)* blooms late spring and tolerates drier soils. Grows larger than most, at 8 to 15 feet. Zone 3+. **American cranberry bush** *(V. opulus var. americanum)* (pictured above) is a fast-growing suckering shrub blooming in late spring/early summer with showy berry clusters. 5 to 15 feet. Zone 2+. **Black haw** *(V. prunifolium)* blooms in early spring. Spreads from roots but can be pruned to a specimen. 8 to 15 feet. Zone 3+

Xanthorhiza simplicissima (Yellowroot*)*

Adaptable, small shrub, excellent for covering a slope or colonizing an area to form a dense mat that smothers weeds. Purplish brown early spring flowers and lacy foliage that turns a beautiful burnished gold in the fall. Height: 12 to 18 inches. Spread: 24 to 48 inches. Zone 3+.

Medium to Large Mast Trees

"Mast" trees are large native trees that supply large numbers of nuts, seeds and other food resources for wildlife.

Abies balsamea (Balsam Fir)

New England's only native fir, the familiar "Christmas tree" grows in our northern forests. Needs cool, acid soil, with decent moisture. Easily stressed by fungal problems, it is not suitable for urban regions or warm, humid areas. Densest growth in full sun. Good winter cover for birds. Height: 60 to 80 feet. Spread: 12 to 18 feet. Zones 3 to 6.

Acer spp. (Maple)

Excellent specimen trees, but shallow roots and dense shade means understory plants may be difficult to establish. Seeds and buds eaten by many birds and mammals. Sap wells are drilled by woodpeckers, providing a sweet drink for birds and insects. Flowers are an early season nectar source. Foliage supports hundreds of butterfly and moth species. Twigs and bark browsed by grouse, pheasant, chipmunks, beaver, squirrel, and snowshoe hare. Nesting sites for robin, vireo, grosbeak, oriole, goldfinch, and prairie warbler. **Red maple** (*A. rubrum*) is suitable for any soil, including poorly drained or intermittently flooded areas. 40 to 75 feet. **Sugar maple** (*A. saccharum*) is famous for its sap and its fall color, but site away from roads where salt is used. 60 to 80 feet. **Silver maple** (*A. saccharinum*) tolerates occasional spring floods but is prone to breakage once mature. Site away from homes or structures. 60 to 75 feet. **Boxelder** (*A. negundo*) grows in dry, disturbed areas. 20 to 40 feet. **Striped maple** (*A. pensylvanicum*) grows in colder, northern, hardwood forests. Its twigs and stems are important to snowshoe hares and moose (another, common name is "moosewood"), and its seeds feed red squirrels, chipmunks, and ruffed grouse. 15 to 20 feet. Zone 3+. **Mountain maple** (*A. spicatum*) is similar, but without the striped bark.

Betula spp. (Birch)

Birch has an attractive multi-trunking habit and casts only light shade, making it an excellent specimen tree for smaller woodland gardens. Birch seeds (catkins), bud, bark, and twigs all provide fall and winter food for chickadees, juncos, kinglets, common redpoll, pine siskins, chickadee, ruffed grouse, and mammals such as deer, snowshoe hare, beaver, and porcupine. Also an important food plant for many butterfly and moths. **River** (*B. nigra*) and **yellow birches** (*B. alleghaniensis*) are large species, of moist areas, growing 60 to 80 feet with interesting exfoliating bark. Both tolerate some shade. Zone 3+. **Bog birch** (*B. pumila*) is short (3 to 10 feet), and suitable to colder, higher-elevation areas. Zone 2+. **Paper** or **canoe birch** (*B. papyrifera*) and its northern New England equivalent the **heartleaf birch** (*B. cordifolia*) are worth growing for their familiar peeling white bark. Best in cool, partly shaded areas with consistent moisture. 60 to 80 feet. Zone 2+. **Gray birch** (*B. populifolia*) is similar to paper birch, but is short-lived, and commonly seen growing in poor, sandy soils or disturbed areas. 20 to 40 feet. Zone 3+.

Carpinus caroliniana (American Hornbeam)

Understory tree with nice fall foliage and hanging catkins. Birds and animals eat the nuts, and leaves host many butterfly caterpillars. A good landscape tree, especially if lower branches are removed to expose interesting slate-gray, smooth bark similar to American beech. Does best in a moist area, tolerates drier soils. Height: 15 to 30 feet. Spread 12 to 18 feet. Zones 3 to 8.

Carya spp. (Hickory)

Important nut trees for red squirrels and chipmunks, plus woodpeckers, wild turkeys, field sparrows, white-breasted nuthatches, yellow-rumped and pine warblers, cardinals, rose-breasted grosbeaks, rufous-sided towhees, and wood ducks. Foliage is eaten by many interesting insects including luna moths and northern walking sticks. Fruits form in early fall. **Shagbark hickory** (*C. ovata*) has interesting peeling bark texture. **Pignut** (*C. glabra*) is the most adaptable hickory, growing in

A single mature tree with a 30-foot crown not only shades the ground underneath, keeping it cool and moist, but its leaves transpire approximately 40 gallons of water per day, reducing nearby air temperatures by several degrees. This shagbark hickory tree is an important host plant for many beautiful New England butterfly and moth caterpillars, including the beautiful luna moth.

most soils. **Bitternut hickory** *(C. cordiformis)* grows in moist soils, often on slopes, in acid or limestone soils. **Mockernut** *(C. tomentosa)*, exhibits a narrower shape, grows in sandy or rocky soils. Height: 60 to 100 feet. Spread: 20 to 40 feet. Zone 4+.

Celtis occidentalis (Northern Hackberry)

Adaptable tree growing in wet or dry soil, sun, or light shade. Good for tough, urban conditions. Fruits are valuable for birds and mammals, and its leaves feed many butterfly caterpillars. Height: 30 to 100 feet. Spread: 20 to 70 feet. Zone 3+.

Chamaecyparis thyoides
(Atlantic White Cedar, False Cypress)

Attractive, soft-textured, evergreen foliage provides good shelter for birds for nesting and winter cover. Native to bogs and wooded swamps on the coastal plain, but becoming rarer in its native range. Asian varieties are readily available. Favored by deer in winter stress periods. Height: 20 to 55 feet. Spread: 6 to 15 feet. Zone 4+.

Fagus grandifolia (American Beech)

Shade-tolerant, stately tree with beautiful fall foliage and smooth bark. Best in moist, fertile soils, but forms clonal colonies that are too aggressive for small gardens. Beechnuts form in the fall, and are important winter food for many birds and mammals. Flower buds feed finches and other birds. Food plant for dusky wing butterfly caterpillars. Height: 50 to 70 feet. Spread: 25 to 50 feet. Zone 4+.

Fraxinus spp. (Ash)

Our native ash species are excellent large shade trees for wetlands and other areas with consistent moisture. Often used as street trees, they require adequate moisture to prevent ash decline, unexplained phenomena killing ash trees across the country. **White ash** *(F. americana)* is the largest ash, growing 60 to 90 feet with a 25 to 60 feet spread. **Black ash** *(F. nigra)* is narrower, growing 30 to 50 feet with a 15 to 25 feet spread. **Green ash** *(F. pensylvanica)* tolerates drier soils and is hardy to Zone 3. Grows 40 to 60+ with a 20 to 30 feet spread. Cultivars are readily available.

Juglans nigra (Black Walnut)

Grow in full sun, in moist, well-drained soil with a pH above 6.5. The trunks are straight with no branches growing on the lower part. Produces juglones that prevent other plants from growing beneath. Valuable nut tree for mammals and birds such as yellow-rumpled warbler, pine warbler, field sparrow, chickadee, tufted titmouse, purple finch, and nuthatch. Fruits can sometimes be messy in fall and early winter. Nuts are a rich source of healthy omega-3s and vitamins. Height: 70 to 90+. Spread 30 to 60 feet. Zone 4+. **Butternut** *(J. cinerea)* is shorter (50 to 70 feet) but dying out across its range from butternut canker, so plant only resistant strains.

Larix laricina (Tamarack, Hackmatack, Larch)

New England's only deciduous conifer, growing in cold, moist soils across the north. Beautiful soft yellow needles are unmistakable in fall. Female cones bloom in dark red in spring. Food plant for many butterflies and moths, including cecropia and sphinx moths. Height: 30 to 60 feet. Spread 10 to 18 feet. Zone 1+.

Liriodendron tulipifera (Tulip Poplar, Tulip Tree)

Enormous, fast-growing tree native to moist woods. Beautiful, 2-inch Willy-Wonka-esque, candy-cup flowers in spring offer a treasure trove for wildlife, with abundant flower nectar and persistent seeds that feed finches, cardinals, quail, mice, squirrels, and rabbits. Its native populations have declined due to the popularity of its wood. Height: 70 to 120 feet. Spread 30 to 60 feet. Zone 4+.

Nyssa sylvatica (Tupelo, Black Gum, Sour Gum)

Good street or landscape tree. for its fall color and winter form. Prefers moisture but will establish in drier soils. Fruit and buds are eaten by many birds and mammals, and foliage feeds many different caterpillars. Height: 30 to 60 feet+. Spread 25 to 35 feet. Zone 4+.

Ostrya virginiana (Hop hornbeam, Ironwood)

An understory tree in the wild, growing in dry woods along with oaks and pines. It has a fairly narrow crown and is tolerant of pollution and dry soil, making it a good tree for tough urban settings. Seeds, catkins, and buds provide winter forage for downy woodpecker, mockingbird, rose-breasted grosbeak, purple finch, common merganser, wild turkey, ruffed grouse, and ring-necked pheasant. Fruits August through October. Height: 20 to 30 feet+. Spread: 10 to 18 feet. Zone 3+.

Photinia spp. (Chokeberry)

Suckering shrub with white spring flowers and clusters of sour berries, which are often ignored by birds until late winter after fermentation has sweetened them. Good for naturalized shrub borders. Fiery fall foliage. Adaptable shrub, doing well in most situations, but flowers and fruits best in at least partial sun. **Red chokeberry** (*A. pyrifolia*) is readily available, growing 5 to 10 feet tall and spreading 4 to 8 feet. Zone 4+. **Black chokeberry** (*A. melanocarpa*) is smaller, hardier and a little more scrubby than the red variety, and grows in sandy soils. Zone 3+. **Purple chokeberry** (*P. floribunda*) is a hybrid of red and black varieties. Formerly *Aronia*.

Picea spp. (Spruce)

Small-needled evergreen for cool, moist acidic soils with some sun. Dense canopy provides shelter and nesting sites. Early winter seeds, bark, and needles are an important food source for northern wildlife such as spruce grouse, crossbill, snowshoe hare, and deer. Fruits from late summer into fall. **White spruce** (*P. glauca*) is hardy in the coldest areas, Zones 1 to 6. Dwarf cultivars available. **Red spruce** (*P. rubens*) grows in Zones 4 to 7. **Black spruce** (*P. mariana*) grow in northern bogs, often alongside larch. **Colorado blue spruce** (*P. pungens*) is native to the west, but blue-needled cultivars are readily available here. Height: 30 to 60 feet+. Spread 8 to 18 feet. Zones 3 to 7.

Pinus spp. (Pine)

Pine trees provide excellent year-round cover for birds who also use their needles for nest building. Pine seeds form a large part of the diet of many birds and mammals, and the twigs and foliage are also a food source for wildlife. Needles are food for hundreds of herbivorous insects, including many that eat only pine. Fruits (cones) form in late summer. **Eastern white pine** (*P. strobus*) is a familiar, majestic, long-needled variety, growing in most soils as long as there is some sun. Intolerant of salt. In shade, it will grow very tall in search of the sun, with lower branches becoming bare, providing great perches for birds. Maine's state tree, it's our tallest pine, growing

60 to 100 feet+. **Red pine** *(P. resinosa)* grows in the colder zones (3 to 6) of New England's mountainous regions. 50 to 80 feet+. **Pitch pine** *(P. rigida)* grows in poor, sandy or salty soil, and is good for the harshest locations. 30 to 50 feet+. Zone 4+. **Jack pine** *(P. banksiana)* is common in poor, sandy, early successional, northern boreal forests from Maine northwards. 30 to 50 feet, Zones 3 to 7.

Platanus occidentalis (Sycamore)

Large size makes it unsuitable for small areas, but grow for its interesting bark and fast growth. Height: 70 to 100 feet+. Spread 40 to 60 feet. Zone 4+.

Populus spp. (Poplar, Cottonwood, Aspen)

Fast growing tree suitable for erosion control. Many ground-feeding birds and mammals eat the flower buds and seeds (catkins), and its foliage are an important host of many butterfly caterpillars. **Eastern cottonwood** *(P. deltoides)* drops cottony seeds and twigs and is somewhat messy for garden use, but is an excellent large tree for moist soil. 60 to 100 feet with a 25 to 50 feet spread. Zone 4+. **Bigtooth aspen** *(P. grandidenta)* and **balsam poplar** *(P. balsamifera)* grow to 80 feet in the coldest northern regions of New England. Zone 1+.

Quercus spp. (Oak)

One of New England's most familiar large native trees, oak is one of our most important wildlife trees. Fall acorns feed winter ground feeding birds such as wild turkey, grouse, ruffed grouse, blue jay, wood duck, various songbirds as well as mammals such as squirrel, deer, bear, flying squirrel, cottontail rabbit. Oak branches and woodpecker holes provide nesting opportunities for many birds. Oak is a food plant for the largest number of butterfly and moth species of any native tree. The best way to grow oaks is to plant acorns, which quickly sprout into locally adapted seedlings. Native oak species that are readily available: **White** *(Q. alba)* and **scarlet oaks** *(Q. coccinea)* grow in any soil, including sand. **Pin oak** *(Q. palustris)* is easily transplanted into a moist, well-drained soil. **Swamp white oak** *(Q. bicolor)* is best for moist to wet soils. **Scrub** or **bear oak** *(Q. ilicifolia)* is a small tree, growing up to 15 feet in sand dunes, pine barrens, and rocky outcrops. **Northern red oak** *(Q. rubra)* is a good street or lawn tree for moist soil. **Bur oak** *(Q. macrocarpa)* grows in alkaline soil.

Sassafras albidum (Sassafras)

Spectacular fall foliage, interesting bark and pretty, light yellow, spring flowers important to native bees. Fatty blue berries fuel many of the migrating birds that you rarely see at birdfeeders (such as catbird, flicker, flycatcher, kingbird, mockingbird, eastern phoebe, sapsucker, brown thrasher, thrush, towhee, vireo, pileated woodpecker, warbler). Food plant for many caterpillars, including spicebush swallowtail and promethea moth. In the wild, it grows in moist sandy or rocky woodland openings in central and southern New England but will also grow in dry soils and on open, eroded slopes. Not easy to dig up and transplant, but easily grown from container seedlings. Height: 30 to 60 feet. Spread: 12 to 25 feet. Zone 4+.

Sorbus americana (Mountain Ash)

Fast-growing tree blooming white in late spring, forming showy fruit clusters in fall and winter that feed many birds and mammals. Twigs are also foraged by mammals. Fruits August to March. **Showy mountain ash** *(S. decora),* native to northern New England forests, blooms later, forming larger fruits. Height: 15 to 35 feet+. Spread: 8 to 20 feet. Zones 2 to 5.

Thuja occidentalis (Northern White Cedar, Eastern Arborvitae)

Popular screening tree suitable for an exposed location with some moisture. Tolerates some soil salinity. Dense, evergreen foliage provides nesting and roosting for birds. Seeds and foliage are eaten by pine siskin, deer, and snowshoe hare. Fruits fall through winter. Many cultivars originate from Europe. Height: 20 to 40 feet+ Spread: 5 to 20 feet. Zones 3 to 6.

Tilia americana (Basswood)

Handsome shade tree for any well-drained soil. Creamy-yellow flowers bloom in spring and early summer are loved by bees. Height: 60 to 80 feet. Spread: 45 feet. Zone 3+.

*Tsuga canadensis (*Eastern or Canada Hemlock)

Large, graceful tree for cool, damp areas such as north-facing slopes. Cones (seeds) are eaten by pine siskin, crossbill, black-capped chickadee, and small mammals such as red squirrel and white-footed mouse. Good cover for deer, wild turkey, and ruffed grouse, and nesting for smaller birds such as veeries, warblers, and juncos. Fruits fall through winter. Height: 60 to 80 feet+. Spread: 25 to 40 feet. Zones 4 to 7.

Ulmus americana (American Elm)

Until the 1950s, most New England Main Streets were lined with American elm, but Dutch elm disease wiped most of them out in one fell swoop. Some survived,

becoming the parentage of the Dutch elm resistant cultivars that you can now buy. Planting a few of these cultivars may increase the chances that we will be able to enjoy the shaded canopy of mature elms once again. Elm leaves feed many butterfly and moth caterpillars. Grows best in good, moist soil in full sun, but tolerates some dryness. Height: 60 to 80 feet+. Spread: 30 to 50 feet. Zone 3+.

Ticks

Green spaces unfortunately offer tick habitat. The **deer tick** (or **black-legged tick**) can transmit **Lyme disease**, which can lead to chronic illnesses that weaken the heart and nervous system. Deer ticks are tiny, with nymphs (babies) only the size of a poppy seed and adults the size of a pinhead. They hide in leafy areas or perch on tall grass, attaching to any warmblooded creature that passes by. They pick up Lyme disease from infected **white-tailed deer** and **mice**, transmitting it to mammals. The larger **American dog tick** does not transmit Lyme disease

Avoiding tick bites:
- Apply insect repellent before going into tick habitat.
- Wear light-colored clothing so you can see ticks and inspect clothes and skin regularly. Have somebody check areas you can't see, such as your hairline.
- Inspect pets, which may carry ticks indoors.

Tick removal:
- Remove ticks as soon as you notice them. Deer ticks must feed for about 24 hours before the Lyme disease bacterium is transmitted.
- Use fine tweezers to grasp the tick as close to the point of attachment as possible, and gently but firmly pull it out of the skin.
- Consult your doctor if you develop a bull's-eye-type rash at the bite site or a fever within a month of being bitten. Early treatment with appropriate antibiotics will kill the bacteria.

New England Plant Hardiness Zones

Don't try to push your plant zone

Recent reclassification of "plant hardiness zones" from warming average temperatures have placed many areas of New England in one zone warmer, which means the list of plants that you can grow in your area now includes plants native to warmer regions than ours. But one of the impacts of climate change is extreme weather fluctuations, including jumps between cold and warm. Some native plants that have historically grown in our climate may be able to adapt to the warmer average temperatures of a higher zone, but plants traditionally native to warmer areas may not tolerate the swings to the cold temperatures that will undoubtedly still occur here.

Hardiness Zones

Approximate Range
of Average Annual
Minimum Temperatures

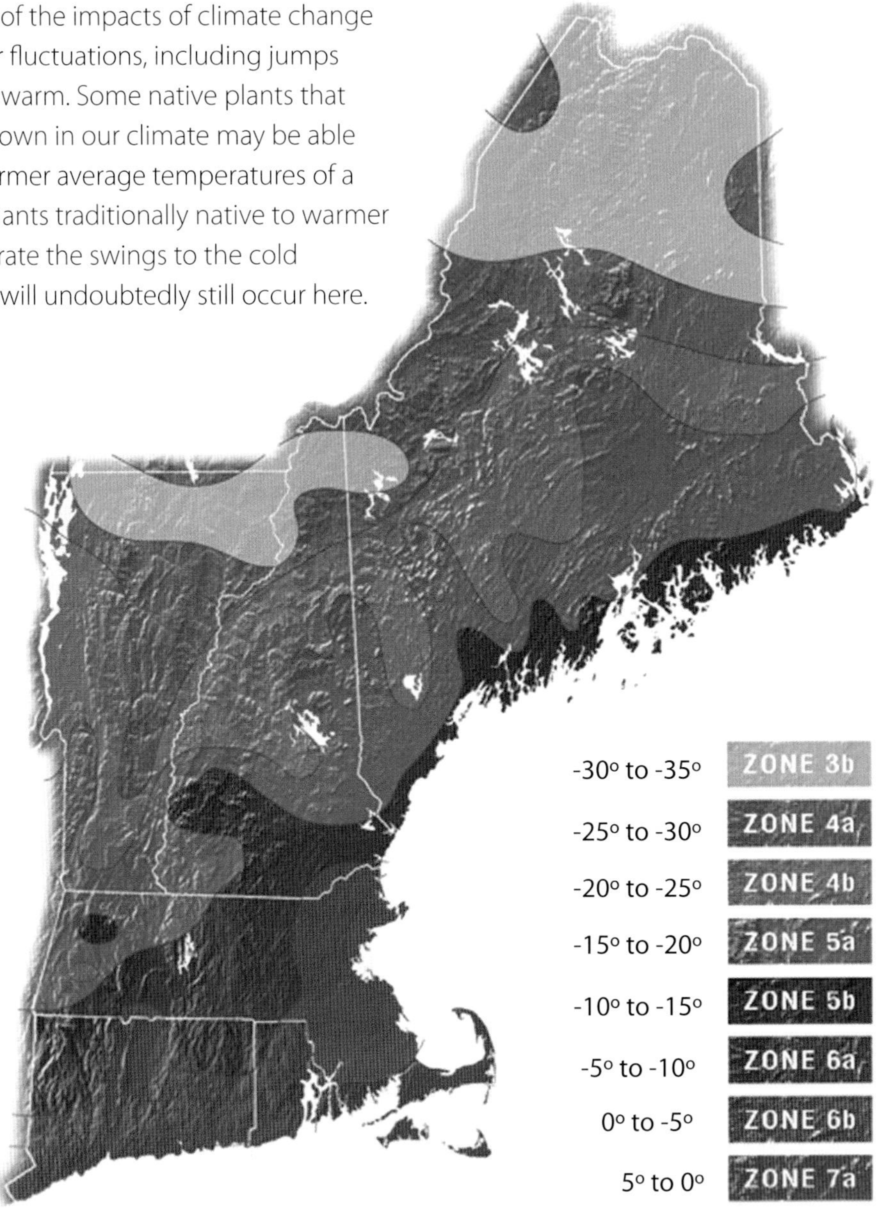

-30° to -35°	ZONE 3b
-25° to -30°	ZONE 4a
-20° to -25°	ZONE 4b
-15° to -20°	ZONE 5a
-10° to -15°	ZONE 5b
-5° to -10°	ZONE 6a
0° to -5°	ZONE 6b
5° to 0°	ZONE 7a

Need More Information?

Often seen congregating in coastal areas during migration periods, the common loon is a bird of special concern to wildlife biologists because they nest on undisturbed edges of large, quiet inland lakes, which is a declining habitat in New England. With a low reproductive rate (usually one chick per year) and predation of chicks by large bass and predatorial birds, loon chicks have many challenges to overcome in order to reach maturity. Loons are very sensitive to mercury poisoning and the ingestion of lead bullets and fishing sinkers, which have now been banned in most of New England.

Sources of Information:
Backyards on the Bay: savebay.org
Brooklyn Botanic Garden: bbg.org
BugGuide.net
Center for Northern Woodlands Mission: northernwoodlands.org
Connecticut Botanical Society: ct-botanical-society.org
GrowNative Massachusetts: grownativemass.org
Invasive Plant Atlas of New England: ipane.org
Lady Bird Johnson Native Plant Database: wildflower.org/plants
Monarch Waystation Program: monarchWatch.org
National Wildlife Federation: nwf.org
New England Wildflower Society: newfs.org
North American Native Plant Society: NANPS.org
Northeast Organic Farming Association (NOFA): nofa.org
Rhode Island Wild Plant Society: RIWPS.org
SafeLawns.org
The Native Fish Conservancy: nativefish.org
Turtle Conservation: turtleconservationproject.org
USDA Plants Database: plants.usda.gov
Wild Ones: for-wild.org
The Xerces Society: xerces.org

Soil Testing:
Connecticut: University of Connecticut Soil Nutrient Analysis Laboratory: soiltest.uconn.edu/
Maine: University of Maine Analytical Laboratory and Maine Soil Testing Service, www.extension.umaine.edu/counties
Massachusetts: University of Massachusetts at Amherst Soil and Plant Tissue Testing Lab: umass.edu/plsoils/soiltest/

New Hampshire: UNH Cooperative Extension Soil Testing Program: extension.unh.edu/Agric/AGPDTS/SoilTest.htm
Rhode Island: uri.edu/ce/factsheets/sheets/soiltest.html
Vermont: The University of Vermont Agricultural and Environmental Testing Lab: uvm.edu/pss/ag_testing/

Where to Buy Native Plants:
Blue Moon Farm, Wakefield, RI: bluemoonfarmperennials.com
City Natives Nursery, Mattapan, MA: bostonnatural.org/citynativesnursery.htm
Evermay Nursery, Old Town, ME: EvermayNursery.com
Found Well Farm, Pembroke, NH: foundwellfarm.com
Garden in the Woods, Framingham & Whately, MA: newfs.org
Mason Hollow Nursery, Mason, NH: MasonHollow.com
Moss Acres, Inc., Honesdale, PA: mossacres.com
The Moss Farm, Raleigh, NC: mossandstonegardens.com
New Hampshire State Forest Nursery: nhnursery.com
Project Native, Housatonic, MA: www.projectnative.org
Sticks and Stones Farms, Newtown, CT: sticksandstonesfarm.com
Twombly Nursery, Monroe, CT: twomblynursery.com
Tripple Brook Farm, Easthampton MA: tripplebrookfarm.com
Vermont Wildflower Farm: vermontwildflowerfarm.com
Wildflower Farm, Coldwater, Ontario: Wildflowerfarm.com

Places to Visit in New England:

Arnold Arboretum, Jamaica Plain, MA

Audubon Sanctuaries across New England

Bartlett Arboretum and Gardens, Stamford, CT

Berkshire Botanical Garden, Stockbridge, MA

Blithewold Mansion, Gardens & Arboretum, Bristol, RI

Coastal Maine Botanic Gardens, Boothbay, ME

Elm Bank, Wellesley, MA

Friends of the Horticulture Farm, Burlington, VT

Garden in the Woods, Framingham, MA

Highstead Arboretum, Redding, CT

McLaughlin Foundation, Garden & Horticultural Center, So. Paris, ME

New England Ecological Garden, Durham, NH

Norcross Wildlife Sanctuary, Monson, MA

Polly Hill Arboretum, Martha's Vineyard

Save The Bay Center, Providence, RI

Tower Hill Botanic Garden, Boylston, MA

"Pick Your Own" Locations and Community Gardens/Agriculture:

American Community Gardening Association: communitygarden.org

Boston Natural Areas Network "Find a Garden" page: bostonnatural.org

Connecticut Community Gardening: ctcommunitygardening.org

Eat Maine Foods: eatmainefoods.ning.com

Farmfresh.org

New Hampshire Community Gardens: extension.unh.edu/HCFG/Map_CommGarden.htm

Vermont Community Garden Network: burlingtongardens.org

Landowner Incentive Programs:

MassWildlife Landowner Incentive Program: mass.gov/dfwele/dfw/habitat/grants/lip/lip_home.htm nrcs.usda.gov/programs/whip

US Fish and Wildlife Service: fws.gov

Sources of Birding Supplies

Duncraft: duncraft.com

New England Birdhouse: newenglandbirdhouse.com

Earth-friendly Garden Supplies and Natural Pest Control

Gardeners' Supply, Burlington, VT: Gardeners.com

Get involved with local land protection and conservation groups

Most development decisions are made at the local level. If big changes are proposed for your neighborhood, even if you can't stop a development, you have the right to visit public meetings to insist that development plans consider the impact to wildlife, and encourage setting aside land for open space to protect wildlife habitat.

Support zoning changes in your town to encourage the preservation of open space. Many towns have opportunities to purchase open land that would otherwise be developed. These purchases sometimes lead to short-term property tax increases, but studies show that preserving open space costs less over time because residential development increases the number of services that the town must provide to its population.

Giant Solomon's Seal (Polygonatum commutatum)

Bibliography

Bird, Richard, 2003. *Companion Planting*. Quantum Publishing Ltd.

Brooklyn Botanic Garden, 1994. *Going Native: Biodiversity in Our Own Backyards.* Brooklyn Botanic Garden Publications.

Cromwell, Nicole, Wenley Ferguson, and Andy Lipsky, 1999. *Backyards on the Bay (A Yard Care Guide for the Coastal Homeowner).* Published by Save the Bay. savebay.org

Cullina, William. *Understanding Perennials, A New Look at an old Favorite.* Houghton Mifflin Harcourt.

ibid. *Wildflowers; Native Trees, Shrubs, and Vines; Understanding Orchids; Native Ferns, Mosses, and Grasses.* All authored for The New England Wild Flower Society. Houghton Mifflin Harcourt.

Cunningham, Sally Jean, 1998. *Great Garden Companions: A Companion Planting System for a Beautiful, Chemical-Free Vegetable Garden.* Rodale Press, Inc.

DiSabato-Aust, Tracy, 1998. *The Well-tended Perennial Garden: Planting & Pruning Techniques.* Timber Press.

Darke, Rick, 2002. *The American Woodland Garden: Capturing the Spirit of the Deciduous Forest.* Timber Press, Inc.

Fedor, John, 2001. *Organic Gardening for the 21st Century.* Reader's Digest Illustrated Reference Books.

Gee, Barbara, 2007. *The Massachusetts Gardener's Companion: An Insider's Guide to Gardening from the Berkshires to the Islands.* The Globe Pequot Press.

Greenlee, John, 2009. *The American Meadow Garden: Creating a Natural Alternative to the Traditional Lawn.* Timber Press.

Grissell, Eric, 2001. *Insects and Gardens: In Pursuit of a Garden Ecology.* Timber Press.

Kingsbury, Noel, 2003. *Natural Gardening in Small Spaces.* Timber Press, Inc.

Lowenfels, Jeff and Wayne Lewis, 2010. *Teaming with Microbes: The Organic Gardener's Guide to the Soil Food Web.* Timber Press.

Massachusetts Butterfly Club. *Mowing Guidelines for Fields and Grasslands:* naba.org/chapters/nabambc/butterfly-conservation.asp (Online publication.)

The Massachusetts Chapter of the Nature Conservancy. *Our Irreplaceable Heritage: Protecting Biodiversity in Massachusetts.* Produced by Natural Heritage & Endangered Species Program, MA, Division of Fisheries & Wildlife, and The Massachusetts Chapter of the Nature Conservancy.

Matson, Tim, 1991. *Earth Ponds: The Country Pond Maker's Guide to Building, Maintenance and Restoration.* Countryman Press.

National Audubon Society Field Guides, various: *Birds, Trees, Wildflowers.*

Plants for a Future. pfaf.org

Primack, Richard, Abraham Miller-Rushing, Dan Primack and Sharda Mukunda, 2007. Using Photographs to Show the Effects of Climate Change on Flowering Times. *Arnoldia, the Magazine of Arnold Arboretum,* Vol 65, No. 1.

Rubin, Carole, 2002. *How to Get Your Lawn off Grass: A North American Guide to Turning off the Water Tap and Going Native.* Harbour Publishing.

Smith, Edward C., 2009. *The Vegetable Gardener's Bible.* Storey Publishing, LLC.

Stuckey, Irene H. and Lisa Lofland Gould, 2001. *Coastal Plants from Cape Cod to Cape Canaveral.* University of North Carolina Press.

Tallamy, Douglas W., 2007. *Bringing Nature Home: How Native Plants Sustain Wildlife in Our Gardens.* Timber Press.

Tukey, Paul, 2007. T*he Organic Lawn Care Manual: A Natural, Low-Maintenance System for a Beautiful, Safe Lawn.* Storey Publishing.

University of New Hampshire Cooperative Extension: *New Hampshire's Native Trees, Shrubs and Vines with Wildlife Value.* Compiled by Wendy Patmos. 3/95.

Wagner, David L., 2005. *Caterpillars of Eastern North America.* Princeton Field Guides. Princeton University Press.

Wells National Estuarine Research Reserve, *Maine's Salt Marshes: Their Functions, Values and Restoration.* www.gulfofmaine.org/council/internal/docs/saltmarsh.pdf (Online publication.)

Zimmerman, Catherine, 2010. *Urban and Suburban Meadows: Bringing Meadowscaping to Big and Small Spaces.* Matrix Media Press.

Photographic credits

Charles Armstrong, 160 (rove beetle); Scott Bauer, USDA Agricultural Research Service, bugwood.org 44, 158 (braconid wasp); Burris & Richards/ButterflyNature.com 67 (cecropia caterpillar); Shawna Coronado/ShawnaCoronado.com 14, 39 (veg. Gardens); William Cullina 23, 44 (hoverfly), 53, 60 (top), 70, 95 (left), 135 (left), 159 (hoverfly), 184 (left); Dcoetzee/Wikimedia 121; Alfredo DiMauro, Assoc AIA 105 (bottom); Richard Felber back cover, 119; Jan Fiala 110 (bottom), 112 (bottom); Ken Gergle Photography/Moss and Stone Gardens 41 (moss), 101 (right), 140; Veronica Guyre 96 (top); Pat D. Hemlepp 1, 43; Alan Hicks 98 (bat); Kent McFarland/Vermont Center for Ecostudies 6, 7; Robert D. McNeill III 129; Leslie J. Mehrhoff/IPANE 147 (bottom), 149 (*ailanthus, ligustrum*), 150 (*phalaris, microstegium, cynanchum*); Moss Acres 90 (top); John J. Mosesso, NBII 135 (top); Tom Murray 49 (towhee), 97 (top), 114 (bottom), 120 (bird), 158 (ladybird, lacewing) 159 (tachinid, soldier beetle), 160 (ground beetle, slug), 215; New England Birdhouse 99 (top); Liz Noffsinger/FreeDigitalPhotos.net 97 (bottom); Andre Karwath/Creative Commons 56 (pussy willow); Tony Kemplen 103 (cobbles); Tom Pawlesh 19 (goldfinch), 26, 34 (flicker), 45 (waxwings), 50 (toad), 52 (butterfly puddling), 54, 59 (rudbeckia), 67 (luna, bottom), 69 (checkerspot), 111, 116 (bluebird), 157 (bottom), 158 (top, tiger beetle, assassin bug), 159 (damselfly); Kevin Prior 143; Randall G. Prostak 36; Jim Rathert/MO Dept. of Conservation 138; Greg Schneider/gschneiderphoto.com 48 (sapsucker); Aubrey Scott 101 (moth); Bill Schmoker back cover flap (cedar waxwing); Jerry Segraves 134 (top); Kelly Senser 52 (cup plant); Joseph Sestili 124 (terrapin); Brian E. Small 112 (top); Robert Sousa back cover (double marigold with bee, nicotiana and sweat bee on aster), 4, 12, 15 (bee), 27 (leaves), 44 (sweat bee), 57, 66 (web), 144, 157 (nicotiana), 158 (spider), 159 (top), 174 (right); Paul Tukey 214; USFWS 47 (thrush), 69 (turtle); Joe Vincent 122 (right); Max Wahrhaftig/Creative Commons 157 (left); Adriaan Walther 96 (leaves), 168; Trudy Walther front cover, 19 (birches, chickadee), 28 (white rose), 31 (hollyhock), 56 (red berries), 58, 64 (top), 68 (top), 72 (top), 78 (top), 80 (right), 81 (top), 83 (top), 91 (acorns), 93 (top), 107 (top), 113 (bottom), 117 (butterfly), 123, 126, 128 (middle, bottom), 134 (right), 137 (left), 142 (left), 148 (rose, iris), 162, 167, 171 (left), 204 (left); Wildflower Farm Inc. 37 (bench); Wikipedia 124 (plover); Ben Young Landscape Architects 87 (top), 95 (right); Victor Young/NHFG back cover and 27 (Karner); all other photographs by Ellen Sousa.

Index